Taste *of* Home
ULTIMATE
OUTDOOR COOKBOOK

TASTE OF HOME BOOKS • RDA ENTHUSIAST BRANDS, LLC • MILWAUKEE, WI

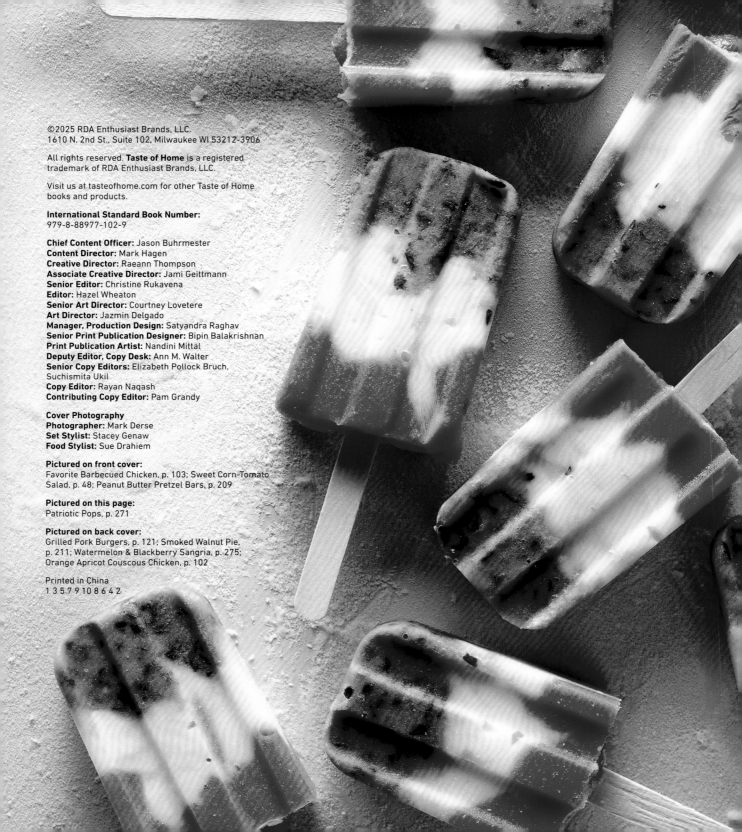

Visit us at tasteofhome.com for other Taste of Home books and products.

International Standard Book Number:
979-8-88977-102-9

Chief Content Officer: Jason Buhrmester
Content Director: Mark Hagen
Creative Director: Raeann Thompson
Associate Creative Director: Jami Geittmann
Senior Editor: Christine Rukavena
Editor: Hazel Wheaton
Senior Art Director: Courtney Lovetere
Art Director: Jazmin Delgado
Manager, Production Design: Satyandra Raghav
Senior Print Publication Designer: Bipin Balakrishnan
Print Publication Artist: Nandini Mittal
Deputy Editor, Copy Desk: Ann M. Walter
Senior Copy Editors: Elizabeth Pollock Bruch, Suchismita Ukil
Copy Editor: Rayan Naqash
Contributing Copy Editor: Pam Grandy

Cover Photography
Photographer: Mark Derse
Set Stylist: Stacey Genaw
Food Stylist: Sue Drahiem

Pictured on front cover:
Favorite Barbecued Chicken, p. 103; Sweet Corn-Tomato Salad, p. 48; Peanut Butter Pretzel Bars, p. 209

Pictured on this page:
Patriotic Pops, p. 271

Pictured on back cover:
Grilled Pork Burgers, p. 121; Smoked Walnut Pie, p. 211; Watermelon & Blackberry Sangria, p. 275; Orange Apricot Couscous Chicken, p. 102

Printed in China
1 3 5 7 9 10 8 6 4 2

TABLE OF CONTENTS

P. 274

P. 236

P. 254

HOW TO KEEP FOOD COLD

Keeping your potluck salads, sides and fresh vegetables cold when eating outside can be tricky. Whether you're packing up to travel to a picnic ground or setting up for a party in the backyard, here are some ways to keep foods cool—and safe to eat—all day long.

PACKING FOR A PICNIC

- Remember that cold foods should be kept at 40° or colder.

- When packing your cooler, it should be about 25% ice and 75% food. Place ice on the bottom and along the sides of the cooler. Then place the heaviest and most perishable foods on top of the ice. Fill in with lighter items.

- Transfer chilled foods directly from the refrigerator to the cooler. Don't use the cooler to chill warm or room-temperature items.

- A full cooler will stay colder longer than one that is partially empty, so choose an appropriate-sized cooler. If food doesn't completely fill your cooler, add more ice.

- Large pieces of ice melt more slowly than ice cubes. If you plan to be gone awhile, use chunks of ice instead of ice cubes. You can also fill clean empty milk cartons with water and freeze them to use as ice packs.

PACKING FOR A COOKOUT

If you plan to cook meats such as chicken, steak, hamburgers or hot dogs, heed these helpful hints:

- Wrap raw meat, poultry or fish separately from cooked foods in airtight plastic containers or resealable bags.

- Do as much prep as possible at home. Marinating your ingredients and draining and discarding the excess marinade before packing will make for an easy and clean transfer from cooler to grill. Shaping patties at home cuts down on the mess of handling uncooked meat on-site.

- Do not partially cook foods at home to speed up cooking at the site; bacteria grows faster in partially cooked foods.

- Freeze meats before packing so they remain cold longer. This is especially important if you're traveling a long distance to a picnic location or campground, or if the foods won't be grilled immediately upon arrival.

BACKYARD DINING

Your celebration may be just a few steps from your kitchen, so there are many things you can do to keep all your food cool and tasting fresh.

CHOOSE A SHADY SPOT
Be sure to shield your food from the sun. If necessary, set up a second table under an umbrella or in the shade of a tree. It will make a huge difference once you set your food out.

PRE-CHILL PLATES AND BOWLS
Put your serving dishes in your fridge or freezer while you prep. Place salads, dips and other cold food into the pre-chilled serving dishes.

PUT DISHES ON ICE
When you set out cold foods, place serving containers in a larger dish filled with ice. For larger plates and platters, add ice to a clean plastic or metal tub and place your dish on top.

DON'T PUT EVERYTHING OUT AT ONCE
Bring dishes out in order of when they'll be eaten. This will ensure everything is fresh when guests are ready to eat.

SERVE OUT OF SMALLER BOWLS
Instead of making one big bowl of potato salad, dish up two or three smaller bowls. Put one on your buffet table and store backups in the fridge to bring out as needed.

KEEP FOOD COVERED
Cover food with a clean dish towel or aluminum foil when you're not passing it around; this will prevent bugs from getting in, and the cold from escaping.

SERVE FROM THE KITCHEN
An alternative to setting all your dishes outside is to have your food station (for everything but the grilled goodies!) in the kitchen. This will make it easier to shift food to and from the refrigerator as needed.

PUT LEFTOVERS AWAY
If guests have moved on from cold apps to other courses, put the apps away. This will ensure nothing goes to waste because it sat out too long.

ROASTED BEETROOT &
GARLIC HUMMUS P. 16

APPETIZERS & BEVERAGES

TOMATO & CORN CHEESY PASTRY BITES

Local veggies and herbs have a magical knack for inspiring me to cook. After my first CSA box arrived, I used the fresh ingredients to create this adorable appetizer.
—*Kristen Heigl, Staten Island, NY*

PREP: 25 min. • **BAKE:** 20 min.
MAKES: 8 pastries

- 1 Tbsp. olive oil
- ½ cup finely chopped onion
- 1 cup fresh corn
- 1 tsp. garlic powder
- ½ tsp. minced fresh parsley
- ¼ tsp. salt
- ⅛ tsp. pepper
- 1 pkg. (17.3 oz.) frozen puff pastry, thawed
- 1 large egg
- 1 Tbsp. water
- ¾ cup quartered cherry tomatoes
- ½ cup crumbled goat cheese
- ½ cup shredded provolone cheese
- 2 Tbsp. minced fresh basil

1. Preheat oven to 375°. In a large skillet, heat oil over medium heat. Add the onion; cook and stir until tender, about 5 minutes. Stir in corn, garlic powder, parsley, salt and pepper; cook until corn is tender, about 2 minutes. Remove from heat.
2. Unfold puff pastry sheets. Using a floured 4-in. round cookie cutter, cut 4 circles in each sheet; place circles on parchment-lined baking sheets. Whisk together egg and water; brush over pastries. Spoon 2 Tbsp. corn mixture onto each circle. Top with tomatoes and cheeses.
3. Bake until pastry is golden brown and the cheese is melted, about 20 minutes. Sprinkle with basil.
1 PASTRY 236 cal., 14g fat (5g sat. fat), 37mg chol., 279mg sod., 22g carb. (2g sugars, 3g fiber), 7g pro.

TROPICAL BERRY SMOOTHIES

This fruity, healthy smoothie is a big hit with kids and adults alike because it tastes like a treat while delivering the vitamins. The recipe is easy to increase based on the number of people you'll be serving.
—*Hillary Engler, Cape Girardeau, MO*

TAKES: 10 min. • **MAKES:** 2 servings

- 1 cup pina colada juice blend
- 1 container (6 oz.) vanilla yogurt
- ⅓ cup frozen unsweetened strawberries
- ¼ cup frozen mango chunks
- ¼ cup frozen unsweetened blueberries

In a blender, combine all ingredients; cover and process for 30 seconds or until smooth. Pour into chilled glasses; serve immediately.
1¼ CUPS 172 cal., 2g fat (1g sat. fat), 4mg chol., 62mg sod., 35g carb. (32g sugars, 2g fiber), 5g pro.

BLUEBERRY ICED TEA

I enjoy coming up with new ways to use my slow cooker. If it's going to take up space, it needs to earn its keep! Pour this refreshing tea over plenty of ice and garnish with blueberries if desired. For extra fun, freeze blueberries in the ice cubes.
—Colleen Delawder, Herndon, VA

PREP: 10 min. • **COOK:** 3 hours + cooling
MAKES: 11 servings (2¾ qt.)

- 12 cups water
- 2 cups fresh blueberries
- 1 cup sugar
- ¼ tsp. salt
- 4 family-sized tea bags
  Ice cubes
  Optional: Lemon slices and fresh mint leaves

1. In a 5-qt. slow cooker, combine water, blueberries, sugar and salt. Cover and cook on low heat for 3 hours.
2. Turn off slow cooker; add tea bags. Cover and let stand 5 minutes. Discard tea bags; cool 2 hours.
3. Strain; discard blueberries. Pour tea into a 3-qt. pitcher; serve over ice cubes. If desired, top with lemon slices, fresh mint and additional fresh blueberries.
1 CUP 73 cal., 0 fat (0 sat. fat), 0 chol., 61mg sod., 19g carb. (18g sugars, 0 fiber), 0 pro.

CREAMY RED PEPPER VEGGIE DIP

I got this recipe from a college roommate. Thick and creamy with just a touch of sweetness, this colorful dip is a winner, especially served with chunky veggies.
—Lynne German, Buford, GA

PREP: 15 min. • **COOK:** 5 min. + chilling
MAKES: 2 ½ cups

- 2 large eggs, slightly beaten
- 2 Tbsp. sugar
- 2 Tbsp. cider vinegar
- 1 Tbsp. butter, softened
- 1 Tbsp. all-purpose flour
- 1 pkg. (8 oz.) cream cheese, softened
- 1 small sweet red pepper, chopped
- 4 green onions (both white and green portions), chopped
  Fresh baby carrots
  Fresh broccoli florets

In a small saucepan over low heat, whisk together the first 5 ingredients. Increase heat to medium; whisk until thickened, 4-5 minutes. Remove from heat. Stir in cream cheese, pepper and onions; mix well. Refrigerate 2 hours; serve with baby carrots and broccoli florets.
¼ CUP 121 cal., 10g fat (6g sat. fat), 63mg chol., 96mg sod., 5g carb. (4g sugars, 0 fiber), 3g pro.

5i

BACON-WRAPPED STUFFED JALAPENOS

Sunday is grill-out day for my husband, and these zesty peppers are one of his specialties. We usually feature them at our annual Daytona 500 party.
—*Therese Pollard, Hurst, TX*

PREP: 1 hour • **GRILL:** 40 min.
MAKES: 2 dozen

- 24   medium jalapeno peppers
- 1   lb. uncooked chorizo or bulk spicy pork sausage
- 2   cups shredded cheddar cheese
- 12   bacon strips, cut in half

1. Make a lengthwise cut in each jalapeno, about ⅛ in. deep; remove seeds. Combine sausage and cheese; stuff into jalapenos. Wrap each with a piece of bacon; secure with toothpicks.
2. Grill, covered, over indirect medium heat for 35-40 minutes or until a thermometer reads 160°, turning once. Grill, covered, over direct heat until bacon is crisp, 1-2 minutes longer.
NOTE Wear disposable gloves when cutting hot peppers; the oils can burn skin. Avoid touching your face.
1 STUFFED JALAPENO 132 cal., 10g fat (4g sat. fat), 30mg chol., 365mg sod., 1g carb. (1g sugars, 0 fiber), 8g pro.

TEST KITCHEN TIPS

For a milder flavor, use pork sausage, Italian sausage or ground beef instead of chorizo. If you like your poppers with cream cheese, cook ½ lb. meat and mix it with 8 oz. softened cream cheese and 1 cup shredded cheddar for the filling.

TEST KITCHEN TIP

Three medium ears of corn will yield about 2 cups of kernels.

CHIPOTLE MEXICAN STREET CORN DIP WITH GOAT CHEESE

I was craving the Mexican street corn that I had during a recent trip to Puerto Vallarta, so I came up with this fabulous dip. It blends the traditional profile of the popular street food with updated flavors for a tasty twist.
—*Joseph Sciascia, San Mateo, CA*

PREP: 30 min. • **BAKE:** 35 min.
MAKES: 3 cups

- 3   medium ears sweet corn
- 1   Tbsp. olive oil
- 1   cup crumbled goat cheese
- ¾   cup mayonnaise
- 1   can (4 oz.) chopped green chiles
- 1   jar (4 oz.) diced pimientos, drained
- 2   green onions, chopped
- 2   Tbsp. finely chopped chipotle peppers in adobo sauce
- 1   Tbsp. minced fresh cilantro
- 1   to 2 Tbsp. lime juice
- 1½ tsp. grated lime zest
- 1   tsp. ground cumin
- 1   tsp. chili powder
    Tortilla chips

1. Brush corn with oil. Grill corn, covered, over medium heat until lightly browned and tender, 10-12 minutes, turning occasionally. Cool slightly.
2. Preheat oven to 350°. Cut corn from cobs; transfer to a large bowl. Stir in the goat cheese, mayonnaise, green chiles, pimientos, green onions, chipotle peppers, cilantro, lime juice, lime zest, cumin and chili powder. Transfer to a greased 1½-qt. baking dish. Bake until bubbly and golden brown, 35-40 minutes. Serve with tortilla chips.
NOTE Wear disposable gloves when cutting hot peppers; the oils can burn skin. Avoid touching your face.
¼ CUP 157 cal., 14g fat (3g sat. fat), 13mg chol., 182mg sod., 7g carb. (2g sugars, 1g fiber), 3g pro.

HEIRLOOM TOMATO GALETTE WITH PECORINO

I found some beautiful heirloom tomatoes at the market and had to show them off. In this easy galette, the tomatoes are tangy and the crust is beyond buttery.
—*Jessica Chang, Playa Vista, CA*

PREP: 10 min. + chilling
BAKE: 25 min. + cooling
MAKES: 6 servings

- 1   cup all-purpose flour
- 1   tsp. baking powder
- ¾   tsp. kosher salt, divided
- ½   cup cold unsalted butter, cubed
- ½   cup sour cream
- 2   cups heirloom cherry tomatoes, halved
- 3   oz. pecorino Romano cheese, thinly sliced

1. Whisk flour, baking powder and ½ tsp. salt; cut in butter until mixture resembles coarse crumbs. Stir in sour cream until the dough forms a ball. Shape into a disk; cover and refrigerate until firm enough to roll, about 2 hours.
2. Meanwhile, place the tomatoes in a colander; toss with the remaining ¼ tsp. salt. Let stand 15 minutes.
3. Preheat oven to 425°. On a floured sheet of parchment, roll dough into a 12-in. circle. Transfer to a baking sheet.
4. Place cheese slices over crust to within 2 in. of edge; arrange tomatoes over cheese. Fold crust edges over filling, pleating as you go and leaving the center uncovered. Bake until the crust is golden brown and the cheese is bubbly, about 25 minutes. Cool for 10 minutes before slicing.
1 PIECE 317 cal., 23g fat (15g sat. fat), 68mg chol., 559mg sod., 19g carb. (2g sugars, 1g fiber), 9g pro.

⏱ 🄳 GRILLED HERBED OLIVES

A few years ago, we hit the olive bar at our local grocery store and were amazed by the grilled olives. I never thought to grill olives before! Use whatever herbs you prefer. You could also use black olives or a combination of each.
—*Debra Keil, Owasso, OK*

TAKES: 30 min. • **MAKES:** 6 servings

- 1   can (6 oz.) pitted green olives, drained
- 1   Tbsp. extra virgin olive oil
- ¾   tsp. each minced fresh marjoram, rosemary and thyme
    Optional: Sea salt and coarsely ground pepper

1. In a small bowl, combine olives, oil and herbs. Let stand for 15 minutes.
2. Transfer olives to a grill wok or open grill basket; place on grill rack. Grill, uncovered, over medium-high heat until lightly charred, 8-10 minutes, stirring frequently. If desired, sprinkle with salt and pepper. Serve warm or at room temperature.
¼ CUP 64 cal., 7g fat (0 sat. fat), 0 chol., 480mg sod., 2g carb. (0 sugars, 0 fiber), 0 pro. **DIABETIC EXCHANGES** 1½ fat.

PERUVIAN CHICHA MORADA

Chicha morada is a nonalcoholic Peruvian beverage made by boiling purple corn (called *maiz morado*) with water, pineapple rinds, cinnamon, cloves, sugar and lime. It can be traced back to the precolonial era in Peru and is considered a staple of Peruvian cuisine. You can find maiz morado in specialty shops and online outlets.
—*Andrea Potischman, Menlo Park, CA*

PREP: 20 min. + chilling • **COOK:** 50 min.
MAKES: 8 servings

- 1 fresh pineapple
- 1 pkg. (15 oz.) dried purple corn on the cob
- 12 cups water
- ¾ cup sugar
- 3 cinnamon sticks (3 in.)
- 10 whole cloves
- ⅓ cup lime juice
- 1 medium green apple, chopped

1. Peel pineapple, removing any eyes from the fruit. Reserve half the peel. Remove and discard core from fruit. Chop pineapple and reserve for garnish.
2. Rinse corn cobs; place in a Dutch oven. Add the water, pineapple peel, sugar, cinnamon and cloves. Bring to a boil; reduce heat. Simmer, uncovered, for 50 minutes.
3. Strain. Refrigerate until chilled, at least 1 hour.
4. Stir in lime juice. Serve over ice with apple and reserved chopped pineapple.
¾ CUP 99 cal., 0 fat (0 sat. fat), 0 chol., 1mg sod., 26g carb. (24g sugars, 1g fiber), 0 pro.

BLACKBERRY BEER COCKTAIL

This refreshing hard lemonade has a mild alcohol flavor. The beer adds just enough fizz to dance on your tongue as you sip. Sorry, adults only!
—*Ginger Sullivan, Cutler Bay, FL*

TAKES: 10 min. • **MAKES:** 10 servings

- 4 bottles (12 oz. each) beer, chilled
- 1 can (12 oz.) frozen raspberry lemonade concentrate, thawed
- ¾ cup fresh or frozen blackberries, thawed
- ½ cup vodka
  Ice cubes
  Lemon slices

In a large pitcher, combine the beer, lemonade concentrate, blackberries and vodka. Serve over ice and garnish with lemon slices.

¾ CUP 151 cal., 0 fat (0 sat. fat), 0 chol., 6mg sod., 21g carb. (19g sugars, 1g fiber), 1g pro.

SLOW-COOKED PEACH SALSA

Fresh peaches and tomatoes make my salsa a hands-down winner. I give my co-workers several jars throughout the year as a special treat.
—*Peggi Stahnke, Cleveland, OH*

PREP: 20 min. • **COOK:** 3 hours + cooling
MAKES: 11 cups

- 4 lbs. tomatoes (about 12 medium), chopped
- 1 medium onion, chopped
- 4 jalapeno peppers, seeded and finely chopped
- ½ to ⅔ cup packed brown sugar
- ¼ cup minced fresh cilantro
- 4 garlic cloves, minced
- 1 tsp. salt
- 4 cups chopped peeled fresh peaches (about 4 medium), divided
- 1 can (6 oz.) tomato paste

1. In a 5-qt. slow cooker, combine the first 7 ingredients; stir in 2 cups peaches. Cook, covered, on low 3-4 hours or until onion is tender.

2. Stir in tomato paste and remaining peaches. Cool. Transfer to covered containers. Refrigerate up to 1 week.

FREEZE OPTION Transfer salsa to freezer-safe containers; fill to within ½ in. of tops. freeze up to 12 months. Thaw in refrigerator before serving.

NOTE Wear disposable gloves when cutting hot peppers; the oils can burn skin. Avoid touching your face.

¼ CUP 28 cal., 0 fat (0 sat. fat), 0 chol., 59mg sod., 7g carb. (5g sugars, 1g fiber), 1g pro. **DIABETIC EXCHANGES** ½ starch.

3. Remove from oven; unwrap. Rinse beets with cold water; peel when cool enough to handle. Squeeze garlic from skins. Place beets and garlic in a food processor. Add the garbanzo beans, lemon juice, tahini, cumin, cayenne pepper and the remaining ¼ cup oil, ¼ tsp. salt and ¼ tsp. ground pepper. Process until smooth.

4. If desired, pulse 2 Tbsp. Greek yogurt with the beet mixture, dolloping the remaining 2 Tbsp. yogurt over finished hummus. Sprinkle with dill or parsley. Serve with vegetables and pita bread.

¼ CUP 87 cal., 5g fat (1g sat. fat), 0 chol., 131mg sod., 8g carb. (3g sugars, 2g fiber), 2g pro. **DIABETIC EXCHANGES** 1 fat, ½ starch.

GRILLED NECTARINES WITH BURRATA & HONEY

Classic Caprese gets a sweet makeover with this inspired summer starter. Burrata, mint and honey are served over nectarine halves—or any stone fruit you like—in this creamy, dreamy dish.
—Anthony Gans, Hawthorne, CA

TAKES: 15 min. • **MAKES:** 6 servings

- 3 medium ripe nectarines, halved and pitted
  Cooking spray
- 8 oz. burrata cheese
- 2 Tbsp. honey
- 12 fresh mint leaves
  Flaky sea salt, such as Maldon

1. Heat a grill pan over medium-high heat. Spritz cut sides of nectarines with cooking spray. Place cut sides down on pan. Grill until just tender, 4-5 minutes. Meanwhile, drain burrata; cut into 6 slices.

2. Arrange nectarine halves, cut side up, on a serving platter. Top with burrata, honey and mint; sprinkle with salt.

1 SERVING 160 cal., 8g fat (5g sat. fat), 27mg chol., 60mg sod., 15g carb. (13g sugars, 1g fiber), 7g pro.

ROASTED BEETROOT & GARLIC HUMMUS

This beetroot hummus is so tasty and healthy, and it's the prettiest pink snack I've ever seen—it's a stunner at garden parties! It's also a great recipe to make in batches and keep in the fridge for weekday lunches and snacks.
—Elizabeth Worndl, Toronto, ON

PREP: 25 min. • **BAKE:** 45 min.
MAKES: 4 cups

- 3 fresh medium beets (about 1 lb.)
- 1 whole garlic bulb
- ½ tsp. salt, divided
- ½ tsp. coarsely ground pepper, divided
- 1 tsp. plus ¼ cup olive oil, divided
- 1 can (15 oz.) garbanzo beans or chickpeas, rinsed and drained
- 3 to 4 Tbsp. lemon juice
- 2 Tbsp. tahini
- ½ tsp. ground cumin
- ½ tsp. cayenne pepper
- ¼ cup plain Greek yogurt, optional
  Minced fresh dill weed or parsley
  Assorted fresh vegetables
  Sliced or torn pita bread

1. Preheat oven to 375°. Pierce beets with a fork; place in a microwave-safe bowl and cover loosely. Microwave on high for 4 minutes, stirring halfway. Cool slightly. Wrap beets in individual foil packets.

2. Remove papery outer skin from garlic, but do not peel or separate cloves. Cut bulb in half crosswise. Sprinkle halves with ¼ tsp. salt and ¼ tsp. pepper; drizzle with 1 tsp. oil. Wrap in individual foil packets. Roast beets and garlic until cloves are soft, about 45 minutes.

BEST DEVILED EGGS

Herbs lend amazing flavor, making these the best deviled eggs you can make!
—*Jesse and Anne Foust, Bluefield, WV*

TAKES: 25 min. • **MAKES:** 2 dozen

- ½ cup mayonnaise
- 2 Tbsp. 2% milk
- 1 tsp. dried parsley flakes
- ½ tsp. dill weed
- ½ tsp. minced chives
- ½ tsp. ground mustard
- ¼ tsp. salt
- ¼ tsp. paprika
- ⅛ tsp. garlic powder
- ⅛ tsp. pepper
- 12 hard-boiled large eggs
  Minced fresh parsley and additional paprika

In a small bowl, combine the first 10 ingredients. Cut eggs lengthwise in half; remove yolks and set whites aside. In another bowl, mash yolks; add to mayonnaise mixture, mixing well. Spoon or pipe filling into egg whites. Sprinkle with parsley and additional paprika. Refrigerate until serving.

1 STUFFED EGG HALF 73 cal., 6g fat (1g sat. fat), 108mg chol., 81mg sod., 0 carb. (0 sugars, 0 fiber), 3g pro.

BACON DEVILED EGGS To mayonnaise, add 3 crumbled cooked bacon strips, 3 Tbsp. finely chopped red onion, 3 Tbsp. sweet pickle relish and ¼ tsp. smoked paprika.

SMOKIN' HOT DEVILED EGGS To mayonnaise, add 3 finely chopped chipotle peppers in adobo sauce, 1 Tbsp. drained capers, 1 Tbsp. stone-ground mustard, ¼ tsp. salt and ¼ tsp. white pepper. Sprinkle stuffed eggs with minced fresh cilantro.

CRABBY DEVILED EGGS Increase mayonnaise to ⅔ cup. Mix in 1 cup finely chopped imitation crabmeat, ½ cup finely chopped celery, ½ cup chopped slivered almonds, 2 Tbsp. finely chopped green pepper and ½ tsp. salt.

GARDEN-FRESH SEAFOOD COCKTAIL

For something cool on a hot day, we mix shrimp and crabmeat with crunchy veggies straight from the garden. Look for adobo seasoning in your grocery's international section.
—*Teri Schloessmann, Tulsa, OK*

PREP: 15 min. + chilling • **MAKES:** 6 cups

- ¾ lb. peeled and deveined cooked shrimp (31-40 per lb.)
- 1 container (8 oz.) refrigerated jumbo lump crabmeat, drained
- 3 celery ribs, chopped
- 1 medium cucumber, peeled, seeded and chopped
- 1 medium sweet orange pepper, chopped
- 2 plum tomatoes, seeded and chopped
- ½ cup red onion, finely chopped
- 1 to 2 jalapeno peppers, seeded and finely chopped
- ¼ cup minced fresh cilantro
- 3 Tbsp. lime juice
- 1 Tbsp. olive oil
- 2¼ tsp. adobo seasoning

Combine the first 9 ingredients. Whisk together lime juice, oil and adobo seasoning; drizzle over shrimp mixture and toss gently to coat. Refrigerate at least 1 hour, tossing gently every 20 minutes. Serve shrimp mixture in cocktail glasses.

NOTE Wear disposable gloves when cutting hot peppers; the oils can burn skin. Avoid touching your face.

¾ CUP 103 cal., 3g fat (0 sat. fat), 92mg chol., 619mg sod., 5g carb. (2g sugars, 1g fiber), 15g pro.

RAINBOW SPRITZER

This drink gets its bubbly goodness from ginger ale and puckery lemonade.
—*Olivia Thompson, Milwaukee, WI*

TAKES: 20 min. • **MAKES:** 4 servings

- ½ cup fresh blueberries
- ½ cup chopped peeled kiwifruit
- ½ cup chopped fresh pineapple
- ½ cup sliced fresh strawberries or fresh raspberries
- 1 cup chilled ginger ale
- ½ cup chilled unsweetened pineapple juice
- ½ cup chilled lemonade

In 4 tall glasses, layer blueberries, kiwi, pineapple and strawberries. In a 2-cup glass measure or small pitcher, mix the remaining ingredients; pour over fruit. Serve immediately.

1 SERVING 91 cal., 0 fat (0 sat. fat), 0 chol., 8mg sod., 23g carb. (18g sugars, 2g fiber), 1g pro.

AVOCADO SALSA

I first set out this recipe at a party, and it was an absolute success. People love the garlic, corn and avocado combination.
—*Susan Vandermeer, Ogden, UT*

PREP: 20 min. + chilling
MAKES: about 7 cups

1⅔ cups (about 8¼ oz.) frozen corn, thawed
2 cans (2¼ oz. each) sliced ripe olives, drained
1 medium sweet red pepper, chopped
1 small onion, chopped
5 garlic cloves, minced
⅓ cup olive oil
¼ cup lemon juice
3 Tbsp. cider vinegar
1 tsp. dried oregano
½ tsp. salt
½ tsp. pepper
4 medium ripe avocados, peeled
   Tortilla chips

1. Combine corn, olives, red pepper and onion. In another bowl, mix the next 7 ingredients. Pour over corn mixture; toss to coat. Refrigerate, covered, overnight.
2. Just before serving, chop avocados and stir gently into salsa. Serve with tortilla chips.
¼ CUP 82 cal., 7g fat (1g sat. fat), 0 chol., 85mg sod., 5g carb. (1g sugars, 2g fiber), 1g pro. **DIABETIC EXCHANGES** 1½ fat.

READER REVIEW

"I simply love this recipe. Every time I want something fresh and healthy for dinner, I prepare this salsa together with a nice piece of meat. It's also a big hit as a snack with tortilla chips."
—GUEST7820, TASTEOFHOME.COM

5i LEMON-BASIL MOJITO MOCKTAILS

In this twist on the classic summer beverage, lemon basil takes the place of mint. For a grown-up version, just add your favorite rum or vodka.
—*Cheryl Perry, Hertford, NC*

PREP: 15 min. + chilling
MAKES: 12 servings

1½ cups sugar
4 cups water
6 cups fresh basil leaves, divided
   Crushed ice, divided
2 bottles (1 liter each) club soda
GARNISH
   Fresh lemon wedges

1. In a small saucepan, bring sugar and water to a boil. Cook and stir until the sugar is dissolved. Place half the basil in a small bowl. With a pestle or wooden spoon, crush basil until its aroma is released. Stir into the sugar mixture. Remove from heat; cool completely. Strain; refrigerate until cold.
2. Place 2 cups crushed ice and the remaining basil in a 4-qt. pitcher. Using a muddler or a wooden spoon, press the basil leaves against the ice until their aroma is released. Stir in basil syrup and soda. Serve over crushed ice in tall glasses; squeeze lemon wedges into drink.
1 SERVING 101 cal., 0 fat (0 sat. fat), 0 chol., 36mg sod., 26g carb. (25g sugars, 0 fiber), 0 pro.

TOMATO-BACON DIP WITH FOCACCIA

For a spread with BLT flavor, mix mayo and sour cream, then add bacon and tomato. We use it as a dip and a zesty sandwich spread.
—*Marsha Postar, Lubbock, TX*

PREP: 20 min. + chilling
MAKES: 12 servings

1 cup mayonnaise
1 cup sour cream
½ lb. bacon strips, cooked and crumbled
1 large tomato, seeded and finely chopped
½ small onion, finely chopped
   Optional: Minced fresh parsley and additional crumbled cooked bacon
   Focaccia bread, sliced and lightly toasted

1. In a small bowl, mix mayonnaise and sour cream. Stir in bacon, tomato and onion. Refrigerate until cold, about 1 hour.
2. If desired, sprinkle with parsley and additional bacon; serve with focaccia.
¼ CUP DIP 211 cal., 21g fat (5g sat. fat), 27mg chol., 228mg sod., 2g carb. (1g sugars, 0 fiber), 3g pro.

PINEAPPLE COCONUT REFRESHER

This refresher is lower in calories and fat than most smoothie recipes. It's quite refreshing and packed with vitamins and minerals.
—*Shelly Bevington, Hermiston, OR*

TAKES: 10 min. • **MAKES:** 4 servings

- 1½ cups pineapple-flavored coconut water
- 1 Tbsp. agave nectar
- ½ tsp. avocado oil
- 2 cups cubed fresh pineapple
- 1 cup crushed ice

Place all ingredients in a blender. Cover and process until smooth. Serve immediately.

1 CUP 78 cal., 1g fat (0 sat. fat), 0 chol., 24mg sod., 19g carb. (16g sugars, 1g fiber), 1g pro.

FROZEN LEMON-BERRY MARGARITAS

I like to cool down with this fantastic alcohol-optional margarita. It's icy, thick and perfect for when you need a break.
—*Julie Hieggelke, Grayslake, IL*

TAKES: 15 min. • **MAKES:** 4 servings

- 4 lime wedges
- 2 Tbsp. coarse sugar
- ⅔ cup thawed lemonade concentrate
- 1 cup frozen unsweetened raspberries
- 2 cups ice cubes
- 2 pkg. (10 oz. each) frozen sweetened sliced strawberries, thawed
- ½ cup frozen blueberries
- 1 Tbsp. sugar
- ½ cup tequila, optional

1. Using lime wedges, moisten the rims of 4 margarita or cocktail glasses. Set aside limes for garnish. Sprinkle coarse sugar on a plate; hold each glass upside down and dip rim into sugar. Set aside. Discard remaining sugar on plate.

2. In a blender, combine the lemonade concentrate and raspberries; cover and process until blended. Press mixture through a fine sieve; discard the seeds. Return raspberry mixture to the blender; add the ice, strawberries, blueberries, sugar and, if desired, tequila. Cover and process until smooth.

3. Pour into prepared glasses. Garnish with reserved limes.

1 CUP 271 cal., 0 fat (0 sat. fat), 0 chol., 6mg sod., 71g carb. (65g sugars, 4g fiber), 1g pro.

MEDITERRANEAN TOMATO BITES

My friend Mary served these lovely appetizers at a summer gathering years ago, and I adapted them to my taste. It's a great recipe for late summer, when tomatoes and herbs are at their freshest.
—*Susan Wilson, Milwaukee, WI*

PREP: 20 min. • **BAKE:** 15 min.
MAKES: 32 pastries

- 1 pkg. (17.3 oz.) frozen puff pastry, thawed
- 1½ cups shredded Gouda cheese
- 6 plum tomatoes, thinly sliced
- ¼ cup pitted ripe olives, coarsely chopped
- 1 cup crumbled feta cheese
  Minced fresh basil
  Minced fresh oregano

1. Preheat oven to 400°. Unfold puff pastry. Cut each sheet into 16 squares; place on parchment-lined baking sheets.
2. Sprinkle with Gouda cheese; top with tomatoes, olives and feta cheese. Bake until golden brown, 14-18 minutes. Sprinkle with herbs.
FREEZE OPTION Cover and freeze unbaked pastries on waxed paper-lined baking sheets until firm. Transfer to freezer containers, separating layers with waxed paper; return to freezer. To use, bake as directed, increasing time as necessary to heat through. Sprinkle with herbs.
1 PASTRY 106 cal., 6g fat (2g sat. fat), 8mg chol., 136mg sod., 9g carb. (0 sugars, 1g fiber), 3g pro.

HEALTH TIP

Puff pastry is convenient, but very rich. Lighten up this appetizer by using toasted French bread slices instead. Decrease the bake time slightly and skip the freeze option.

SESAME CHICKEN DIP

I can't tell you how many times I'm asked to bring this easy dip to holidays, birthday parties or girls' weekend getaways. It's fresh and light, and it has the Asian flavors that make it stand out. The rice crackers are a must!
—*Dawn Schutte, Sheboygan, WI*

PREP: 30 min. + chilling
MAKES: 36 servings

- 2 Tbsp. reduced-sodium soy sauce
- 4 tsp. sesame oil
- 2 garlic cloves, minced
- 4 cups shredded cooked chicken breast
- 3 pkg. (8 oz. each) reduced-fat cream cheese
- 1 jar (10 oz.) sweet-and-sour sauce
- 2 cups chopped fresh baby spinach
- 1 cup thinly sliced green onions (about 8)
- ½ cup chopped salted peanuts
  Sesame rice crackers

1. Mix soy sauce, sesame oil and garlic; toss with chicken. Refrigerate, covered, at least 1 hour.
2. Spread cream cheese onto a large serving plate; top with sweet-and-sour-sauce, spinach and chicken. Sprinkle with green onions and peanuts. Refrigerate, covered, at least 2 hours. Serve with crackers.
¼ CUP DIP 97 cal., 6g fat (3g sat. fat), 25mg chol., 176mg sod., 4g carb. (2g sugars, 0 fiber), 7g pro.

READER REVIEW
"Just made this for a neighborhood get-together, and everyone loved it! Sesame oil adds a fabulous aroma to a cold dip ... yum!"
—LOUISEINNC, TASTEOFHOME.COM

⑤ᵢ
LUSCIOUS LIME SLUSH

Guests really go for this sweet-tart refresher. If you like, you can swap in lemonade concentrate for the limeade.
—*Bonnie Jost, Manitowoc, WI*

PREP: 20 min. + freezing
MAKES: 28 servings

- 9 cups water
- 4 green tea bags
- 2 cans (12 oz. each) frozen limeade concentrate, thawed
- 2 cups sugar
- 2 cups lemon rum or rum
- 7 cups lemon-lime soda, chilled
  Lime slices, optional

1. In a Dutch oven, bring the water to a boil. Remove from the heat; add tea bags. Cover and steep for 3-5 minutes. Discard tea bags. Stir in the limeade concentrate, sugar and rum.
2. Transfer to a 4-qt. freezer container; cool. Cover and freeze for 6 hours or overnight.
3. To use: Combine limeade mixture and soda in a 4-qt. pitcher. Or for 1 serving, combine ½ cup limeade mixture and ¼ cup soda in a glass. If desired, garnish with lime slices. Serve immediately.
¾ CUP 177 cal., 0 fat (0 sat. fat), 0 chol., 7mg sod., 36g carb. (35g sugars, 0 fiber), 0 pro.

FRESH SHRIMP & AVOCADO NACHOS

Since I'm such a fan of shrimp any which way and my family loves nachos, I combined my fresh-from-the-garden ingredients with shrimp and avocado for a cool yet satisfying take on the classic party snack.
—*Teri Schloessmann, Tulsa, OK*

PREP: 30 min. + chilling
MAKES: 10 servings

4 plum tomatoes, chopped
3 tomatillos, husked and chopped
4 jalapeno peppers, seeded and finely chopped
1 small onion, chopped
¼ cup minced fresh cilantro
3 Tbsp. olive oil
3 Tbsp. lime juice, divided
2 Tbsp. seasoned rice vinegar
2 garlic cloves, minced
1½ tsp. sea salt
½ tsp. dried oregano
1 lb. peeled and deveined cooked shrimp (31-40 per lb.), coarsely chopped
2 medium ripe avocados, peeled and pitted, divided
½ cup sour cream
8 cups tortilla chips
1 cup shredded lettuce

1. In a large bowl, combine tomatoes, tomatillos, peppers, onion, cilantro, oil, 1 Tbsp. lime juice, the vinegar, garlic, sea salt and oregano. Cover and refrigerate until chilled, at least 30 minutes. Stir in shrimp.

2. For avocado cream, mash 1 avocado with sour cream and 1 Tbsp. lime juice until smooth. Cube the remaining avocado and toss with the remaining 1 Tbsp. lime juice.

3. To serve, arrange chips on a large platter. Top with the shrimp mixture, cubed avocado, lettuce and avocado cream. Serve immediately.

NOTE Wear disposable gloves when cutting hot peppers; the oils can burn skin. Avoid touching your face.

1 SERVING 264 cal., 16g fat (3g sat. fat), 72mg chol., 542mg sod., 20g carb. (3g sugars, 3g fiber), 12g pro.

TEST KITCHEN TIPS

The avocado cream makes a great topping for tacos, quesadillas and burgers. Seasoned rice vinegar is different from regular rice vinegar. It has added sugar and salt.

DILL VEGETABLE DIP

A friend gave me this zesty dip recipe many years ago, and now I serve it at our annual holiday open house. To let your guests keep circulating, make individual servings by spooning dip into a small cup, then garnishing with fresh veggies.
—Karen Gardiner, Eutaw, AL

PREP: 5 min. + chilling • **MAKES:** 1½ cups

- 1 cup sour cream
- ½ cup mayonnaise
- 1 Tbsp. finely chopped onion
- 2 tsp. dried parsley flakes
- 1 tsp. dill weed
- 1 tsp. seasoned salt
  Assorted fresh vegetables

Combine the first 6 ingredients; mix well. Cover and refrigerate. Serve with vegetables.

2 TBSP. 107 cal., 11g fat (3g sat. fat), 17mg chol., 187mg sod., 1g carb. (1g sugars, 0 fiber), 1g pro.

READER REVIEW

"Very simple and refreshing! I love making dips from scratch. It's so easy and you can control the sodium and other ingredients to ensure you're getting a quality dish!"
—JMSCANLAN, TASTEOFHOME.COM

PINEAPPLE RUM PUNCH

I created this with my favorite Bahamian juices. I got the inspiration for it from other Bahama punches I have sampled.
—*Pamela Vitti Knowles, Hendersonville, NC*

TAKES: 10 min. • **MAKES:** 12 servings

 3½ cups unsweetened pineapple juice
 1½ cups orange juice
  1 cup coconut water
  1 cup coconut rum
  1 cup orange peach mango juice
  1 cup dark rum
  ¼ cup Key lime juice
  3 Tbsp. Campari liqueur or
     grenadine syrup
     Ice cubes
     Optional: Orange slices and
     pineapple fronds

In a pitcher, combine first 8 ingredients. Serve over ice. If desired, garnish with orange slices and pineapple fronds.
¾ CUP 157 cal., 0 fat (0 sat. fat), 0 chol., 23mg sod., 16g carb. (13g sugars, 0 fiber), 1g pro.

READER REVIEW
"We had these while on an RV trip and everyone in our group enjoyed them next to a warm campfire! Will be making again!"
—XXCSKIER, TASTEOFHOME.COM

CUCUMBER GIN SMASH

It doesn't get more refreshing than this gin cocktail. If you like your drinks on the sweet side, top yours off with lemon-lime soda instead of club soda.
—*Taste of Home Test Kitchen*

TAKES: 5 min. • **MAKES:** 1 serving

  1 tsp. sugar
  2 slices cucumber
  4 basil sprigs
  2 oz. gin
     Crushed ice
     Club soda

Muddle sugar, cucumber and basil in an old-fashioned glass. Add gin and crushed ice. Top with club soda and stir.
1 SERVING 146 cal., 0 fat (0 sat. fat), 0 chol., 1mg sod., 5g carb. (4g sugars, 0 fiber), 0 pro.

MAPLE BLACKBERRY MOJITO

This refreshing cocktail is how you take advantage of prime berry season during the summer months. I've also used other types of fruit, including raspberries, kiwi and strawberries.
—*Donna Noel, Gray, ME*

TAKES: 10 min. • **MAKES:** 1 serving

  4 fresh or frozen blackberries, thawed
  5 fresh mint leaves
  1 Tbsp. maple syrup
  1 lime wedge
  ¼ cup club soda, chilled
 1½ oz. light rum
  ½ to ¾ cup ice cubes

In a glass, muddle the blackberries and mint with maple syrup. Squeeze lime wedge into the glass. Stir in club soda and rum. Strain into a chilled glass; serve with ice.
½ CUP 160 cal., 0 fat (0 sat. fat), 0 chol., 18mg sod., 16g carb. (13g sugars, 1g fiber), 0 pro.

TIPSY ICED COFFEE

My family loves this frozen coffee with amaretto and whipped cream. Serve it at a brunch or as an after-dinner treat.
—*Sonya Labbe, West Hollywood, CA*

PREP: 10 min. + freezing
MAKES: 8 servings

  4 cups strong brewed coffee
  ½ cup amaretto
  ¼ cup plus 3 Tbsp. sugar, divided
  ⅔ cup heavy whipping cream

1. In a large bowl, whisk the coffee, amaretto and ¼ cup sugar. Cool to room temperature.
2. Transfer to an 8-in. square dish. Freeze for 1 hour. Stir with a fork. Freeze 2-3 hours longer or until completely frozen, stirring every 30 minutes.
3. In a small bowl, beat cream until it begins to thicken. Add remaining 3 Tbsp. sugar; beat until stiff peaks form. Cover and refrigerate until serving.
4. To serve, stir mixture with a fork; spoon into glasses. Top with whipped cream. Serve immediately.
1 CUP WITH 2 TBSP. WHIPPED CREAM 165 cal., 7g fat (5g sat. fat), 23mg chol., 7mg sod., 17g carb. (17g sugars, 0 fiber), 1g pro.

MANGO ORANGE QUENCHER

Serve this beautiful beverage at your next brunch in place of mimosas. Just chill the base an hour before adding the club soda.
—Taste of Home *Test Kitchen*

PREP: 10 min. + chilling
MAKES: 13 servings (about 2½ qt.)

    4   cups mango nectar
    2   cups orange juice
    2   Tbsp. lime juice
    1   bottle (1 liter) club soda, chilled
        Lime slices, optional

1. In a large pitcher, combine the nectar and juices. Refrigerate at least 1 hour.
2. Just before serving, stir in club soda. Serve in champagne flutes or wine glasses. Garnish with lime slices if desired.
¾ CUP 58 cal., 0 fat (0 sat. fat), 0 chol., 19mg sod., 14g carb. (12g sugars, 0 fiber), 0 pro. **DIABETIC EXCHANGES** 1 fruit.

WASABI CRAB CAKES

With wasabi in both the crab cakes and the dipping sauce, this festive appetizer brings its own heat to any party.
—*Marie Rizzio, Interlochen, MI*

PREP: 35 min. • **BAKE:** 15 min.
MAKES: 2 dozen (½ cup sauce)

    1   medium sweet red pepper, finely
        chopped
    1   celery rib, finely chopped
    ⅓   cup plus ½ cup dry bread crumbs,
        divided
    3   green onions, finely chopped
    2   large egg whites
    3   Tbsp. fat-free mayonnaise
    ¼   tsp. prepared wasabi
    1½ cups lump crabmeat, drained
        Cooking spray

SAUCE
    1   celery rib, finely chopped
    ⅓   cup fat-free mayonnaise
    1   green onion, finely chopped
    1   Tbsp. sweet pickle relish
    ½   tsp. prepared wasabi

1. Preheat oven to 425°. Combine red pepper, celery, ⅓ cup bread crumbs, green onions, egg whites, mayonnaise and wasabi. Fold in crab.
2. Place remaining ½ cup bread crumbs in a shallow bowl. Drop a heaping tablespoonful of the crab mixture into crumbs. Gently coat and shape into a ¾-in.-thick patty; place on a baking sheet coated with cooking spray. Repeat with the remaining mixture.
3. Spritz crab cakes with cooking spray. Bake until golden brown, 15-18 minutes, turning once. Meanwhile, combine sauce ingredients. Serve with crab cakes.
1 CRAB CAKE WITH 1 TSP. SAUCE 31 cal., 1g fat (0 sat. fat), 8mg chol., 148mg sod., 4g carb. (1g sugars, 1g fiber), 2g pro.

CONTEST-WINNING GRILLED MUSHROOMS

Mushrooms cooked over hot coals always taste good, but this easy recipe makes them taste fantastic! As the mother of two, I love to cook entire meals on the grill. It's fun spending time outdoors with the kids.
—*Melanie Knoll, Marshalltown, IA*

TAKES: 15 min. • **MAKES:** 4 servings

½ lb. medium fresh mushrooms
¼ cup butter, melted
½ tsp. dill weed
½ tsp. garlic salt
  Grilled lemon wedges, optional

1. Thread mushrooms on 4 metal or soaked wooden skewers. Combine butter, dill and garlic salt; brush over mushrooms.
2. Grill, covered, over medium-high heat until tender, 10-15 minutes, basting and turning every 5 minutes. Serve with grilled lemon wedges if desired.
1 SKEWER 77 cal., 8g fat (5g sat. fat), 20mg chol., 230mg sod., 2g carb. (1g sugars, 0 fiber), 1g pro.

TEST KITCHEN TIP

Skewers make these ready-to-serve and fun to eat, but you can cook them in a grill basket instead—it'll save prep time and let you "rescue" smaller mushrooms from overcooking.

GRILLED BRUSCHETTA

This is my go-to appetizer in the summer when tomatoes and basil are fresh from the garden. The balsamic glaze takes this recipe over the top. I like to use an olive oil infused with basil or Tuscan herbs, but the recipe works well with plain olive oil too.
—*Brittany Allyn, Mesa, AZ*

PREP: 30 min. • **GRILL:** 5 min.
MAKES: 16 servings

- ½   cup balsamic vinegar
- 1½ cups chopped and seeded plum tomatoes
- 2   Tbsp. finely chopped shallot
- 1   Tbsp. minced fresh basil
- 2   tsp. plus 3 Tbsp. olive oil, divided
- 1   garlic clove, minced
- 16 slices French bread baguette (½ in. thick)
      Sea salt
      Grated Parmesan cheese

1. In a small saucepan, bring vinegar to a boil; cook until liquid is reduced to 3 Tbsp., 8-10 minutes. Remove from heat. Meanwhile, combine tomatoes, shallot, basil, 2 tsp. olive oil and garlic. Cover and refrigerate until serving.
2. Brush remaining 3 Tbsp. olive oil over both sides of baguette slices. Grill, uncovered, over medium heat until golden brown on both sides.
3. Top toasts with the tomato mixture. Drizzle with balsamic syrup; sprinkle with sea salt and Parmesan. Serve immediately.
1 PIECE 58 cal., 3g fat (0 sat. fat), 0 chol., 49mg sod., 7g carb. (3g sugars, 0 fiber), 1g pro. **DIABETIC EXCHANGES** ½ starch, ½ fat.

SANTORINI LAMB SLIDERS

I love lamb burgers, so I created a crowd-friendly slider version. The tzatziki sauce is best made a day or two in advance to allow the flavors to mingle.
—*Cristina Certano, Colorado Springs, CO*

PREP: 30 min. + chilling • **GRILL:** 10 min.
MAKES: 10 sliders

- 1   cup plain Greek yogurt
- ½   cup shredded peeled cucumber
- 1¼   tsp. salt, divided
- 1   lb. ground lamb
- 1   Tbsp. grated lemon zest
- 4   garlic cloves, minced and divided
- 2   tsp. dried oregano
- ¼   tsp. plus ⅛ tsp. pepper, divided
- 1   tsp. lemon juice
- 1   tsp. dill weed
- 10   mini buns or mini ciabatta buns
- 10   Bibb lettuce leaves or Boston lettuce leaves
- 1   medium red onion, thinly sliced
- 1   cup crumbled feta cheese

1. Line a strainer or colander with 4 layers of cheesecloth or 1 coffee filter; place over a bowl. Place yogurt in the prepared strainer; cover with sides of cheesecloth. Refrigerate 2-4 hours. Meanwhile, place the cucumber in a colander over a plate; sprinkle with ¼ tsp. salt and toss. Let stand 30 minutes.
2. For burgers, in a large bowl, combine lamb, lemon zest, half the minced garlic, oregano, ¾ tsp. salt and ¼ tsp. pepper, mixing lightly but thoroughly. Shape mixture into ten ½-in.-thick patties. Refrigerate 30 minutes.
3. For sauce, remove yogurt from cheesecloth to a bowl; discard strained liquid. Squeeze cucumber and blot dry with paper towels. Add cucumber, lemon juice, dill, and the remaining minced garlic, ¼ tsp. salt and ⅛ tsp. pepper to yogurt, stirring until combined.
4. Grill burgers, covered, over medium heat 3-4 minutes on each side or until a thermometer reads 160°. Grill buns over medium heat, cut sides down, for 30-60 seconds or until toasted. Serve burgers on buns with lettuce, red onion, feta and sauce.
1 SLIDER 228 cal., 12g fat (5g sat. fat), 43mg chol., 531mg sod., 16g carb. (3g sugars, 1g fiber), 14g pro.

BERRY-BEET SALAD P. 54

SALADS &
DRESSINGS

MEATLESS TACO SALAD

This colorful salad brings together all your favorite taco ingredients—minus the ground beef. And you won't miss the meat at all! The guacamole dressing is thick and creamy.
—*Kimberly Dray, Pflugerville, TX*

TAKES: 20 min. • **MAKES:** 2 servings

- ⅓ cup guacamole
- ¼ cup sour cream
- 1 Tbsp. prepared Italian salad dressing
- 1 Tbsp. chopped green onions
- 2 Tbsp. chopped green pepper
- ¼ tsp. pepper
- ¼ tsp. chili powder
- 3 cups shredded lettuce
- 8 cherry tomatoes, halved
- ½ cup canned kidney beans, rinsed and drained
- ¼ cup sliced ripe olives
- ½ cup crushed corn chips
- ½ cup shredded cheddar cheese

1. In a small bowl, combine the first 7 ingredients; set aside.
2. In a large bowl, combine the lettuce, tomatoes, beans and olives.
3. Arrange lettuce mixture on 2 serving plates; top with guacamole mixture. Sprinkle with corn chips and cheese.
1 SERVING 486 cal., 33g fat (12g sat. fat), 35mg chol., 849mg sod., 34g carb. (7g sugars, 9g fiber), 16g pro.

READER REVIEW

"Love, love, love this recipe as one can use a variety of beans (kidney, chili, red beans). Same with the dressing: Russian, Catalina, etc."
—MS11145, TASTEOFHOME.COM

ORZO VEGETABLE SALAD

Heading to a cookout and need something to share? Tangy lemon dressing over cool orzo and fresh vegetables is everything you could want in a summer dish.
—*Terri Crandall, Gardnerville, NV*

TAKES: 30 min. • **MAKES:** 6 servings

- ½ cup uncooked orzo pasta
- 3 plum tomatoes, chopped
- 1 cup marinated quartered artichoke hearts, chopped
- 1 cup coarsely chopped fresh spinach
- 2 green onions, chopped
- ½ cup crumbled feta cheese
- 1 Tbsp. capers, drained

DRESSING
- ⅓ cup olive oil
- 4 tsp. lemon juice
- 1 Tbsp. minced fresh tarragon or 1 tsp. dried tarragon
- 2 tsp. grated lemon zest
- 2 tsp. rice vinegar
- ½ tsp. salt
- ¼ tsp. pepper

1. Cook orzo according to the package directions.
2. Meanwhile, in a large bowl, combine the tomatoes, artichokes, spinach, onions, cheese and capers. In a small bowl, whisk the dressing ingredients.
3. Drain orzo and rinse in cold water. Add to the vegetable mixture.
4. Pour dressing over salad; toss to coat. Chill until serving.
⅔ CUP 259 cal., 19g fat (4g sat. fat), 5mg chol., 460mg sod., 18g carb. (2g sugars, 2g fiber), 4g pro.

TANGY BLUE CHEESE DRESSING

Caramelized onions add a depth of flavor you won't find in a store-bought dressing. Keep this mixture on hand to add zip as needed to a sandwich spread, crostini topper or celery dip.
—*Alisha Goins, Sabin, MN*

PREP: 10 min. • **COOK:** 35 min.
MAKES: 2½ cups

- 1 cup chopped sweet onion
- 2 tsp. canola oil
- 1 cup reduced-fat mayonnaise
- ½ cup reduced-fat sour cream
- ½ cup buttermilk
- 1 tsp. hot pepper sauce
- ¼ tsp. Worcestershire sauce
- ½ cup crumbled blue cheese

1. In a large skillet, saute onion in oil until softened. Reduce heat to medium-low; cook, uncovered, for 30-35 minutes or until deep golden brown, stirring occasionally. Set aside to cool.
2. In a small bowl, whisk the mayonnaise, sour cream, buttermilk, pepper sauce and Worcestershire sauce. Stir in cheese and onion. Store in an airtight container in the refrigerator for up to 2 weeks.
2 TBSP. 70 cal., 6g fat (2g sat. fat), 9mg chol., 156mg sod., 3g carb. (2g sugars, 0 fiber), 1g pro. **DIABETIC EXCHANGES** 1 fat.

FIRE & ICE TOMATOES

You won't miss the salt in this refreshing tomato salad! It's well-seasoned with cayenne pepper, mustard seed and vinegar but not the least bit spicy. This dish is always a hit at potlucks.
—*Nan Rickey, Yuma, AZ*

PREP: 10 min. • **COOK:** 5 min. + chilling
MAKES: 8 servings

- 5 large tomatoes, cut into wedges
- 1 medium onion, sliced
- ¾ cup white vinegar
- 6 Tbsp. sugar
- 3 tsp. mustard seed
- ¼ tsp. cayenne pepper
- 1 large cucumber, sliced

1. Place tomatoes and onion in a large heatproof nonreactive bowl. In a small saucepan, combine vinegar, sugar, water, mustard seed and cayenne; bring to a boil. Cook 1 minute, stirring to dissolve sugar; pour carefully over tomato mixture. Cool completely.
2. Stir in cucumber. Refrigerate, covered, overnight.
¾ CUP 72 cal., 1g fat (0 sat. fat), 0 chol., 7mg sod., 17g carb. (14g sugars, 2g fiber), 2g pro. **DIABETIC EXCHANGES** 1 vegetable, ½ starch.

POPPY SEED DRESSING

The best way to dress up fruit all year long is with this sweet and tangy topping.
—*Patricia Staudt, Marble Rock, IA*

TAKES: 5 min. • **MAKES:** 12 servings

- 1 cup canola oil
- ⅓ cup white vinegar
- ¾ cup sugar
- 1½ tsp. onion salt
- 1 tsp. ground mustard
- 1 Tbsp. poppy seeds
  Fresh fruit or salad greens of choice

Place the first 5 ingredients in a blender; cover and process until the sugar is dissolved. Stir in the poppy seeds. Refrigerate, covered, until serving. Serve with fruit or salad greens.
2 TBSP. DRESSING 219 cal., 19g fat (1g sat. fat), 0 chol., 225mg sod., 13g carb. (13g sugars, 0 fiber), 0 pro.

TEST KITCHEN TIP

Drizzle this poppy seed dressing on top of coleslaw, a strawberry salad or a side of fruit. Switch things up by adding fresh or frozen raspberries to the blended ingredients for a lovely raspberry poppy seed dressing.

DAD'S GREEK SALAD

The heart of a Greek salad is in the olives, feta and fresh veggies. This is the time to splurge on some gorgeous Greek olives!
—*Arge Salvatori, Waldwick, NJ*

TAKES: 20 min. • **MAKES:** 8 servings

- 4 large tomatoes, seeded and coarsely chopped
- 2½ cups thinly sliced English cucumbers
- 1 small red onion, halved and thinly sliced
- ¼ cup olive oil
- 3 Tbsp. red wine vinegar
- ¼ tsp. salt
- ⅛ tsp. pepper
- ¼ tsp. dried oregano, optional
- ¾ cup pitted Greek olives
- ¾ cup crumbled feta cheese

Place tomatoes, cucumbers and onion in a large bowl. In a small bowl, whisk oil, vinegar, salt and pepper and, if desired, oregano until blended. Drizzle over salad; toss to coat. Top with olives and cheese.

¾ CUP 148 cal., 12g fat (2g sat. fat), 6mg chol., 389mg sod., 7g carb. (3g sugars, 2g fiber), 3g pro. **DIABETIC EXCHANGES** 2 vegetable, 2 fat.

READER REVIEW

"We thoroughly enjoyed this salad! It is very flavorful. I love oregano dressings, and the feta was just right. Colorful too. This is a keeper!"
—ANNRMS, TASTEOFHOME.COM

SUMMERTIME SLAW

As a change from mayonnaise-laden slaw, I created this refreshing alternative. It uses many of the garden vegetables I grow, so it's also economical. I serve it at our family reunion each Fourth of July, and it's always a big hit at get-togethers.
—*Sharon Payne, Mayfield, KY*

PREP: 25 min. + cooling
COOK: 10 min. + chilling
MAKES: 12 servings

- ¾ cup sugar
- ¾ cup white vinegar
- ⅓ cup canola oil
- 1 Tbsp. water
- 1 tsp. salt
- 1 tsp. pepper
- ½ tsp. crushed red pepper flakes, optional
- 1 pkg. (14 oz.) coleslaw mix
- 2 medium tomatoes, peeled, seeded and chopped
- 1 large onion, chopped
- 1 small green pepper, chopped
- 1 small sweet red pepper, chopped
- ½ cup sweet pickle relish

1. For dressing, in a large saucepan, combine the sugar, vinegar, oil, water, salt, pepper and, if desired, pepper flakes. Cook and stir over medium heat until the mixture comes to a boil. Cook 2 minutes longer or until sugar is dissolved. Cool to room temperature, stirring several times.
2. In a large salad bowl, combine the coleslaw mix, tomatoes, onion, peppers and pickle relish. Add the dressing and toss to coat. Cover and refrigerate overnight. Serve with a slotted spoon.
¾ CUP 138 cal., 6g fat (1g sat. fat), 0 chol., 291mg sod., 21g carb. (17g sugars, 2g fiber), 1g pro.

TZATZIKI POTATO SALAD

My son has an egg allergy, so this egg-free potato salad is perfect for him. For extra color, add radishes, apple and garlic dill pickles.
—*Cindy Romberg, Mississauga, ON*

PREP: 25 min. + chilling
MAKES: 12 servings

- 3 lbs. small red potatoes, halved
- 1 carton (12 oz.) refrigerated tzatziki sauce
- 2 celery ribs, thinly sliced
- ½ cup plain Greek yogurt
- 2 green onions, chopped
- 2 Tbsp. snipped fresh dill
- 2 Tbsp. minced fresh parsley
- ½ tsp. salt
- ¼ tsp. celery salt
- ¼ tsp. pepper
- 1 Tbsp. minced fresh mint, optional

1. Place potatoes in a Dutch oven; add water to cover. Bring to a boil. Reduce heat; cook, uncovered, until potatoes are tender, 10-15 minutes. Drain; cool completely.
2. In a small bowl, mix tzatziki sauce, celery, yogurt, green onions, dill, parsley, salt, celery salt, pepper and, if desired, mint. Spoon over potatoes; toss to coat. Refrigerate, covered, until cold.
¾ CUP 128 cal., 3g fat (2g sat. fat), 7mg chol., 190mg sod., 21g carb. (3g sugars, 2g fiber), 4g pro. **DIABETIC EXCHANGES** 1½ starch, ½ fat.

SUMMER HARVEST GRILLED PANZANELLA SALAD

This colorful and healthy salad is a delicious twist on the classic Italian dish. It makes the most of simple, seasonal ingredients, combining the smoky flavors of grilled vegetables, juicy tomatoes, crusty bread and a zesty vinaigrette. Panzanella salad is best enjoyed after the bread has soaked up the flavors and juices from the veggies and dressing.
—Olga Kouloufakos, Lake Pleasant, MA

PREP: 20 min. • **GRILL:** 5 min. + standing
MAKES: 8 servings

- 1   medium eggplant, quartered lengthwise
- 1   medium zucchini, quartered lengthwise
- 1   medium red onion, sliced into ¼-in. slices
- 3   cups cubed ciabatta bread
- 2   cups cherry tomatoes
- 1   can (14 oz.) large water-packed artichoke hearts, drained and halved lengthwise
- ¼   cup extra virgin olive oil
- 2   Tbsp. chopped fresh basil or thyme
- ½   tsp. salt
- ¼   tsp. pepper

DRESSING
- 2   Tbsp. red wine vinegar
- 2   Tbsp. extra virgin olive oil
- 1   tsp. Dijon mustard
- 1   garlic clove, minced
- ½   tsp. salt
- ¼   tsp. pepper

1. Brush the first 6 ingredients with oil. Place onion slices, artichoke hearts, tomatoes and bread into grill basket. Grill, along with eggplant and zucchini, covered, over medium-high heat until lightly charred, 4-6 minutes, turning occasionally.
2. Remove eggplant and zucchini to a cutting board. Cut into bite-sized pieces. Transfer to a large serving bowl with the other grilled items. Sprinkle with basil, salt and pepper; toss gently.

3. In a small bowl, whisk the dressing ingredients; drizzle over salad. Toss gently to coat. Let stand for 10 minutes before serving.
1 CUP 263 cal., 12g fat (2g sat. fat), 0 chol., 643mg sod., 37g carb. (6g sugars, 4g fiber), 6g pro.

HOMEMADE RANCH DRESSING & DIP MIX

Keep this versatile mix on hand to use for stirring together either a dip or a salad dressing. They're both delicious!
—Taste of Home Test Kitchen

TAKES: 5 min.
MAKES: about ¾ cup mix
(for 4 batches dressing/dip)

- ⅓   cup buttermilk blend powder
- ¼   cup dried parsley flakes
- 2   Tbsp. dried minced onion
- 2   tsp. salt
- 2   tsp. garlic powder

ADDITIONAL INGREDIENTS FOR SALAD DRESSING
- 1   cup reduced-fat mayonnaise
- 1   cup plus 6 Tbsp. buttermilk

ADDITIONAL INGREDIENTS FOR DIP
- 2   cups reduced-fat sour cream

1. Combine the first 5 ingredients. Store in an airtight container in a cool, dry place for up to 1 year.
2. For 1 batch salad dressing: In a small bowl, whisk mayonnaise, buttermilk and 3 Tbsp. mix. Refrigerate at least 1 hour. Yield: about 2 cups.
3. For 1 batch dip: In a small bowl, combine sour cream and 3 Tbsp. mix. Refrigerate at least 2 hours. Serve with assorted crackers and fresh vegetables.
2 TBSP. DRESSING/DIP 62 cal., 5g fat (1g sat. fat), 7mg chol., 219mg sod., 3g carb. (2g sugars, 0 fiber), 1g pro.

VERMICELLI PASTA SALAD

I started making this salad because it's loaded with peppers, my husband's favorite. Don't be surprised when there are no leftovers to take home after the family reunion, picnic or church potluck.
—Janie Colle, Hutchinson, KS

PREP: 20 min. + chilling
MAKES: 10 servings

- 12 oz. uncooked vermicelli
- 1   bottle (16 oz.) creamy Italian salad dressing
- 1   small green pepper, chopped
- 1   small sweet red pepper, chopped
- 6   green onions, chopped
- 1   tsp. dill seed
- 1   tsp. caraway seeds
- 1   tsp. poppy seeds

Cook vermicelli according to the package directions. Drain; transfer to a large bowl. Add the remaining ingredients; toss to coat. Refrigerate until cold.
¾ CUP 309 cal., 18g fat (3g sat. fat), 0 chol., 404mg sod., 30g carb. (5g sugars, 2g fiber), 5g pro.

GUACAMOLE TOSSED SALAD

The fresh blend of avocados, tomatoes, red onion and greens in this salad gets additional pizazz from crumbled bacon and a slightly spicy vinaigrette.
—*Lori Fischer, Chino Hills, CA*

TAKES: 15 min. • **MAKES:** 4 servings

- 2 medium tomatoes, seeded and chopped
- ½ small red onion, sliced and separated into rings
- 6 bacon strips, cooked and crumbled
- ⅓ cup canola oil
- 2 Tbsp. cider vinegar
- 1 tsp. salt
- ¼ tsp. pepper
- ¼ tsp. hot pepper sauce
- 2 large ripe avocados, peeled and cubed
- 4 cups torn salad greens

1. In a large bowl, combine the tomatoes, onion and bacon; set aside.
2. In a small bowl, whisk the oil, vinegar, salt, pepper and hot pepper sauce. Pour over the tomato mixture; toss gently. Add avocados.
3. Place greens in a large salad bowl; add avocado mixture and toss to coat.
1 SERVING 531 cal., 51g fat (7g sat. fat), 12mg chol., 868mg sod., 17g carb. (3g sugars, 10g fiber), 9g pro.

AVOCADO SALAD DRESSING

Buttermilk and plain yogurt create the base for this thick dressing, which gets its color from avocado and parsley. The mild mixture is refreshing when dolloped over a tossed green salad.
—Taste of Home *Test Kitchen*

TAKES: 5 min. • **MAKES:** 2 cups

- 1 cup buttermilk
- ½ cup fat-free plain yogurt
- 1 medium ripe avocado, peeled and sliced
- 2 green onions, chopped
- ¼ cup minced fresh parsley
- ½ tsp. salt
- ½ tsp. garlic powder
- ¼ tsp. dill weed
- ⅛ tsp. pepper
  Salad greens and vegetables of your choice

Combine the first 9 ingredients in a food processor; cover and process until smooth. Serve over salad. Store in the refrigerator.
2 TBSP. 25 cal., 1g fat (0 sat. fat), 1mg chol., 109mg sod., 2g carb. (1g sugars, 1g fiber), 1g pro.

AVOCADO SALAD DRESSING TIPS

What kind of lettuce is this dressing good with? Spring greens and hearty lettuces like romaine go well with this slightly thick dressing. For a double dose of avocado, pair it with Guacamole Tossed Salad (recipe at left).

How long does this salad dressing last? Avocado salad dressing will last for up to 5 days when stored in an airtight container in the refrigerator.

Will the avocado go brown in a salad? Avocado will naturally turn brown when it's exposed to air. To keep the dressing's pretty green color, add a splash of fresh squeezed lime juice.

DELI-STYLE PASTA SALAD

Pasta provides a base for this tongue-tingling make-ahead salad. It has lots of fresh and satisfying ingredients topped with a flavorful dressing. It's terrific to serve to company or take to a potluck.
—*Joyce McLennan, Algonac, MI*

PREP: 20 min. + chilling
MAKES: 12 servings

- 7 oz. tricolor spiral pasta
- 6 oz. thinly sliced hard salami, julienned
- 6 oz. provolone cheese, cubed
- 1 can (2¼ oz.) sliced ripe olives, drained
- 1 small red onion, thinly sliced
- 1 small zucchini, halved and thinly sliced
- ½ cup chopped green pepper
- ½ cup chopped sweet red pepper
- ¼ cup minced fresh parsley
- ¼ cup grated Parmesan cheese

DRESSING
- ½ cup olive oil
- ¼ cup red wine vinegar
- 1 garlic clove, minced
- 1½ tsp. ground mustard
- 1 tsp. dried basil
- 1 tsp. dried oregano
- ¼ tsp. salt
  Dash pepper
- 2 medium tomatoes, cut into wedges

1. Cook the pasta according to the package directions; rinse in cold water and drain. Place in a large bowl; add the next 9 ingredients.
2. In a jar with tight-fitting lid, combine oil, vinegar, garlic, mustard, basil, oregano, salt and pepper; shake well.
3. Pour dressing over salad; toss to coat. Cover and chill 8 hours or overnight. Toss before serving. Garnish with tomatoes.
1 CUP 273 cal., 18g fat (6g sat. fat), 25mg chol., 536mg sod., 17g carb. (3g sugars, 1g fiber), 11g pro.

SUMMER BUZZ FRUIT SALAD

For picnics, cookouts and showers, we make a sweet salad of watermelon, cherries, blueberries and microgreens. No matter where I take it, it always delivers on the wow factor.
—*Kaliska Russell, Talkeetna, AK*

TAKES: 15 min. • **MAKES:** 6 servings

- 2 cups watermelon balls
- 2 cups fresh sweet cherries, pitted and halved
- 1 cup fresh blueberries
- ½ cup cubed English cucumber
- ½ cup microgreens or torn mixed salad greens
- ½ cup crumbled feta cheese
- 3 fresh mint leaves, thinly sliced
- ¼ cup honey
- 1 Tbsp. lemon juice
- 1 tsp. grated lemon zest

Combine the first 7 ingredients. In a small bowl, whisk together remaining ingredients. Drizzle over salad; toss.
¾ CUP 131 cal., 2g fat (1g sat. fat), 5mg chol., 94mg sod., 28g carb. (24g sugars, 2g fiber), 3g pro. **DIABETIC EXCHANGES** 1 starch, 1 fruit.

GRILLED ROMAINE SALAD

For a great-tasting salad, try this recipe on the grill! It's equally good with any dressing of your choice.
—*Susan Court, Pewaukee, WI*

TAKES: 20 min. • **MAKES:** 12 servings

- ⅓ cup plus 3 Tbsp. olive oil, divided
- 2 Tbsp. white wine vinegar
- 1 Tbsp. dill weed
- ½ tsp. garlic powder
- ⅛ tsp. crushed red pepper flakes
- ⅛ tsp. salt
- 6 green onions
- 4 plum tomatoes, halved
- 1 large cucumber, peeled and halved lengthwise
- 2 romaine hearts, halved lengthwise

1. For dressing, in a small bowl, whisk together ⅓ cup olive oil with the white wine vinegar, dill, garlic powder, red pepper flakes and salt.
2. Brush the onions, tomatoes, cucumber and romaine with remaining 3 Tbsp. oil. Grill the onions, tomatoes and cucumber, uncovered, over medium heat until onions are crisp-tender, 4-5 minutes on each side. Grill romaine until heated through, 30 seconds on each side.
3. Place romaine on a serving platter. Chop vegetables and sprinkle over romaine. Drizzle salad with dressing. Serve immediately.
¾ CUP 98 cal., 10g fat (1g sat. fat), 0 chol., 30mg sod., 3g carb. (1g sugars, 1g fiber), 1g pro.

GRILLED THREE-POTATO SALAD

Everyone in our extended family loves to cook, so I put together all our favorite recipes in a cookbook to be handed down from generation to generation. This delicious twist on traditional potato salad comes from that cookbook.
—*Suzette Jury, Keene, CA*

PREP: 25 min. + cooling • **GRILL:** 10 min.
MAKES: 6 servings

- ¾ lb. Yukon Gold potatoes
- ¾ lb. red potatoes
- 1 medium sweet potato, peeled
- ½ cup thinly sliced green onions
- ¼ cup canola oil
- 2 to 3 Tbsp. white wine vinegar
- 1 Tbsp. Dijon mustard
- 1 tsp. salt
- ½ tsp. celery seed
- ¼ tsp. pepper

1. Place potatoes and sweet potato in a Dutch oven; cover with water. Bring to a boil. Reduce heat; cover and simmer for 15-20 minutes or until tender. Drain and cool. Cut into 1-in. chunks.
2. Place potato mixture in an oiled grill wok or basket. Grill, uncovered, over medium heat for 8-12 minutes or until browned, stirring frequently. Transfer to a large salad bowl; add onions.
3. Whisk the oil, vinegar, mustard, salt, celery seed and pepper. Drizzle over potato mixture and toss to coat. Serve warm or at room temperature.
NOTE If you do not have a grill wok or basket, use a disposable foil pan. Poke holes in the bottom of the pan with a meat fork to allow liquid to drain.
¾ CUP 191 cal., 10g fat (1g sat. fat), 0 chol., 466mg sod., 24g carb. (3g sugars, 3g fiber), 3g pro. **DIABETIC EXCHANGES** 2 fat, 1½ starch.

OVERNIGHT SLAW

Think of slaw as a side for all seasons—but especially summer—no matter what you're serving. Use your food processor for even easier prep.
—*Nancy Brown, Janesville, WI*

PREP: 15 min. + chilling
MAKES: 8 servings

- 1   medium head cabbage, shredded
- 4   mild white onions, thinly sliced
- 2   large carrots, shredded
- ½   cup vinegar
- ½   cup sugar
- 1   tsp. ground mustard
- 1   tsp. celery seed
- 1   tsp. salt
- ⅛   tsp. pepper
- ½   cup canola oil

1. Combine cabbage, onions and carrots; set aside.
2. In a saucepan, combine vinegar, sugar, mustard, celery seed, salt and pepper; bring to a boil, stirring until the sugar is dissolved. Remove from heat and stir in oil. Pour over cabbage mixture. Cool to room temperature. Cover and refrigerate overnight; stir several times before serving.
¾ CUP 238 cal., 14g fat (2g sat. fat), 0 chol., 325mg sod., 28g carb. (21g sugars, 5g fiber), 3g pro.

SWEET CORN-TOMATO SALAD

I always make this for family events and parties. It reminds me of all the fun barbecues and picnics over the years. Fresh corn and basil make a huge difference in this recipe.
—*Jessica Kleinbaum, Plant City, FL*

PREP: 15 min. • **COOK:** 10 min. + chilling
MAKES: 10 servings

- 8   medium ears sweet corn, husked
- 1   large sweet red pepper, chopped
- 2   cups cherry tomatoes, halved
- 1   small red onion, finely chopped
- ¼   cup coarsely chopped fresh basil

DRESSING
- ½   cup canola oil
- ¼   cup rice vinegar
- 2   Tbsp. lime juice
- 1¼ tsp. salt
- ½   to 1 tsp. hot pepper sauce
- ½   tsp. garlic powder
- ½   tsp. grated lime zest
- ¼   tsp. pepper

1. Place corn in a large stockpot; add water to cover. Bring to a boil. Cook, covered, until crisp-tender, 6-8 minutes; drain. Cool slightly. Cut corn from cobs and place in a large bowl. Stir in red pepper, tomatoes, onion and basil.
2. In a small bowl, whisk the dressing ingredients until blended. Pour over the corn mixture; toss to coat. Refrigerate, covered, at least 1 hour.
¾ CUP 192 cal., 12g fat (1g sat. fat), 0 chol., 407mg sod., 21g carb. (9g sugars, 3g fiber), 3g pro. **DIABETIC EXCHANGES** 2 fat, 1 starch, 1 vegetable.

GRILLED MEDITERRANEAN ZUCCHINI SALAD

This zucchini salad is the best side dish. I also like to add summer squash for a variation, or crumbled goat cheese when I want some extra creaminess.
—*Rashanda Cobbins, Aurora, CO*

TAKES: 20 min. • **MAKES:** 4 servings

3 medium zucchini, thinly sliced
¼ cup olive oil, divided
¼ tsp. salt
¼ tsp. pepper
¼ cup chopped red onion
3 Tbsp. minced fresh mint
2 Tbsp. minced fresh parsley
1 medium lemon, juiced and zested
⅓ cup crumbled feta cheese
3 Tbsp. pine nuts, toasted

1. In a large bowl, combine zucchini and 2 Tbsp. olive oil. Add salt and pepper; toss to coat. Transfer to a grill wok or open grill basket; place on grill rack. Grill, covered, over medium-high heat until the zucchini is crisp-tender, 5-10 minutes, turning occasionally.
2. Transfer zucchini to a serving bowl; sprinkle with the remaining 2 Tbsp. olive oil and the red onion. When zucchini has cooled slightly, sprinkle with mint, parsley, lemon juice, lemon zest and cheese. Stir gently. Sprinkle with pine nuts before serving.
1 CUP 220 cal., 20g fat (3g sat. fat), 5mg chol., 252mg sod., 8g carb. (4g sugars, 3g fiber), 5g pro.

TEST KITCHEN TIPS

Try adding a touch of honey to the dressing if your melon isn't super sweet. It will wake it right up!

English cucumbers are firmer and less watery than regular cukes. If you use a traditional cucumber, halve it lengthwise and use a spoon to scoop out the seeds before cubing it.

WATERMELON & SPINACH SALAD

Summer is the perfect time to toss up this watermelon salad. You'd never expect it, but the spinach is awesome here. Eat it and feel cool on even the hottest days.
—*Marjorie Au, Honolulu, HI*

TAKES: 30 min. • **MAKES:** 8 servings

- ¼ cup rice vinegar or white wine vinegar
- 1 Tbsp. grated lime zest
- 2 Tbsp. lime juice
- 2 Tbsp. canola oil
- 4 tsp. minced fresh gingerroot
- 2 garlic cloves, minced
- ½ tsp. salt
- ¼ tsp. sugar
- ¼ tsp. pepper

SALAD
- 4 cups fresh baby spinach or arugula
- 3 cups cubed seedless watermelon
- 2 cups cubed cantaloupe
- 2 cups cubed English cucumber
- ½ cup chopped fresh cilantro
- 2 green onions, chopped

For dressing, in a small bowl, whisk the first 9 ingredients. In a large bowl, combine the salad ingredients. Drizzle with the dressing and toss to coat; serve immediately.

1 CUP 84 cal., 4g fat (0 sat. fat), 0 chol., 288mg sod., 13g carb. (10g sugars, 1g fiber), 1g pro. **DIABETIC EXCHANGES** 1 vegetable, 1 fat, ½ fruit.

ZUCCHINI & SUMMER SQUASH SALAD

I came up with this colorful, tasty slaw years ago for a recipe contest, and I was delighted when it won honorable mention! The recipe easily doubles and is a perfect dish to take to potlucks or family gatherings.
—*Paula Wharton, El Paso, TX*

PREP: 25 min. + chilling
MAKES: 12 servings

- 4 medium zucchini
- 2 yellow summer squash
- 1 medium sweet red pepper
- 1 medium red onion
- 1 cup fresh sugar snap peas, trimmed and halved

DRESSING
- ⅓ cup olive oil
- ¼ cup balsamic vinegar
- 2 Tbsp. reduced-fat mayonnaise
- 4 tsp. fresh sage or 1 tsp. dried sage leaves
- 2 tsp. honey
- 1 tsp. garlic powder
- 1 tsp. celery seed
- 1 tsp. dill weed
- ½ tsp. salt
- ½ tsp. pepper

1. Thinly slice zucchini, squash, red pepper and onion; place in a large bowl. Add snap peas.
2. In a small bowl, whisk the dressing ingredients until blended. Pour over vegetables; toss to coat. Refrigerate, covered, at least 3 hours.

¾ CUP 101 cal., 7g fat (1g sat. fat), 1mg chol., 124mg sod., 8g carb. (6g sugars, 2g fiber), 2g pro. **DIABETIC EXCHANGES** 1½ fat, 1 vegetable.

ROASTED GARLIC VINAIGRETTE

Roasted garlic blends with Italian seasoning, Dijon mustard, tarragon vinegar and lemon juice in this zesty dressing. Try it over greens or tomatoes.
—*Taste of Home Test Kitchen*

PREP: 40 min. + cooling • **MAKES:** ¾ cup

- 3 whole garlic bulbs
- 1 tsp. plus 2 Tbsp. olive oil, divided
- 3 Tbsp. tarragon vinegar
- 2 Tbsp. water
- 1 Tbsp. sugar
- 1 Tbsp. lemon juice
- 1½ tsp. Italian seasoning
- ½ tsp. Dijon mustard
- ¼ tsp. salt
- ⅛ tsp. pepper

1. Remove papery outer skin from garlic (do not peel or separate cloves). Cut tops off garlic bulbs. Brush cut sides with 1 tsp. oil. Wrap each bulb in heavy-duty foil. Bake at 425° for 30-35 minutes or until softened. Cool for 10-15 minutes.
2. Squeeze softened garlic into a blender. Add vinegar, water, sugar, lemon juice, Italian seasoning, mustard, salt, pepper and the remaining 2 Tbsp. oil; cover and process until smooth. Store in the refrigerator.

2 TBSP. 83 cal., 5g fat (1g sat. fat), 0 chol., 112mg sod., 8g carb. (2g sugars, 0 fiber), 1g pro. **DIABETIC EXCHANGES** 1 vegetable, 1 fat, ½ starch.

CLASSIC FRENCH DRESSING

Making salad dressings at home is easy! This recipe uses pantry staples, so it's a snap to whip up any time. It tastes wonderful on any type of greens.
—*Maron Craig Bielovitz, Elmhurst, PA*

TAKES: 10 min. • **MAKES:** 1⅔ cups

- ½ cup ketchup
- ⅓ cup sugar
- ¼ cup white vinegar
- 1 small onion, minced
- 1 garlic clove, minced
- 1 Tbsp. paprika
- ½ to 1 tsp. salt
- ½ cup vegetable oil

In a blender or food processor, combine the first 7 ingredients; cover and process until blended. While processing, gradually add the oil in a steady stream. Process until thickened. Store in the refrigerator.

2 TBSP. 100 cal., 8g fat (1g sat. fat), 0 chol., 186mg sod., 8g carb. (6g sugars, 0 fiber), 0 pro.

CRUNCHY LEMON-PESTO GARDEN SALAD

I love using vegetables straight from the garden to prepare this salad. If I pick the squash and cucumbers early enough, the skins are so tender that there's no need to remove them! Best of all, it's easily adaptable—you can use almost any garden veggies with delicious results.
—*Carmell Childs, Orangeville, UT*

TAKES: 25 min. • **MAKES:** 6 servings

- 5 Tbsp. prepared pesto
- 1 Tbsp. lemon juice
- 2 tsp. grated lemon zest
- 1½ tsp. Dijon mustard
- ¼ tsp. garlic salt
- ¼ tsp. pepper
- 2½ cups thinly sliced yellow summer squash
- 1¾ cups thinly sliced mini cucumbers
- ¾ cup fresh peas
- ½ cup shredded Parmesan cheese
- ¼ cup thinly sliced green onions
- 5 thick-sliced bacon strips, cooked and crumbled

1. In a bowl, whisk together the first 6 ingredients until blended.
2. In another bowl, combine the squash, cucumbers, peas, Parmesan and green onions.
3. Pour dressing over salad; toss to coat. Top with bacon to serve.

¾ CUP 159 cal., 11g fat (3g sat. fat), 13mg chol., 586mg sod., 8g carb. (4g sugars, 2g fiber), 8g pro. **DIABETIC EXCHANGES** 2 fat, 1 vegetable.

GINGER DRESSING

I love this flavorful dressing because it's super easy to make and uses pantry staples. It's a speedy recipe to serve with salad greens or veggies on a weeknight.
—*Rashanda Cobbins, Aurora, CO*

TAKES: 10 min. • **MAKES:** 1½ cups

- ⅓ cup rice vinegar
- 3 Tbsp. finely chopped onion
- 2 Tbsp. minced fresh gingerroot
- 2 Tbsp. soy sauce
- 1 Tbsp. honey
- ¼ tsp. pepper
- ¾ cup olive oil or peanut oil

In a blender, combine first 6 ingredients; cover and process until blended. While processing, gradually add oil in a steady stream. Chill until serving.
2 TBSP. 137 cal., 14g fat (2g sat. fat), 0 chol., 260mg sod., 4g carb. (4g sugars, 0 fiber), 0 pro.

TEST KITCHEN TIP

Ginger dressing tastes great on salads, as a meat marinade or in a stir-fry dish. It will last for up to a week in the refrigerator.

BERRY-BEET SALAD

Here's a delightfully different salad that balances the earthy flavor of beets with the natural sweetness of berries. If you prefer, substitute crumbled feta for the goat cheese.
—Amy Lyons, Mounds View, MN

PREP: 20 min. • **BAKE:** 30 min. + cooling
MAKES: 4 servings

1	each fresh red and golden beets
¼	cup balsamic vinegar
2	Tbsp. walnut oil
1	tsp. honey
	Dash salt
	Dash pepper
½	cup sliced fresh strawberries
½	cup fresh raspberries
½	cup fresh blackberries
3	Tbsp. chopped walnuts, toasted
1	shallot, thinly sliced
4	cups torn mixed salad greens
1	oz. fresh goat cheese, crumbled
1	Tbsp. fresh basil, thinly sliced

1. Place beets in an 8-in. square baking dish; add 1 in. of water. Cover and bake at 400° for 30-40 minutes or until tender.
2. Meanwhile, in a small bowl, whisk the vinegar, oil, honey, salt and pepper; set aside. Cool beets; peel and cut into thin slices.
3. In a large bowl, combine the beets, berries, walnuts and shallot. Pour the dressing over the beet mixture; toss gently to coat. Divide salad greens among 4 serving plates. Top with beet mixture; sprinkle with cheese and basil.
1 SERVING 183 cal., 12g fat (2g sat. fat), 5mg chol., 124mg sod., 18g carb. (11g sugars, 5g fiber), 4g pro. **DIABETIC EXCHANGES** 2 fat, 1 starch.

VEGETABLE COUSCOUS SALAD

This salad is great as a side with any kind of grilled meat or fish. If you want to serve it as a vegetarian main, add some crumbled goat cheese or tangy feta cheese.

—*Patricia Levenson, Santa Ana, CA*

PREP: 35 min. • **GRILL:** 10 min.
MAKES: 10 servings

- ½ cup olive oil
- ⅓ cup balsamic vinegar
- 4 tsp. capers, drained
- 4 tsp. lemon juice
- 2 garlic cloves, minced
- ¾ tsp. Dijon mustard
- 1¼ tsp. minced fresh rosemary or ½ tsp. dried rosemary, crushed
- 1¼ tsp. minced fresh thyme or ½ tsp. dried thyme
- ⅛ tsp. salt
- ⅛ tsp. pepper

SALAD
- 1 pkg. (10 oz.) uncooked couscous
- 2 medium zucchini or yellow summer squash, halved lengthwise
- 2 medium sweet yellow or red peppers, quartered
- 1 Japanese eggplant, halved lengthwise
- 2 Tbsp. olive oil
- ¼ tsp. salt
- ¼ tsp. pepper
- 1 cup grape tomatoes, halved
- ½ cup Greek olives, pitted and sliced
- 1 Tbsp. minced fresh parsley or 1 tsp. dried parsley flakes
- 1 Tbsp. minced fresh basil or 1 tsp. dried basil

1. For the dressing, in a small bowl, whisk the first 10 ingredients. Refrigerate until serving.

2. Cook couscous according to package directions. Meanwhile, brush the zucchini, peppers and eggplant with oil; sprinkle with salt and pepper. Grill, covered, over medium heat until crisp-tender, 10-12 minutes, turning once.

3. Chop grilled vegetables; place in a large bowl. Add the tomatoes, olives, parsley, basil and couscous. Pour dressing over salad and toss to coat. Serve warm or chilled.

NOTE Greek olives are also known as kalamata olives, They are almond shaped and deep purple, and range from ½ in. to 1 in. long. Rich and fruity in flavor, they can be found packed in either vinegar brine or olive oil.

¾ CUP 272 cal., 16g fat (2g sat. fat), 0 chol., 244mg sod., 29g carb. (5g sugars, 3g fiber), 5g pro. **DIABETIC EXCHANGES** 2 fat, 1½ starch, 1 vegetable.

TEST KITCHEN TIPS

Since this salad can be served warm or chilled, it's a smart make-and-take for potlucks and picnics.

The flavorful and versatile balsamic vinaigrette is great on lettuce salads too.

BALSAMIC THREE-BEAN SALAD

Here's my little girl's favorite salad. She eats it just about as fast as I can make it. Prepare it ahead so the flavors have plenty of time to get to know each other.
—*Stacey Feather, Jay, OK*

PREP: 25 min. + chilling
MAKES: 12 servings

- 2 lbs. fresh green beans, trimmed and cut into 2-in. pieces
- ½ cup balsamic vinaigrette
- ¼ cup sugar
- 1 garlic clove, minced
- ¾ tsp. salt
- 2 cans (16 oz. each) kidney beans, rinsed and drained
- 2 cans (15 oz. each) cannellini beans, rinsed and drained
- 4 fresh basil leaves, torn

1. Fill a Dutch oven three-fourths full with water; bring to a boil. Add green beans; cook, uncovered, until crisp-tender, 3-6 minutes. Drain and immediately drop into ice water. Drain and pat dry.

2. Whisk vinaigrette, sugar, garlic and salt until sugar is dissolved. Add canned beans and green beans; toss to coat. Refrigerate, covered, at least 4 hours. Stir in basil just before serving.

¾ CUP 190 cal., 3g fat (0 sat. fat), 0 chol., 462mg sod., 33g carb. (8g sugars, 9g fiber), 9g pro. **DIABETIC EXCHANGES** 1½ starch, 1 very lean meat, 1 vegetable, ½ fat.

BURRATA CAPRESE

Creamy burrata cheese and ripe tomatoes are a match made in heaven. This is a perfect appetizer for the summer months when tomatoes and basil are in season. Serve by itself or with crostini.
—*Taste of Home Test Kitchen*

TAKES: 10 min. • **MAKES:** 6 servings

- 4 oz. burrata cheese
- 4 medium tomatoes, cut into ¼-in. slices
- 10 to 12 fresh basil leaves
- 3 Tbsp. olive oil
- 1 Tbsp. balsamic vinegar
- ½ tsp. salt
- ¼ tsp. coarsely ground pepper

Place burrata in the center of a serving platter. Arrange tomato slices around the cheese; sprinkle with basil. Drizzle with oil and vinegar. Sprinkle with salt and pepper.

1 SERVING 131 cal., 11g fat (4g sat. fat), 13mg chol., 231mg sod., 5g carb. (3g sugars, 1g fiber), 4g pro.

COOL BEANS SALAD

This protein-filled dish could be served as a colorful side dish or a meatless entree. When you make it, double the recipe—because it will be gone in a flash! The basmati rice adds flavor and texture, and the dressing gives it a bit of a tang.
—*Janelle Lee, Appleton, WI*

TAKES: 20 min. • **MAKES:** 6 servings

- ½ cup olive oil
- ¼ cup red wine vinegar
- 1 Tbsp. sugar
- 1 garlic clove, minced
- 1 tsp. salt
- 1 tsp. ground cumin
- 1 tsp. chili powder
- ¼ tsp. pepper
- 3 cups cooked basmati rice
- 1 can (16 oz.) kidney beans, rinsed and drained
- 1 can (15 oz.) black beans, rinsed and drained
- 1½ cups frozen corn, thawed
- 4 green onions, sliced
- 1 small sweet red pepper, chopped
- ¼ cup minced fresh cilantro

In a large bowl, whisk the first 8 ingredients. Add the remaining ingredients; toss to coat. Chill until serving.
1⅓ CUPS 440 cal., 19g fat (3g sat. fat), 0 chol., 659mg sod., 58g carb. (5g sugars, 8g fiber), 12g pro.

STRAWBERRY VINAIGRETTE

I enjoy using strawberries in a variety of ways, including in this pretty and sweet-tart dressing. It will keep in the refrigerator for up to three days.
—*Carolyn McMunn, San Angelo, TX*

TAKES: 10 min. • **MAKES:** 2½ cups

- 1 pkg. (16 oz.) frozen unsweetened strawberries, thawed
- 6 Tbsp. lemon juice
- ¼ cup sugar
- 2 Tbsp. cider vinegar
- 2 Tbsp. olive oil
- ⅛ tsp. poppy seeds

Place strawberries in a blender; cover and process until pureed. Add lemon juice and sugar; cover and process until blended. While processing, add cider vinegar, then gradually add olive oil in a steady stream; process until thickened. Stir in poppy seeds. Transfer to a large bowl or jar; cover and store in an airtight container in the refrigerator.
2 TBSP. 31 cal., 1g fat (0 sat. fat), 0 chol., 1mg sod., 5g carb. (4g sugars, 0 fiber), 0 pro.

SOUTHERN POTATO SALAD

This potato salad with a southern twist is perfect for a church supper or potluck. The pickles add extra sweetness.
—*Gene Pitts, Wilsonville, AL*

PREP: 30 min. + chilling
MAKES: 8 servings

- 5 medium potatoes, peeled and cubed
- 6 hard-boiled large eggs, chopped
- ½ cup thinly sliced green onions
- ¼ cup chopped sweet pickles
- 1 tsp. prepared mustard
- 1 tsp. celery seed
- 1 cup mayonnaise
   Salt and pepper to taste

Place potatoes in a large saucepan; add water to cover. Bring to a boil. Reduce heat; cook, uncovered, until tender, 10-15 minutes. Drain; refrigerate until cold. Add eggs, onions and pickles; toss well. Stir in mustard, celery seed and mayonnaise. Season with salt and pepper; mix well. Refrigerate until cold.
¾ CUP 377 cal., 26g fat (4g sat. fat), 169mg chol., 275mg sod., 28g carb. (5g sugars, 2g fiber), 8g pro

SOUTHERN POTATO SALAD TIPS

What types of potatoes should I use? You can use any waxy potato, including fingerlings, red potatoes and Yukon Gold potatoes.

Can I use different pickles? We recommend sweet pickles, but you can also use dill.

How should I store this salad? Store it in an airtight container in the fridge; it'll last 3-4 days when stored this way.

ISRAELI PEPPER TOMATO SALAD

This Israeli salad, which is traditionally eaten at breakfast, lends itself to endless variations ... you can add olives, beets or potatoes.
—*Sandy Long, Lees Summit, MO*

PREP: 25 min. + chilling
MAKES: 9 servings

- 6 medium tomatoes, seeded and chopped
- 1 each medium green, sweet red and yellow peppers, chopped
- 1 medium cucumber, seeded and chopped
- 1 medium carrot, chopped
- 3 green onions, thinly sliced
- 1 jalapeno pepper, seeded and chopped
- 2 Tbsp. each minced fresh cilantro, parsley, dill and mint

DRESSING
- ¼ cup lemon juice
- 2 Tbsp. olive oil
- 3 garlic cloves, minced
- ½ tsp. salt
- ¼ tsp. pepper

1. In a large bowl, combine the tomatoes, peppers, cucumber, carrot, green onions, jalapeno and herbs.
2. In a small bowl, whisk together the dressing ingredients. Pour over the tomato mixture; toss to coat evenly.
3. Refrigerate, covered, at least 1 hour. Serve with a slotted spoon.
NOTE Wear disposable gloves when cutting hot peppers; the oils can burn skin. Avoid touching your face.
1 CUP 64 cal., 3g fat (0 sat. fat), 0 chol., 143mg sod., 8g carb. (5g sugars, 3g fiber), 2g pro. **DIABETIC EXCHANGES** 1 vegetable, ½ fat.

GRILLED CORN
IN HUSKS P. 81

TOP VEGGIE DISHES

SUMMER SQUASH & ZUCCHINI SIDE DISH

I'm trying to cut my risk for cardiac disease by changing the way I eat. This colorful side dish is packed with both nutrition and fresh-picked flavor.
—*Marlene Agnelly, Ocean Springs, MS*

TAKES: 30 min. • **MAKES:** 6 servings

- 1 Tbsp. olive oil
- 1 medium yellow summer squash, quartered and sliced
- 1 medium zucchini, quartered and sliced
- 1 medium onion, chopped
- 1 medium sweet red pepper, cut into 1-in. pieces
- 2 garlic cloves, minced
- ½ tsp. salt-free spicy seasoning blend
- ¼ tsp. salt
- ⅛ tsp. pepper
- 1 medium tomato, chopped

In a large skillet, heat oil over medium heat; add yellow squash, zucchini, onion and red pepper. Cook and stir 5 minutes. Add garlic and seasonings; cook until vegetables are crisp-tender, 2-3 minutes. Stir in tomato; heat through.

⅔ CUP 50 cal., 3g fat (0 sat. fat), 0 chol., 106mg sod., 6g carb. (4g sugars, 2g fiber), 1g pro. **DIABETIC EXCHANGES** 1 vegetable, ½ fat.

TEST KITCHEN TIP

The best squash should be firm with smooth skin and full of vibrant color. Don't just reach for the largest ones—smaller squash can be more tender and flavorful.

SOUTHERN FRIED OKRA

Golden brown with a little fresh green showing through, these okra nuggets are crunchy and addicting! My sons like to dip them in ketchup.
—*Pam Duncan, Summers, AR*

TAKES: 30 min. • **MAKES:** 2 servings

- 1½ cups sliced fresh or frozen okra, thawed
- 3 Tbsp. buttermilk
- 2 Tbsp. all-purpose flour
- 2 Tbsp. cornmeal
- ¼ tsp. salt
- ¼ tsp. garlic herb seasoning blend
- ⅛ tsp. pepper
  Oil for deep-fat frying
  Optional: Additional salt and pepper

1. Pat the okra dry with paper towels. Place the buttermilk in a shallow bowl. In another shallow bowl, combine the flour, cornmeal, salt, seasoning blend and pepper. Dip okra in the buttermilk, then roll in the cornmeal mixture.

2. In an electric skillet or deep-fat fryer, heat 1 in. oil to 375°. Fry okra, a few pieces at a time, 1½-2½ minutes on each side or until golden brown. Drain on paper towels. Season with additional salt and pepper if desired.

¾ CUP 200 cal., 12g fat (1g sat. fat), 1mg chol., 430mg sod., 20g carb. (4g sugars, 3g fiber), 5g pro.

SPINACH-TOPPED TOMATOES

This side dish is classic for a reason.
It provides a perfect taste of summer
when garden-fresh tomatoes are in
season, but we enjoy it year-round.
My daughter especially loves this dish.
—*Ila Mae Alderman, Galax, VA*

PREP: 20 min. • **BAKE:** 15 min.
MAKES: 6 servings

1 pkg. (10 oz.) frozen chopped spinach
2 chicken bouillon cubes
  Salt
3 large tomatoes, halved
1 cup soft bread crumbs
½ cup grated Parmesan cheese
½ cup chopped onion
½ cup butter, melted
1 large egg, lightly beaten
1 garlic clove, minced
¼ tsp. pepper
⅛ tsp. cayenne pepper
  Shredded Parmesan cheese,
  optional

1. Preheat oven to 350°. In a large
saucepan, cook the spinach according
to package directions with bouillon;
drain well. Cool slightly; press out
excess liquid.
2. Lightly salt the tomato halves; place
with cut side down on a paper towel for
15 minutes to absorb excess moisture.
3. Meanwhile, in a small bowl, combine
the spinach, bread crumbs, cheese,
onion, butter, egg, garlic, pepper and
cayenne pepper.
4. Place the tomato halves, cut side up, in
a shallow baking dish. Divide the spinach
mixture over tomatoes. Sprinkle with
shredded cheese if desired. Bake for
about 15 minutes or until heated through.
NOTE To make soft bread crumbs, tear
bread into pieces and place in a food
processor or blender. Cover and pulse
until crumbs form. One slice of bread
yields ½-¾ cup crumbs.
½ TOMATO 236 cal., 19g fat (11g sat. fat),
78mg chol., 649mg sod., 12g carb. (4g
sugars, 3g fiber), 7g pro.

CHILLED ASPARAGUS WITH BASIL CREAM

This recipe is an all-time family favorite that has been served at most of our holiday meals. I like it because it's simple and can be prepared ahead of time.
—*Melissa Puccetti, Rohnert Park, CA*

TAKES: 20 min. • **MAKES:** 8 servings

- 2 lbs. fresh asparagus, trimmed
- 1 cup mayonnaise
- ¼ cup heavy whipping cream
- 4 Tbsp. minced fresh basil, divided
- 2 garlic cloves, peeled and halved
- ½ tsp. salt
- ¼ tsp. pepper
- 2 Tbsp. pine nuts, toasted
- 1 Tbsp. grated lemon zest

1. In a large saucepan, bring 8 cups water to a boil. Add half the asparagus; cook, uncovered, just until crisp-tender, 2-4 minutes. Remove and immediately drop into ice water. Drain and pat dry. Repeat with the remaining asparagus. Arrange on a serving platter.

2. Place mayonnaise, cream, 3 Tbsp. basil, garlic, salt and pepper in a food processor; cover and process until blended. Spoon over asparagus (or serve on the side). Garnish with pine nuts, lemon zest and remaining 1 Tbsp. minced basil.

1 SERVING 235 cal., 24g fat (5g sat. fat), 10mg chol., 296mg sod., 3g carb. (1g sugars, 1g fiber), 2g pro.

GRILLED POTATOES WITH RANCH

These potatoes are tender and good all by themselves, but pairing them with the sauce creates a perfect combination.
—*Craig Carpenter, Coraopolis, PA*

TAKES: 30 min. • **MAKES:** 5 servings

- 2 Tbsp. olive oil
- 1 Tbsp. barbecue seasoning
- 2 garlic cloves, minced
- 2 tsp. lemon juice
- 1½ lbs. small potatoes, quartered

SAUCE

- ⅔ cup ranch salad dressing
- 4 tsp. bacon bits
- 2 tsp. minced chives
  Dash hot pepper sauce

1. In a large bowl, combine oil, barbecue seasoning, garlic and lemon juice. Add potatoes; toss to coat. Place on a double thickness of heavy-duty foil (about 28 in. square). Fold foil around potato mixture and seal tightly. Grill, covered, over medium heat 20-25 minutes or until potatoes are tender.

2. In a small bowl, combine the sauce ingredients. Serve with potatoes.

¾ CUP WITH 2 TBSP. SAUCE 365 cal., 23g fat (4g sat. fat), 7mg chol., 879mg sod., 37g carb. (3g sugars, 3g fiber), 4g pro.

PESTO-CORN PEPPERS

We grill almost daily and enjoy using fresh produce from our garden. These pepper halves filled with a basil-seasoned corn mixture are my husband's favorite.
—*Rachael Marrier, Star Prairie, WI*

TAKES: 30 min. • **MAKES:** 8 servings

- ½   cup plus 2 tsp. olive oil, divided
- ¾   cup grated Parmesan cheese
- 2   cups packed basil leaves
- 2   Tbsp. sunflower kernels or walnuts
- 4   garlic cloves
- ½   cup finely chopped sweet red pepper
- 4   cups fresh or frozen corn, thawed
- 4   medium sweet red, yellow or green peppers
- ¼   cup shredded Parmesan cheese, optional

1. For pesto, combine ½ cup oil, grated cheese, basil, sunflower kernels and garlic in a blender; cover and process until blended.
2. In a large skillet, heat remaining 2 tsp. oil over medium-high heat. Add chopped red pepper; cook and stir until tender. Add corn and pesto; heat through.
3. Halve peppers lengthwise; remove seeds. Grill peppers, covered, over medium heat, cut side down, 8 minutes. Turn; fill with corn mixture. Grill until tender, 4-6 minutes longer. If desired, sprinkle with shredded cheese.
1 STUFFED PEPPER HALF 287 cal., 19g fat (4g sat. fat), 6mg chol., 168mg sod., 26g carb. (4g sugars, 4g fiber), 7g pro.

TEST KITCHEN TIP

Use various colored sweet peppers—red, yellow, orange, green or even purple—for a beautiful presentation for any summer barbecue.

GRILLED LOADED POTATO ROUNDS

My go-to recipe for outdoor potlucks is an awesome potato side. I prep everything beforehand, then assemble and grill at the party. Pass with sour cream, cheese, bacon and chives.
—*Fay Moreland, Wichita Falls, TX*

TAKES: 30 min. • **MAKES:** 16 appetizers

- 4   large potatoes, baked and cooled
- ¼   cup butter, melted
- ¼   tsp. salt
- ¼   tsp. pepper
- 1   cup sour cream
- 1½ cups shredded cheddar cheese
- 8   bacon strips, cooked and crumbled
- 3   Tbsp. minced chives

1. Trim the ends of the potatoes. Slice potatoes into 1-in.-thick rounds. Brush one side with half the butter; sprinkle with salt and pepper.
2. Place potatoes on grill rack, buttered side down. Grill , covered, over medium heat or broil 4 in. from heat until browned, 5-7 minutes. Brush with the remaining butter; turn. Grill or broil until browned, 5-7 minutes longer.
3. To serve, top with sour cream, cheese, bacon and chives.
1 POTATO ROUND 188 cal., 11g fat (6g sat. fat), 26mg chol., 212mg sod., 17g carb. (1g sugars, 2g fiber), 6g pro.

GARDEN-FRESH RAINBOW CHARD

Chard is a member of the beet family, prized for its green leaves and celery-like stalks. Stir up these good-for-you greens with garlic and red onion.
—Taste of Home *Test Kitchen*

TAKES: 20 min. • **MAKES:** 4 servings

- 2 Tbsp. olive oil
- 1 medium red onion, halved and sliced
- 3 garlic cloves, sliced
- ¼ cup chicken broth
- 2 bunches rainbow Swiss chard, coarsely chopped (about 16 cups)
- 2 Tbsp. lemon juice
- ¼ tsp. salt
- ¼ tsp. pepper

1. In a 6-qt. stockpot, heat oil over medium-high heat. Add onion; cook and stir until tender, 2-3 minutes. Add garlic; cook 1 minute longer.
2. Add broth and chard; cook and stir until chard is tender, 5-6 minutes. Remove from heat; stir in lemon juice, salt and pepper.
½ CUP 115 cal., 7g fat (1g sat. fat), 0 chol., 631mg sod., 11g carb. (4g sugars, 4g fiber), 4g pro. **DIABETIC EXCHANGES** 2 vegetable, 1½ fat.

TOMATO PIE

Make sure your tomatoes are firm and not too ripe. Ripe tomatoes will add too much moisture to the pie.
—*Lois Morgan, Edisto Beach, SC*

PREP: 50 min. + chilling
BAKE: 30 min. + standing
MAKES: 8 servings

- 1 cup plus 2 Tbsp. all-purpose flour
- ¼ tsp. salt
- ½ cup cold butter, cubed
- 2 to 3 Tbsp. ice water

FILLING
- ¾ cup mayonnaise
- ½ cup shredded cheddar cheese
- ⅓ cup thinly sliced green onions
- 1 Tbsp. minced fresh oregano
- ½ tsp. ground coriander
- ¼ tsp. salt
- ¼ tsp. pepper
- 6 medium tomatoes (1¾ lbs.), cut into ¼-in. slices
- 4 bacon strips, cooked and crumbled

1. In a large bowl, mix flour and salt; cut in the butter until crumbly. Gradually add ice water, tossing with a fork until dough holds together when pressed. Shape into a disk; cover and refrigerate 30 minutes or overnight.
2. Preheat oven to 350°. On a lightly floured surface, roll dough to a ⅛-in.-thick circle; transfer to a 9-in. pie plate. Trim crust to ½ in. beyond rim of plate; flute edge. Line unpricked crust with a double thickness of foil. Fill with pie weights, dried beans or uncooked rice.
3. Bake until bottom is lightly browned, 20-25 minutes. Remove foil and weights; bake until light brown, 5-10 minutes longer. Cool on a wire rack.
4. For filling, in a small bowl, combine the mayonnaise, cheese, green onions and seasonings. Arrange a third of the tomatoes in the crust; spread with a third of the mayonnaise mixture. Repeat layers twice. Bake 25 minutes.
5. Top with bacon; bake until filling is bubbly, 5-10 minutes longer. Let stand 10 minutes before cutting.
1 PIECE 396 cal., 32g fat (12g sat. fat), 49mg chol., 466mg sod., 22g carb. (5g sugars, 3g fiber), 7g pro.

RAW CAULIFLOWER TABBOULEH

This recipe is super easy and quick to make. I love that I can offer it to my guests with special dietary restrictions.
—*Maiah Miller, Montclair, VA*

PREP: 10 min. + chilling • **MAKES:** 6 cups

- 1 medium head cauliflower
- ½ cup oil-packed sun-dried tomatoes
- 12 pitted Greek olives
- 2 cups fresh parsley leaves
- 1 cup fresh cilantro leaves
- 1 Tbsp. white wine vinegar or cider vinegar
- ¼ tsp. salt
- ¼ tsp. pepper

1. Core and coarsely chop cauliflower. In batches, pulse cauliflower in a food processor until it resembles rice (do not overprocess). Transfer to a large bowl.
2. Add the remaining ingredients to the food processor; pulse until finely chopped. Add to cauliflower; toss to combine. Refrigerate 1 hour before serving to allow flavors to blend.
¾ CUP 55 cal., 3g fat (0 sat. fat), 0 chol., 215mg sod., 7g carb. (2g sugars, 2g fiber), 2g pro. **DIABETIC EXCHANGES** 1 vegetable, ½ fat.

AIR-FRIED RADISHES

Radishes aren't just for salads anymore. This abundant springtime veggie makes a colorful side for any meal.
—Taste of Home *Test Kitchen*

TAKES: 25 min. • **MAKES:** 6 servings

- 2¼ lbs. radishes, trimmed and quartered (about 6 cups)
- 3 Tbsp. olive oil
- 1 Tbsp. minced fresh oregano or 1 tsp. dried oregano
- ¼ tsp. salt
- ⅛ tsp. pepper

Preheat air fryer to 375°. Toss radishes with remaining ingredients. Place radishes on greased tray in air-fryer basket. Cook 12-15 minutes or until crisp-tender, stirring occasionally.
⅔ CUP 88 cal., 7g fat (1g sat. fat), 0 chol., 165mg sod., 6g carb. (3g sugars, 3g fiber), 1g pro. **DIABETIC EXCHANGES** 1½ fat, 1 vegetable.

TEST KITCHEN TIP

If you don't have an air fryer, you can make this recipe in an oven.

TEST KITCHEN TIPS
If ripe, fresh tomatoes
are not available, a
14.5-oz. can of petite diced
tomatoes with juice can be
substituted. For a lovely
variation, add a handful
of chopped, pulled or
shredded pork.

CARAMELIZED KALE & APPLES SAUTE

My garden and my vegetarian daughter inspired me to create this nutritious, quick and easy dish. No one will ever guess that the restaurant-quality dish is made in under 30 minutes! A teaspoon of bacon drippings is a perfect addition to the saute step if you keep a supply in the fridge.
—Cindy Beberman, Orland Park, IL

TAKES: 30 min. • **MAKES:** 4 servings

- 2 Tbsp. olive oil
- 1 large sweet onion, halved and thinly sliced
- 1 large Gala or Honeycrisp apple, peeled and sliced
- 6 cups chopped fresh kale, stems removed and lightly packed
- ½ cup vegetable broth
- 2 Tbsp. cider vinegar
- 1 Tbsp. honey
- 1 Tbsp. lemon juice
- 1 cup diced fresh tomatoes with juice
- ½ tsp. salt

1. In a large skillet, heat oil over medium heat. Add onion and apple; saute, stirring frequently, until tender and starting to brown, 8-10 minutes.
2. Add kale to skillet. In a small bowl, stir together broth, vinegar, honey and lemon juice; pour over kale. Bring to a boil. Reduce heat; cook, covered, stirring occasionally, until kale is wilted, about 10 minutes longer.
3. Stir in the tomatoes and salt. Cook, covered, just until tomatoes are heated through, about 2 minutes longer. Remove from heat; serve with cooking juices.
1 SERVING 146 cal., 7g fat (1g sat. fat), 0 chol., 396mg sod., 21g carb. (14g sugars, 2g fiber), 2g pro.

EGGPLANT FRIES

My kids love this snack—and I like that it's healthy. Coated with Italian seasoning, Parmesan cheese and garlic salt, these veggie sticks are broiled, not fried, so there's no guilt when you crunch into them.
—Mary Murphy, Atwater, CA

TAKES: 20 min. • **MAKES:** 6 servings

- 2 large eggs
- ½ cup grated Parmesan cheese
- ½ cup toasted wheat germ
- 1 tsp. Italian seasoning
- ¾ tsp. garlic salt
- 1 medium eggplant (about 1¼ lbs.) Cooking spray
- 1 cup meatless pasta sauce, warmed

1. Preheat broiler. In a shallow bowl, whisk together eggs. In another shallow bowl, mix cheese, wheat germ and seasonings.
2. Trim ends of eggplant; cut eggplant lengthwise into ½-in.-thick slices. Cut slices lengthwise into ½-in. strips. Dip strips in the eggs, then coat with cheese mixture. Place on a baking sheet coated with cooking spray.
3. Spritz eggplant strips with additional cooking spray. Broil 4 in. from heat 3 minutes. Turn eggplant; spritz with additional cooking spray. Broil until golden brown, 1-2 minutes. Serve immediately with pasta sauce.
1 SERVING 135 cal., 5g fat (2g sat. fat), 68mg chol., 577mg sod., 15g carb. (6g sugars, 4g fiber), 9g pro. **DIABETIC EXCHANGES** 1 vegetable, 1 medium-fat meat, ½ starch.

CHARD WITH BACON-CITRUS SAUCE

Chard is a leafy veggie often used in Mediterranean cooking. I dress it with orange juice and bacon, and my family gobbles it up.
—Teri Schloessmann, Tulsa, OK

TAKES: 25 min. • **MAKES:** 6 servings

- ½ lb. thick-sliced peppered bacon strips
- 2 lbs. rainbow Swiss chard, chopped
- 1 cup orange juice
- 2 Tbsp. butter
- 4 tsp. grated orange zest
- ⅛ tsp. salt
- ⅛ tsp. pepper

1. In a large cast-iron or other heavy skillet, cook bacon over medium heat until crisp; drain on paper towels. Discard all but 1 Tbsp. drippings. Cut bacon into small pieces.
2. Add chard to drippings in pan; cook and stir just until wilted, 5-6 minutes. Add the remaining ingredients; cook 1-2 minutes, stirring occasionally. Top with bacon.
½ CUP 162 cal., 11g fat (5g sat. fat), 22mg chol., 655mg sod., 10g carb. (5g sugars, 3g fiber), 7g pro.

MARINATED CUCUMBERS

Dressed with a light, tangy oil and vinegar mixture, and seasoned with herbs, these cucumber slices make a cool summer side dish. The refreshing salad is perfect alongside sandwiches and a variety of meats.

—Mary Helen Hinson, Lamberton, NC

PREP: 10 min. + marinating
MAKES: 12 servings

```
6   medium cucumbers, thinly sliced
1   medium onion, sliced
1   cup white vinegar
¼   to ⅓ cup sugar
¼   cup olive oil
1   tsp. salt
1   tsp. dried oregano
½   tsp. garlic powder
½   tsp. dried marjoram
½   tsp. lemon-pepper seasoning
½   tsp. ground mustard
```

In a large bowl, combine the cucumbers and onion. In a jar with a tight-fitting lid, combine the remaining ingredients; cover and shake well. Pour over the cucumber mixture; toss to coat. Cover and refrigerate at least 4 hours. Serve with a slotted spoon.

¾ CUP 48 cal., 2g fat (0 sat. fat), 0 chol., 106mg sod., 6g carb. (4g sugars, 2g fiber), 2g pro.

AIR-FRYER PLANTAINS

Having grown up in Puerto Rico, I've had so much amazing Caribbean food, but tostones have always been a favorite of mine. Traditionally they are deep fried, but this version gives me the same fabulous taste without some of the calories.

—Leah Martin, Gilbertsville, PA

PREP: 15 min. + soaking
COOK: 15 min./batch • **MAKES:** 3 dozen

```
3     garlic cloves, minced
1     Tbsp. garlic salt
½     tsp. onion powder
6     green plantains, peeled and
      cut into 1-in. slices
      Cooking spray
```
SEASONING MIX
```
1     Tbsp. garlic powder
1½    tsp. garlic salt
½     tsp. onion powder
½     tsp. kosher salt
      Optional: Guacamole and
      pico de gallo
```

1. Combine garlic, garlic salt and onion powder. Add plantains; cover with cold water. Soak 30 minutes. Drain plantains; place on paper towels and pat dry.
2. Preheat air fryer to 375°. In batches, place plantains in a single layer on greased tray in air-fryer basket; spritz with cooking spray. Cook until lightly browned, 10-12 minutes.
3. Place plantains between 2 sheets of aluminum foil. With the bottom of a glass, flatten to ½-in. thickness. Increase air-fryer temperature to 400°. Return flattened plantains to air fryer; cook until golden brown, 2-3 minutes longer.
4. Combine the 4 seasoning mix ingredients; sprinkle over tostones. Serve with guacamole or pico de gallo if desired.

1 PIECE 39 cal., 0 fat (0 sat. fat), 0 chol., 110mg sod., 10g carb. (4g sugars, 1g fiber), 0 pro.

⑤ⓘ GRILLED BROCCOLI

I started using this recipe in 1987, when I began cooking light, and it's been a favorite side dish ever since. With its lemon and Parmesan flavors, it once took second place in a cooking contest.
—*Alice Nulle, Woodstock, IL*

PREP: 5 min. + standing • **GRILL:** 20 min.
MAKES: 6 servings

- 6 cups fresh broccoli spears
- 2 Tbsp. plus 1½ tsp. lemon juice
- 2 Tbsp. olive oil
- ¼ tsp. salt
- ¼ tsp. pepper
- ¾ cup grated Parmesan cheese
  Optional: Grilled lemon slices and red pepper flakes

1. Place broccoli in a large bowl. Combine lemon juice, oil, salt and pepper; drizzle over broccoli and toss to coat. Let stand for 30 minutes.

2. Toss broccoli, then drain, discarding marinade. Place cheese in a small shallow bowl. Add broccoli, a few pieces at a time, tossing to coat.

3. Prepare grill for indirect heat using a drip pan. Place broccoli over drip pan on an oiled grill rack. Grill, covered, over indirect medium heat for 8-10 minutes on each side or until crisp-tender. If desired, garnish with grilled lemon slices and red pepper flakes.

1 CUP 107 cal., 8g fat (3g sat. fat), 8mg chol., 304mg sod., 5g carb. (2g sugars, 2g fiber), 6g pro. **DIABETIC EXCHANGES** 1½ fat, 1 vegetable.

READER REVIEW

"So good! I'm not sure I'll eat broccoli any other way now. I did put the broccoli in a disposable foil pan to make it easy."
—AMSM, TASTEOFHOME.COM

LATTICE CORN PIE

This unique side dish is brimming with old-fashioned goodness, with tender diced potatoes and a fresh sweet corn flavor. Once you've tasted this delicious pie, you'll never want to serve corn any other way!
—Kathy Spang, Manheim, PA

PREP: 25 min. • **BAKE:** 35 min.
MAKES: 8 servings

- 1   cup diced peeled potatoes
- ⅓   cup 2% milk
- 2   large eggs
- 2   cups fresh or frozen corn, thawed
- 1   tsp. sugar
- ½   tsp. salt
- 2   sheets refrigerated pie crust

1. Preheat oven to 375°. Place potatoes in a small saucepan and cover with water. Bring to a boil. Reduce heat; cover and cook until tender, 6-8 minutes. Drain.
2. In a blender, combine the milk, eggs, corn, sugar and salt; cover and process until blended.
3. Unroll 1 sheet crust into a 9-in. pie plate. Trim to ½ in. beyond rim of plate; flute the edge. Spoon the potatoes into crust; top with the corn mixture (crust will be full). Roll out the remaining crust; make a lattice top. Seal and flute edge.
4. Bake until the crust is golden brown and the filling is bubbly, 35-40 minutes.
1 PIECE 308 cal., 16g fat (7g sat. fat), 57mg chol., 373mg sod., 37g carb. (5g sugars, 1g fiber), 5g pro.

TEST KITCHEN TIP

Recipes for Pennsylvania Dutch corn pie often include hard-boiled eggs instead of raw; you can also add hard-boiled eggs for more texture if you'd like. For a more meal-like pie, add cubed cooked chicken.

CEDAR-PLANK STUFFED PORTOBELLOS

When we were newlyweds, my father-in-law made us stuffed portobello mushrooms. I've tweaked the recipe for our tastes. I like to serve it with salad and potato wedges.
—Katie Stemp, Tacoma, WA

PREP: 30 min. + soaking • **GRILL:** 15 min.
MAKES: 6 servings

- 6   cedar grilling planks
- ½   lb. fresh chorizo or bulk spicy pork sausage
- 10   bacon strips, diced
- 1   large sweet red pepper, finely chopped
- 1   medium onion, finely chopped
- 2   garlic cloves, minced
- ¼   tsp. crushed red pepper flakes
- ⅛   tsp. cayenne pepper
- ½   cup grated Parmesan cheese
- 6   large portobello mushrooms (4 to 4½ in.)

1. Soak planks in water at least 1 hour. In a large skillet, cook chorizo and bacon over medium heat for 10-12 minutes or until chorizo is fully cooked and bacon is crisp. Remove with a slotted spoon; drain on paper towels. Discard drippings, reserving 1 Tbsp. in pan.
2. Add pepper and onion to drippings; cook and stir over medium-high heat 3-4 minutes or until tender. Add garlic, pepper flakes and cayenne; cook 30 seconds longer. In a large bowl, combine the meat mixture, vegetable mixture and cheese; set aside.
3. Remove and discard stems from the mushrooms; with a spoon, scrape and remove gills. Fill caps with meat mixture.
4. Place planks on grill rack over direct medium heat. Cover and heat for 3-4 minutes or until light to medium smoke comes from the planks and the wood begins to crackle. (This indicates the planks are ready.) Turn planks over; place mushroom caps on planks. Grill, covered, over medium heat 8-10 minutes or until mushrooms are tender.
1 STUFFED MUSHROOM 404 cal., 32g fat (11g sat. fat), 70mg chol., 896mg sod., 9g carb. (3g sugars, 2g fiber), 18g pro.

WILTED CURLY ENDIVE

This warm salad is a deliciously different way to serve lettuce. Unlike other wilted versions, this one is not sweet. Vinegar and bacon give it old-fashioned savory goodness.
—*Chere Bell, Colorado Springs, CO*

TAKES: 20 min. • **MAKES:** 6 servings

- 12 bacon strips, diced
- 3 large bunches curly endive
- 2¼ tsp. salt, divided
- 2 to 3 Tbsp. cider vinegar
- 3 Tbsp. finely chopped onion
- ¼ tsp. pepper

1. Cook bacon until crisp; remove with a slotted spoon to paper towels to drain. Reserve 3 Tbsp. drippings. Cut or tear endive leaves from center stalks; discard the stalks.
2. In a large saucepan or Dutch oven, bring 4 qt. water and 1½ tsp. salt to a boil. Add the endive; cover and cook until wilted, about 3 minutes. Drain. Stir in bacon, vinegar, onion, pepper, reserved drippings and remaining ¾ tsp. salt.
½ CUP 256 cal., 26g fat (10g sat. fat), 30mg chol., 1216mg sod., 1g carb. (1g sugars, 0 fiber), 4g pro.

ZUCCHINI PANCAKES

Made with zucchini, these are a tasty change of pace from ordinary potato pancakes. Add a little shredded onion to give them a savory kick.
—*Charlotte Goldberg, Honey Grove, PA*

TAKES: 20 min. • **MAKES:** 2 servings

- 1½ cups shredded zucchini
- 1 large egg, lightly beaten
- 3 Tbsp. grated Parmesan cheese
- 2 Tbsp. biscuit/baking mix
   Dash pepper
- 1 Tbsp. canola oil
   Sour cream, optional

1. Place zucchini in a colander over a bowl; let stand to drain. Squeeze and blot dry with paper towels.
2. In a bowl, mix egg, cheese, baking mix and pepper. Add zucchini; toss to coat.
3. In a large skillet, heat oil over medium heat. Drop 4 pancakes into skillet; press lightly to flatten. Cook until golden brown, about 2 minutes per side. If desired, serve with sour cream.
2 PANCAKES 174 cal., 13g fat (3g sat. fat), 99mg chol., 256mg sod., 9g carb. (2g sugars, 1g fiber), 7g pro.

TEST KITCHEN TIP

For a quick and easy way to get excess water out of shredded zucchini, try using a French press.

EDDIE'S FAVORITE FIESTA CORN

When fresh sweet corn is available, I love making this splurge of a side dish. Frozen corn works, but be sure to taste as you go and add sugar if needed.
—*Anthony Bolton, Bellevue, NE*

PREP: 15 min. • **COOK:** 25 min.
MAKES: 8 servings

½ lb. bacon strips, chopped
5 cups fresh or frozen super sweet corn
1 medium sweet red pepper, finely chopped
1 medium sweet yellow pepper, finely chopped
1 pkg. (8 oz.) reduced-fat cream cheese
½ cup half-and-half cream
1 can (4 oz.) chopped green chiles, optional
2 tsp. sugar
1 tsp. pepper
¼ tsp. salt

1. In a 6-qt. stockpot, cook bacon over medium heat until crisp, stirring occasionally. Remove with a slotted spoon; drain on paper towels. Discard drippings, reserving 1 Tbsp. in pan.
2. Add corn, red pepper and yellow pepper to the drippings; cook and stir over medium-high heat until tender, 5-6 minutes. Stir in cream cheese, half-and-half, chiles if desired, sugar, pepper and salt until blended; bring to a boil. Reduce heat; simmer, covered, until thickened, 8-10 minutes.
⅔ CUP 249 cal., 14g fat (7g sat. fat), 39mg chol., 399mg sod., 22g carb. (9g sugars, 2g fiber), 10g pro.

EASY GRILLED SQUASH

This is one of the best ways to prepare butternut squash and is great alongside grilled steak or chicken. As a bonus, butternut squash is full of vitamin A.
—*Esther Horst, Monterey, TN*

TAKES: 20 min. • **MAKES:** 4 servings

3 Tbsp. olive oil
2 garlic cloves, minced
¼ tsp. salt
¼ tsp. pepper
1 small butternut squash, peeled and cut lengthwise into ½-in. slices

1. In a small bowl, combine the oil, garlic, salt and pepper. Brush over the squash slices.
2. Grill squash, covered, over medium heat or broil 4 in. from the heat on each side or until tender, 4-5 minutes.
2 PIECES 178 cal., 10g fat (1g sat. fat), 0 chol., 156mg sod., 23g carb. (5g sugars, 7g fiber), 2g pro. **DIABETIC EXCHANGES** 1½ starch, 1½ fat.

STUFFED GRILLED ZUCCHINI

Pair these zucchini boats with charred pork chops, smoked fish or other grilled greats.
—*Nancy Zimmerman,
Cape May Court House, NJ*

PREP: 25 min. • **GRILL:** 10 min.
MAKES: 4 servings

- 4 medium zucchini
- 5 tsp. olive oil, divided
- 2 Tbsp. finely chopped red onion
- ¼ tsp. minced garlic
- ½ cup dry bread crumbs
- ½ cup shredded part-skim mozzarella cheese
- 1 Tbsp. minced fresh mint
- ½ tsp. salt
- 3 Tbsp. grated Parmesan cheese

1. Cut zucchini in half lengthwise; scoop out flesh, leaving ¼-in. shells. Brush with 2 tsp. oil; set aside. Chop zucchini flesh.
2. In a large skillet, saute flesh and onion in the remaining oil. Add the garlic; cook 1 minute longer. Add the bread crumbs; cook and stir until golden brown, about 2 minutes.
3. Remove from heat. Stir in mozzarella cheese, mint and salt. Spoon mixture into zucchini shells. Sprinkle with grated Parmesan cheese.
4. Grill, covered, over medium heat until zucchini is tender, 8-10 minutes.
2 STUFFED ZUCCHINI HALVES 186 cal., 10g fat (3g sat. fat), 11mg chol., 553mg sod., 17g carb. (4g sugars, 3g fiber), 9g pro. **DIABETIC EXCHANGES** 1 vegetable, 1 lean meat, 1 fat, ½ starch.

HOW TO GRILL VEGETABLES

Here's a quick guide for grilling a few of our favorite veggies. Unless a recipe calls for a specific marinade, just toss them with a little olive oil. A sprinkle of salt and pepper is really all you need to bring out their flavor.

Grill over direct medium heat and be sure to turn once halfway through the grill time for even cooking—and those gorgeous grill lines.

Bell Peppers
Seed and slice into quarters.
6-8 min.

Cherry Tomatoes
Leave whole. (try on-the-vine tomatoes for easier moving!)
3 min.

Mushrooms
Leave whole. For easier flipping, run a skewer down center of stem and cap.
8-10 min.

Onions
Cut into ½-in. slices.
8-12 min.

Summer Squash & Zucchini
Cut into ½-in. slices.
8-10 min.

VEGETABLE KABOBS

Grilling is a delightful way to prepare the season's freshest produce. The zesty Italian marinade adds just the right amount of spice to the appealing assortment of vegetables.
—Taste of Home *Test Kitchen*

TAKES: 30 min. • **MAKES:** 4 servings

- 1 garlic clove, peeled
- 1 tsp. salt
- ⅓ cup olive oil
- 3 Tbsp. lemon juice
- 1 tsp. Italian seasoning
- ¼ tsp. pepper
- 8 medium fresh mushrooms
- 2 small zucchini, cut into ½-in. slices
- 2 small onions, cut into 6 wedges
- 8 cherry tomatoes

1. In a small bowl, mash the garlic with salt to form a paste. Stir in the oil, lemon juice, Italian seasoning and pepper.
2. Thread vegetables alternately onto metal or soaked wooden skewers; place in a shallow pan. Pour garlic mixture over kabobs; let stand for 15 minutes.
3. Grill kabobs, covered, over medium heat for 10-15 minutes or just until the vegetables are tender, turning frequently.
¾ CUP 202 cal., 18g fat (2g sat. fat), 0 chol., 598mg sod., 9g carb. (5g sugars, 2g fiber), 3g pro.

BRUSSELS SPROUTS & KALE SAUTE

This colorful side dish is filled with healthy greens. It pairs well with turkey, potatoes and other holiday staples. The crispy salami—my kid's favorite ingredient—makes it over-the-top delicious.
—*Jennifer McNabb, Brentwood, TN*

TAKES: 30 min. • **MAKES:** 12 servings

- ¼ lb. thinly sliced hard salami, cut into ¼-in. strips
- 1½ tsp. olive oil
- 2 Tbsp. butter
- 2 lbs. fresh Brussels sprouts, thinly sliced
- 2 cups shredded fresh kale
- 1 large onion, finely chopped
- ½ tsp. kosher salt
- ⅛ tsp. cayenne pepper
- ¼ tsp. coarsely ground pepper
- 1 garlic clove, minced
- ½ cup chicken broth
- ½ cup chopped walnuts
- 1 Tbsp. balsamic vinegar

1. In a Dutch oven, cook and stir salami in oil over medium-high heat until crisp, 3-5 minutes. Remove to paper towels with a slotted spoon; reserve drippings in pan.
2. Add butter to the drippings; heat over medium-high heat. Add the Brussels sprouts, kale, onion, salt, cayenne and black pepper; cook and stir until vegetables are crisp-tender. Add garlic; cook 1 minute longer.
3. Stir in the broth; bring to a boil. Reduce heat; cover and cook until the Brussels sprouts are tender, 4-5 minutes. Stir in walnuts and vinegar. Serve with salami strips.
½ CUP 126 cal., 9g fat (3g sat. fat), 14mg chol., 341mg sod., 9g carb. (3g sugars, 3g fiber), 6g pro. **DIABETIC EXCHANGES** 2 fat, 1 vegetable.

GRILLED CORN IN HUSKS

Seasoned with butter, Parmesan cheese and parsley, grilled corn is especially good. Be sure to give the ears a long soak before putting them on the grill. Hot off the grate, the kernels are moist and tender with a wonderful, sweet flavor.
—*Nancy Zimmerman, Cape May Court House, NJ*

PREP: 20 min. + soaking • **GRILL:** 20 min.
MAKES: 4 servings

- 4 large ears sweet corn in husks
- ¼ cup butter, softened
- 2 Tbsp. minced fresh parsley
- ¼ cup grated Parmesan cheese

1. Carefully peel back husks from corn to within 1 in. of bottom; remove the silk. Soak in cold water for 20 minutes; drain. Pat corn dry. Combine the butter and parsley; spread over corn. Rewrap corn in husks and secure with string.
2. Grill corn, covered, over medium heat 20-25 minutes or until tender, turning often. Sprinkle with cheese.
1 EAR GRILLED CORN 196 cal., 9g fat (5g sat. fat), 24mg chol., 186mg sod., 28g carb. (9g sugars, 4g fiber), 8g pro. **DIABETIC EXCHANGES** 2 starch, 1 fat.

TEST KITCHEN TIP

It's essential to soak your corn in cold water for about 20 minutes before grilling to prevent burning. This also adds extra moisture so the interior of the corn steams as the whole ear is grilled.

GRILLED ZUCCHINI WITH ONIONS

Wondering what to do with all your garden-grown zucchini in the summer? Give it a sizzle and a little heat with this healthy side. It's also an easy recipe to double or triple for summer cookouts.
—*Alia Shuttleworth, Auburn, CA*

TAKES: 20 min. • **MAKES:** 4 servings

- 6 small zucchini, halved lengthwise
- 4 tsp. olive oil, divided
- 2 green onions, thinly sliced
- 2 Tbsp. lemon juice
- ½ tsp. salt
- ⅛ tsp. crushed red pepper flakes

1. Drizzle the zucchini with 2 tsp. oil. Grill, covered, over medium heat until tender, 8-10 minutes, turning once.
2. Place in a large bowl. Add the green onions, lemon juice, salt, pepper flakes and remaining oil; toss to coat.
3 ZUCCHINI HALVES 73 cal., 5g fat (1g sat. fat), 0 chol., 314mg sod., 7g carb. (3g sugars, 2g fiber), 2g pro. **DIABETIC EXCHANGES** 1 vegetable, 1 fat.

GRILLED GREATS

GRILLING SAFETY

Grill on a level surface. Avoid hills or areas with bumpy soil; place the grill on concrete or stone.

Don't use lighter fluid. Lighter fluid adds a chemical taste to your food, and it's easy for the flame to get out of control. Adding lighter fluid to lit coals is an especially bad idea. Use a charcoal starter to get things going.

Keep the lid open when starting a gas grill. Lighting a gas grill with a closed lid can cause a buildup of gas, creating a fireball. If the flame goes out, turn the grill and gas off, and wait at least 5 minutes before relighting.

Give the grill enough space. Avoid awnings and tree branches—floating embers can spark a fire. Your grill should be at least 10 feet away from deck railings and any structures.

Don't leave the grill unattended. Keep kids and pets at least 3 feet away from the grill, even after you're finished cooking—it's easy for them to bump into a hot surface.

Don't overload the grill. Flare-ups can occur if too much fat drips onto the flames, so cook in batches to avoid overloading, particularly with fatty meats.

Be prepared. Have baking soda on hand to control a grease fire, and a fire extinguisher nearby for other types of fires. Never use water to put out a grease fire.

Shut it down. As soon as you're done cooking, turn off the burners on your gas grill and close down the propane supply. If you're using charcoal, close the air vents to shut off the air supply to the embers. Then let the coals cool completely before disposing of them in a metal container.

Keep it clean. Clean the grill after each use, and regularly remove grease and fat buildup from grill grates and drip trays to reduce the danger of flare-ups. Besides, food won't stick as easily to a clean grill.

Check for leaks. After cleaning a gas grill, add some soapy water to the propane hose and turn on the gas. If you see bubbles growing, you have a leak in the hose.

TURN YOUR GRILL INTO A SMOKER

Transform your grill into backyard smoker just by adding some wood chips

1. Soak the wood chips. Soak chips at least 30 minutes; soaking means smoke, and smoke means flavor. Wood scents range from hickory to pecan to spicy apple; choose one that complements the dish you're cooking.

2. Fire up the grill. For both charcoal or gas, the temperature should be around 225° for most recipes. For charcoal, start by filling a chimney starter about a third of the way full with charcoal. Once the coals are hot, pour them off to one side of the grill, and let them burn down until the optimal temperature is reached. Preheating takes 30-60 minutes.

3. Add the chips. Once the grill is at temperature, strain the wood chips.

For charcoal, dump the chips directly onto the coals. For gas, wrap the chips in foil, poke holes to allow steam to escape, lay the foil packet directly on the unlit cooking grate, and then fire it up again. You're ready to start once you see smoke!

4. Start smoking! Smoking meat can take anywhere from 1 to 6 hours. If you're using charcoal, add more coals every hour or so to maintain the desired temperature.

More tips from our Test Kitchen:
• **Avoid softwoods,** which are full of sap and can make your food taste strange and can even make you sick. Stick to hardwoods: hickory, cherry, mesquite, pecan or oak.

• **Don't add too much wood.** It's tempting to add extra, but too much can result in a bitter flavor.

• **Open the vent** above the meat (which should be on the opposite side of the coals and wood)—the airflow will keep the coals hot and will evenly smoke your food.

• **Add a water pan** to the grill to keep meat moist.

• **Don't overdo the seasonings**— you don't want to mask that smoky flavor you spent hours achieving!

GRILLING MARINADES

Prepare to become a pit master! Mix your sauce in a shallow dish, add the main ingredient and let it rest in the fridge (times in the chart are the maximum marinating time).

1 HULI HULI

1 cup packed **brown sugar**, ¾ cup **ketchup**, ¾ cup **reduced-sodium soy sauce**, ⅓ cup **sherry** or **chicken broth**, 2½ tsp. minced **fresh gingerroot** and 1½ tsp. minced **garlic**.
—*Sharon Boling, San Diego, CA*

2 NORTHWOODS

6 Tbsp. **maple syrup**, 6 Tbsp. **balsamic vinegar**, ¾ tsp. **salt** and ¾ tsp. coarsely **ground pepper**.
—*Nicholas King, Duluth, MN*

3 ORANGE-SPICE

½ cup thawed **orange juice concentrate**, ¼ cup **honey**, ¼ cup **soy sauce**, 1 tsp. **Chinese five-spice powder** and ½ tsp. **garlic powder**.
—*Debra Stevens, Lutz, FL*

4 HONEY-GARLIC

¼ cup **lemon juice**, ¼ cup **honey**, 2 Tbsp. **soy sauce** and 2 minced **garlic cloves**.
—*Helen Carpenter, Albuquerque, NM*

5 RANCH

2 cups **sour cream**, 1 envelope **ranch salad dressing mix**, 4 tsp. **lemon juice**, 4 tsp. **Worcestershire sauce**, 2 tsp. **celery salt**, 2 tsp. **paprika**, 1 tsp. **garlic salt** and 1 tsp. **pepper**.
—*Barbee Decker, Whispering Pines, NC*

6 HEAVENLY GREEK

3 cup **lemon juice**, 2 Tbsp. **olive oil**, 4 tsp. grated **lemon zest**, 2 minced **garlic cloves**, 1 tsp. **dried oregano**, ¼ tsp. **salt** and ¼ tsp. **pepper**.
—*Meagan Jensen, Reno, NV*

7 SOUTHWEST CHILI

2 Tbsp. **olive oil**, 1 Tbsp. **chili powder**, 1 tsp. **garlic salt**, 1 tsp. **ground coriander**, 1 tsp. **dried oregano**, ½ tsp. **ground cumin** and ½ tsp. **pepper**.
—*Lindsay Matuszak, Reno, NV*

8 BALSAMIC MUSTARD

1¼ cups **balsamic vinaigrette**, 4 tsp. **ground mustard**, 2¼ tsp. **Worcestershire sauce** and 2 minced **garlic cloves**.
—*Gail Garcelon, Beaverton, OR*

9 GINGER-PEACH

¼ cup **peach preserves**, 1 Tbsp. **lemon juice**, 1 Tbsp. finely chopped **crystallized ginger**, 2 tsp. grated **lemon zest** and ⅛ tsp **ground cloves**.
—*Jacqueline Correa, Landing, NJ*

10 TANGY BARBECUE

1 cup **barbecue sauce**, ½ cup **Burgundy wine** or **beef broth** and ¼ cup **lemon juice**.
—*Beverly Dietz, Surprise, AZ*

Match the Marinade	
Beef	8 hours
Pork	6 hours
Chicken	4 hours
Fruit	1 hour
Seafood	30 min.

GRILLED GREATS: BEEF

SWEET COFFEE-RUBBED RIBEYES

My husband and I love cooking together. He's an Old West chuck wagon enthusiast and I like cooking foods from around the world. This steak is a favorite in our household!
—*Kylie Hatmaker, Knoxville, TN*

PREP: 15 min. + marinating
GRILL: 10 min.
MAKES: 2 servings

- 4 tsp. ground coffee
- 1 Tbsp. sugar
- ½ tsp. salt
- ½ tsp. pepper
- ½ tsp. garlic powder
- ½ tsp. smoked paprika
- ½ tsp. ground chipotle pepper
- 2 Tbsp. olive oil
- 2 Tbsp. Worcestershire sauce
- 2 beef ribeye steaks (¾ lb. each)
- 2 Tbsp. butter

1. In a small bowl, combine the first 7 ingredients. In a shallow dish, combine oil and Worcestershire sauce. Coat the steaks in the oil mixture. Rub coffee mixture over both sides of steaks. Let stand at room temperature for 30 minutes, turning once.
2. Grill, covered, over medium-high heat until meat reaches desired doneness (for medium-rare, a thermometer should read 135°; medium, 140°; medium-well, 145°), 4-6 minutes on each side. Top each steak with 1 Tbsp. butter. Let steaks stand 5 minutes before serving.
1 STEAK 1010 cal., 79g fat (31g sat. fat), 231mg chol., 1025mg sod., 12g carb. (8g sugars, 1g fiber), 61g pro.

SPINACH STEAK PINWHEELS

Bacon and spinach bring plenty of flavor to these sirloin steak spirals. It's an easy dish to make and great to grill at a backyard cookout. I get lots of compliments on it, no matter how many times I serve it.
—*Helen Vail, Glenside, PA*

TAKES: 25 min. • **MAKES:** 6 servings

- 1½ lbs. beef top sirloin steak
- 8 bacon strips, cooked
- 1 pkg. (10 oz.) frozen chopped spinach, thawed and squeezed dry
- ¼ cup grated Parmesan cheese
- ½ tsp. salt
- ⅛ tsp. cayenne pepper

1. Lightly score steak by making shallow diagonal cuts into the top of the steak at 1-in. intervals; repeat cuts in opposite direction. Cover steak with plastic wrap; pound with a meat mallet to ½-in. thickness. Remove plastic.
2. Place bacon widthwise at the center of the steak. In a bowl, mix remaining ingredients; spoon over bacon. Starting at a short side, roll up steak jelly-roll style; secure with toothpicks. Cut into 6 slices.
3. Place pinwheels on an oiled grill rack. Grill, covered, over medium heat until beef reaches desired doneness (for medium-rare, a thermometer should read 145°; medium, 160°, well-done, 170°), 5-6 minutes on each side. Discard toothpicks before serving.
1 PINWHEEL 227 cal., 10g fat (4g sat. fat), 60mg chol., 536mg sod., 3g carb. (0 sugars, 1g fiber), 31g pro. **DIABETIC EXCHANGES** 4 lean meat, 1 fat.

BACON-BLUE CHEESE STUFFED BURGERS

These loaded burgers are one hearty meal in a bun. They're sure to satisfy the biggest appetites.
—Christine Keating, Norwalk, CA

PREP: 30 min. • **GRILL:** 10 min.
MAKES: 4 burgers

1½ lbs. lean ground beef (90% lean)
3 oz. cream cheese, softened
⅓ cup crumbled blue cheese
⅓ cup bacon bits
½ tsp. salt
½ tsp. garlic powder
¼ tsp. pepper
1 lb. sliced fresh mushrooms
1 Tbsp. olive oil
1 Tbsp. water
1 Tbsp. Dijon mustard
4 whole wheat hamburger buns, split
¼ cup mayonnaise
4 romaine leaves
1 medium tomato, sliced

1. Shape beef into 8 thin patties. Combine the cream cheese, blue cheese and bacon bits; spoon onto the center of 4 patties. Top with the remaining patties; press edges firmly to seal. Combine the salt, garlic powder and pepper; sprinkle over patties.
2. Grill burgers, covered, over medium heat or broil 4 in. from the heat on each side until a thermometer reads 160° and juices run clear, 5-7 minutes.
3. Meanwhile, in a large skillet, saute the mushrooms in oil until tender. Stir in the water and mustard.
4. Serve the burgers on buns with mayonnaise, romaine, tomato and the mushroom mixture.

1 BURGER 701 cal., 43g fat (15g sat. fat), 149mg chol., 1280mg sod., 31g carb. (7g sugars, 5g fiber), 48g pro.

HERB & CHEESE-STUFFED BURGERS
Omit blue cheese and bacon bits. Mix cream cheese with ¼ cup shredded cheddar cheese, 2 Tbsp. minced fresh parsley and 1 tsp. Dijon mustard. Season meat with ¾ tsp. crushed dried rosemary and ¼ dried sage leaves. Proceed as recipe directs.

GREEK STUFFED BURGERS Omit cream cheese, blue cheese and bacon bits. Mix ⅓ cup feta cheese, ⅓ cup chopped tomato, 2 Tbsp. chopped red onion, 4 tsp. chopped ripe olives, 2 tsp. olive oil and ¼ tsp. dried oregano. Stuff burgers with feta mixture and proceed as recipe directs.

READER REVIEW

"Our family would give this one six stars if we could. We prepared the filling and the patties the day before. It was a cinch to put together and hand over to my son for grilling while we sauteed the mushrooms and got the side dishes ready."
—CAWALTERS, TASTEOFHOME.COM

THE BEST GRILLED SIRLOIN TIP ROAST

If you're looking for a flavorful cut of meat that's still pretty lean, give this sirloin tip roast recipe a try. I like to cook it slowly over indirect heat, mopping it frequently with red wine sauce.

—James Schend, Pleasant Prairie, WI

PREP: 40 min. + chilling
GRILL: 1½ hours + standing
MAKES: 6 servings

- 1   beef sirloin tip roast or beef tri-tip roast (2 to 3 lbs.)
- 1   Tbsp. kosher salt
- 2   tsp. dried thyme
- 2   tsp. garlic powder
- 1   tsp. coarsely ground pepper
- 1   small onion, chopped
- 2   Tbsp. olive oil, divided
- 1   bottle (750 milliliters) dry red wine
- 6   fresh thyme sprigs
- 1   garlic cloves, crushed
- ½   tsp. whole peppercorns
- 3   whole cloves

HORSERADISH-THYME BUTTER (OPTIONAL)
- 6   Tbsp. softened butter
- 2   Tbsp. prepared horseradish
- 3   Tbsp. fresh thyme leaves

1. Sprinkle roast with salt, thyme, garlic powder and ground pepper. Cover and refrigerate at least 8 hours or up to 24 hours. Meanwhile, in a saucepan, saute onion in 1 Tbsp. oil until tender, about 5 minutes. Add the wine, thyme, garlic, peppercorns and cloves. Simmer until reduced to ¾ cup. Cool; strain, discarding solids, and refrigerate.
2. Remove roast from the refrigerator 1 hour before grilling. Prepare grill for indirect heat, using a drip pan. Add wood chips according to the manufacturer's directions.
3. Pat roast dry with paper towels. Brush with remaining 1 Tbsp. oil; place over drip pan. Grill, covered, over medium-low indirect heat, brushing with sauce every 20 minutes, until the meat reaches desired doneness (for medium-rare, a thermometer should read 135°; medium, 140°; medium-well, 145°), 1½-2 hours. Let stand 15 minutes before slicing.
4. If desired, in a small bowl, stir together butter, horseradish and thyme. Serve on top of roast.

4 OZ. COOKED BEEF 262 cal., 13g fat (4g sat. fat), 91mg chol., 1027mg sod., 3g carb. (1g sugars, 1g fiber), 32g pro.

TEST KITCHEN TIP

Serve this sirloin tip roast with mashed potatoes, balsamic Brussels sprouts, sauteed mushrooms or cubed sweet potatoes.

CRUNCHY BURGER QUESADILLAS

We adore all kinds of burgers, and we also love quesadillas and tacos. I combined all the above to make scrumptious, filling burgers that my whole family enjoys.
—*Ann Marie Eberhart, Gig Harbor, WA*

TAKES: 30 min. • **MAKES:** 4 servings

- 1 lb. ground beef
- 2 tsp. canola oil
- 1 cup mayonnaise
- ⅓ cup salsa
- 4 flour tortillas (12 in.), warmed
- 4 slices pepper jack or cheddar cheese
- 4 tostada shells

1. Gently shape beef into 4 balls, shaping just enough to keep together (do not compact). In a large skillet, heat oil over medium heat. Working in batches, add beef. With a heavy metal spatula, flatten to ¼- to ½-in. thickness. Cook until edges start to brown, about 1½ minutes. Turn burgers; cook until well browned and a thermometer reads at least 160°, about 1 minute. Repeat with remaining beef. Remove from skillet; wipe skillet clean.
2. Combine mayonnaise and salsa; reserve half for serving. Spread remaining mixture over tortillas. On the center of each tortilla, place 1 slice cheese, 1 burger and 1 tostada shell. Fold sides of tortilla over burger; fold the top and bottom to close, pleating as you go.
3. In batches, place wraps in skillet, seam side down. Cook on medium heat 1-2 minutes on each side or until golden brown. Serve with remaining sauce.
1 SERVING 912 cal., 69g fat (17g sat. fat), 93mg chol., 1144mg sod., 41g carb. (2g sugars, 5g fiber), 31g pro.

COWBOY GRILLED MEAT LOAF

I came up with this recipe after eating grilled meat loaf at a restaurant years ago. I loved the idea and developed a recipe that we like even more! Using indirect heat allows the centers to cook through before the outsides of the loaves get too dark.
—Karin Gatewood, Josephine, TX

PREP: 20 min. • **GRILL:** 30 min. + standing
MAKES: 2 loaves (3 servings each)

- 1 large egg, lightly beaten
- 1 medium onion, finely chopped
- ¾ cup Italian-style panko bread crumbs
- ½ cup finely chopped seeded jalapeno pepper or green pepper
- ½ cup ketchup
- 3 Tbsp. Worcestershire sauce
- 1 lb. lean ground beef (90% lean)
- ½ lb. spicy bulk pork sausage

GLAZE

- ⅔ cup ketchup
- 2 Tbsp. brown sugar
- 2 Tbsp. spicy brown mustard

1. In a large bowl, combine the first 6 ingredients. Add beef and sausage; mix lightly but thoroughly. Shape into two 6x4-in. loaves.
2. Prepare grill for indirect heat. Grill loaves, covered, over indirect medium heat for 20 minutes. Meanwhile, in a small bowl, combine glaze ingredients.
3. Brush top and sides of loaves with glaze. Grill until a thermometer reads 160°, another 10-15 minutes. Let stand for 10 minutes before slicing.
NOTE Wear disposable gloves when cutting hot peppers; the oils can burn skin. Avoid touching your face.
1 PIECE 373 cal., 18g fat (5g sat. fat), 99mg chol., 1208mg sod., 29g carb. (19g sugars, 1g fiber), 21g pro.

BALSAMIC-GLAZED BEEF SKEWERS

With only five simple ingredients, these mouthwatering kabobs are a summertime favorite. To prevent the skewers from burning, soak them in water 30 minutes before threading on the meat and tomatoes.
—Carole Fraser, Toronto, ON

TAKES: 25 min. • **MAKES:** 4 servings

- ¼ cup balsamic vinaigrette
- ¼ cup barbecue sauce
- 1 tsp. Dijon mustard
- 1 lb. beef top sirloin steak, cut into 1-in. cubes
- 2 cups cherry tomatoes

1. In a large bowl, whisk vinaigrette, barbecue sauce and mustard until blended. Reserve ¼ cup mixture for basting. Add beef to the remaining mixture; toss to coat.
2. Alternately thread beef and tomatoes on 4 metal or soaked wooden skewers. Grill, covered, over medium heat on a lightly greased grill rack or broil 4 in. from heat 6-9 minutes or until beef reaches desired doneness, turning occasionally and basting frequently with reserved vinaigrette mixture during the last 3 minutes.
1 SKEWER 194 cal., 7g fat (2g sat. fat), 46mg chol., 288mg sod., 7g carb. (5g sugars, 1g fiber), 25g pro. **DIABETIC EXCHANGES** 3 lean meat, 1½ fat, ½ starch.

WHISKEY CHEDDAR BURGERS

This juicy burger has big flavors to satisfy even the heartiest appetites. It always impresses at our cookouts.
—*Amber Nicholson, Winooski, VT*

TAKES: 30 min. • **MAKES:** 8 servings

- ¼ cup whiskey
- 1 Tbsp. reduced-sodium soy sauce
- 1 Tbsp. Worcestershire sauce
- 1 cup shredded sharp cheddar cheese
- ¼ cup finely chopped onion
- 2 Tbsp. seasoned bread crumbs
- 3 garlic cloves, minced
- ½ tsp. salt
- ½ tsp. paprika
- ½ tsp. dried basil
- ½ tsp. pepper
- 1½ lbs. lean ground beef (90% lean)
- 8 onion rolls or hamburger buns, split
  Optional: Lettuce leaves, sliced tomato, cheddar cheese slices and barbecue sauce

1. Combine the first 11 ingredients. Add beef; mix lightly but thoroughly. Shape into eight ½-in.-thick patties.

2. On a greased grill, cook burgers, covered, over medium heat or broil 4 in. from heat for 4-5 minutes on each side or until a thermometer reads 160°. Serve burgers on rolls with toppings as desired.

FREEZE OPTION Place patties on a waxed paper-lined baking sheet; wrap and freeze until firm. Remove from pan and transfer to an airtight container; return to freezer. To use, grill frozen patties as directed, increasing time as necessary for a thermometer to read 160°.

1 BURGER 370 cal., 14g fat (6g sat. fat), 67mg chol., 654mg sod., 28g carb. (4g sugars, 1g fiber), 26g pro.

SRIRACHA-MARINATED SKIRT STEAK

I developed this recipe when looking for ways to use up a bottle of Sriracha. I knew I wanted something quick and easy but with a lot of flavor. It can also be cooked on the stovetop in a cast-iron skillet over medium-high heat. Avoid overcooking, and cut the steak across the grain for the most tender result. Flank steak can be used in place of skirt steak.
—*Kristen Streepey, Geneva, IL*

PREP: 10 min. + marinating
GRILL: 10 min. • **MAKES:** 8 servings

- ½ cup canola oil
- ¼ cup Sriracha chili sauce
- 1 Tbsp. lime juice
- 1 tsp. grated lime zest
- ½ tsp. kosher salt
- ¼ tsp. ground cumin
- ¼ tsp. smoked paprika
- 1 beef skirt steak (2 lbs.)

1. In a small bowl, whisk the first 7 ingredients until blended. Pour into a shallow dish. Add beef; turn to coat. Cover and refrigerate at least 4 hours or overnight.

2. Drain beef, discarding marinade. Grill, covered, over medium-high heat until meat reaches desired doneness (for medium-rare, a thermometer should read 135°; medium, 140°; medium-well, 145°), 4-6 minutes on each side. Let steak stand 5 minutes.

3. Cut diagonally across the grain into thin slices.

4 OZ. COOKED STEAK 286 cal., 17g fat (5g sat. fat), 67mg chol., 230mg sod., 1g carb. (1g sugars, 0 fiber), 30g pro.

STEAK & POTATO FOIL PACKS

As a park ranger, I often assemble foil packs and toss them into my backpack with some ice. When I set up camp, I cook them over a campfire. If I'm at home, I use my grill, and the food is just as good.
—Ralph Jones, San Diego, CA

PREP: 20 min. • **GRILL:** 20 min.
MAKES: 8 servings

- 2 beef top sirloin steaks (1½ lbs. each)
- 3 lbs. red potatoes, cut into ½-in. cubes
- 1 medium onion, chopped
- 4 tsp. minced fresh rosemary
- 1 Tbsp. minced garlic
- 2 tsp. salt
- 1 tsp. pepper

1. Prepare grill for medium heat or preheat oven to 450°. Cut each steak into 4 pieces. In a large bowl, combine steak, potatoes, onion, rosemary, garlic, salt and pepper.
2. Divide mixture among eight 18x12-in. pieces of heavy-duty foil, placing food on the dull side of the foil. Fold foil around potato mixture, sealing tightly.
3. Place packets on grill or in oven; cook until potatoes are tender, 8-10 minutes on each side. Open packets carefully to allow steam to escape. If desired, sprinkle with additional rosemary.

1 PACKET 348 cal., 7g fat (3g sat. fat), 69mg chol., 677mg sod., 29g carb. (2g sugars, 3g fiber), 40g pro. **DIABETIC EXCHANGES** 5 lean meat, 2 starch.

GRILLED MEAT LOAF

This recipe is the perfect twist on a comforting family favorite. Shape the meat into loaves and bake them on a grill. Ketchup brushed over the meat lends a little sweetness to each slice.
—Catherine Carpenter, Barnesville, OH

PREP: 10 min. • **GRILL:** 50 min. + standing
MAKES: 2 loaves (4 servings each)

- ½ cup ketchup
- ½ cup quick-cooking oats
- ¼ cup chopped green pepper
- 1 large egg
- 1 tsp. dried parsley flakes
- 1 tsp. Worcestershire sauce
- ½ tsp. garlic powder
- ½ tsp. dried basil
- ¼ tsp. pepper
- 2 lbs. lean ground beef (90% lean)

1. In a large bowl, combine the first 9 ingredients. Crumble beef over the mixture and mix lightly but thoroughly. Shape into 2 loaves.
2. Prepare grill for indirect heat. Grill loaves on a piece of heavy-duty foil (do not seal foil around loaves), covered, over indirect medium heat 50 minutes or until meat is no longer pink and a thermometer reads 160°. If desired, brush tops with additional ketchup. Let stand 10 minutes before slicing.

1 PIECE 223 cal., 10g fat (4g sat. fat), 94mg chol., 266mg sod., 8g carb. (4g sugars, 1g fiber), 23g pro. **DIABETIC EXCHANGES** 3 lean meat, ½ starch.

GRUYERE & EGG BURGERS

These burgers were a huge hit with our friends during football season. Regular mayo can easily be substituted for the garlic aioli if desired.

—*Melissa Pelkey Hass, Waleska, GA*

PREP: 30 min. • **COOK:** 20 min.
MAKES: 8 servings

- ½ cup mayonnaise
- 2 garlic cloves, minced
- 1 tsp. lemon juice
- ½ tsp. grated lemon zest

CHEESEBURGERS

- 2 lbs. lean ground beef (90% lean)
- 1 Tbsp. stone-ground mustard
- 1 Tbsp. olive oil
- 1 tsp. dried thyme
- ½ tsp. salt
- ½ tsp. pepper
- 8 slices Gruyere or aged Swiss cheese
- 8 mini pretzel buns, split

FRIED EGGS

- 2 Tbsp. butter
- 8 large eggs

TOPPINGS

- 2 medium tomatoes, sliced
  Fresh arugula
  Additional stone-ground mustard, optional

1. Whisk mayonnaise, garlic, lemon juice and zest until blended. Refrigerate.
2. For burgers, combine the next 6 ingredients, mixing lightly but thoroughly (do not overmix). Shape into 8 patties. Grill, covered, over medium direct heat until a thermometer reads 160°, 5-7 minutes on each side. Top with cheese; grill, covered, until the cheese is melted, 1-2 minutes longer. Place burgers on bun bottoms. Keep warm.
3. Melt 1 Tbsp. butter over medium heat in each of 2 large skillets (on grill or stovetop). Break eggs, 1 at a time, into a custard cup or saucer, then gently slide into pans. Immediately reduce heat to low. To prepare eggs sunny-side up, cover pan and cook until yolks thicken but are not hard. To make basted eggs, spoon the butter in pan over eggs while cooking. For over-easy, carefully turn eggs to cook both sides but do not cover the pan.
4. To serve, spread mayonnaise mixture over bun tops. Add tomatoes, arugula and, if desired, additional mustard to burgers. Top with fried eggs. Replace bun tops.

1 BURGER 595 cal., 38g fat (13g sat. fat), 289mg chol., 729mg sod., 23g carb. (3g sugars, 1g fiber), 39g pro.

TERIYAKI SIRLOIN STEAK

Since a co-worker shared this recipe with me, I seldom make steak any other way. It's an excellent entree for folks like my husband who really savor tasty meat, and it's earned me many compliments on my cooking.

—*Nilah Lewis, Calgary, AB*

PREP: 10 min. + marinating
GRILL: 10 min. • **MAKES:** 6 servings

- ½ cup soy sauce
- ¼ cup canola oil
- ¼ cup packed brown sugar
- 2 tsp. ground mustard
- 2 tsp. ground ginger
- 1 tsp. garlic powder
- 1 beef top sirloin steak (1½ lbs.)

1. In a shallow dish, combine the first 6 ingredients; add the steak and turn to coat. Cover and refrigerate 8 hours or overnight.
2. Drain steak, discarding marinade. Grill steak, covered, over medium heat until meat reaches desired doneness (for medium-rare, a thermometer should read 135°; medium, 140°; medium-well, 145°), 5-8 minutes on each side.

3 OZ. COOKED BEEF 178 cal., 7g fat (2g sat. fat), 46mg chol., 370mg sod., 2g carb. (2g sugars, 0 fiber), 25g pro **DIABETIC EXCHANGES** 3 lean meat, ½ fat.

KOREAN SHORT RIBS

These ribs are cut across the bone lengthwise, or flanken-style. The ginger gives the sweet and savory marinade a nice freshness.

—Taste of Home *Test Kitchen*

PREP: 10 min. + marinating
GRILL: 10 min. • **MAKES:** 6 servings

- ½ cup soy sauce
- ⅓ cup packed brown sugar
- ¼ cup mirin (sweet rice wine)
- 2 tsp. sesame oil
- ½ tsp. pepper
- 1 Asian pear, peeled, cored and quartered
- 1 medium onion, quartered
- 8 garlic cloves
- 1-in. piece fresh gingerroot

- 3 lbs. bone-in beef short ribs, cut flanken-style
  Sesame seeds and sliced green onions

1. In a 13x9-in. dish, combine the first 5 ingredients. Place the pear, onion, garlic and ginger in a blender; process until smooth. Whisk into the soy sauce mixture. Add ribs; turn to coat. Cover and refrigerate for 4 hours.
2. Drain and discard marinade. Grill ribs, covered, over medium heat 4-5 minutes on each side or until the meat reaches desired doneness (for medium-rare, a thermometer should read 135°; medium, 140°; medium-well, 145°). Garnish with sesame seeds and green onions.
1 SERVING 238 cal., 12g fat (5g sat. fat), 55mg chol., 650mg sod., 12g carb. (9g sugars, 1g fiber), 20g pro.

GRILLED STEAK TACOS

Spicy aioli brings a zesty kick to steak tacos, and the ribeye is a nice upgrade from typical ground beef. Grab one and enjoy the burst of flavor in each bite!
—*Michael Compean, Los Angeles, CA*

PREP: 25 min. • **GRILL:** 15 min.
MAKES: 4 servings

SPICY AIOLI
- ¼ cup mayonnaise
- 2 tsp. Sriracha chili sauce or 1 tsp. hot pepper sauce
- ⅛ tsp. sesame oil

AVOCADO-CORN SALSA
- 1 medium ripe avocado, peeled and finely chopped
- ½ medium tomato, seeded and chopped
- 3 Tbsp. sliced ripe olives
- 2 Tbsp. canned whole kernel corn
- 2 Tbsp. chopped sweet red pepper
- 2 Tbsp. lime juice
- 4 tsp. minced fresh cilantro
- 1 tsp. kosher salt
- 1 tsp. finely chopped onion
- 1 garlic clove, minced
- ¼ tsp. ground cumin

STEAKS
- 2 tsp. pepper
- 2 tsp. olive oil
- 1 tsp. kosher salt
- 1 tsp. seafood seasoning
- 1 beef ribeye steak (1 lb.), trimmed
- 8 flour tortillas (6 in.)
  Optional: Shredded lettuce, cheddar and Cotija cheese

1. In a small bowl, combine the aioli ingredients. In another bowl, combine the salsa ingredients. Refrigerate until serving.

2. For the steaks, combine the pepper, oil, salt and seafood seasoning; rub over both sides of steak.

3. Grill, covered, over medium heat until meat reaches desired doneness (for medium-rare, a thermometer should read 135°; medium, 140°; medium-well, 145°), 6-8 minutes on each side. Let stand for 5 minutes.

4. Meanwhile, grill tortillas until warm, about 45 seconds on each side. Thinly slice steak; place on tortillas. Serve with aioli, salsa and toppings of your choice.

NOTE Hot pepper sauce is prepared from red chili peppers, vinegar and salt, and is often aged in wooden casks like wine and specialty vinegars. Hot pepper sauce is used in cooking or as a condiment when a spicy, hot flavor is desired.

2 TACOS 650 cal., 45g fat (10g sat. fat), 72mg chol., 1843mg sod., 35g carb. (2g sugars, 4g fiber), 28g pro.

READER REVIEW
"Really nummy! The aioli is so, so good! I will make that in the future for a veggie dip. And the grilled steak with tacos is a welcome change to burgers and hot dogs. Thank you!"
—CALLIE067, TASTEOFHOME.COM

KEY WEST FLANK STEAK

My husband, Jason, is the cook in our family. This is his recipe, inspired by his Colombian roots and our visits to Key West. Serve with sides of rice and fried plantains.
—*Gretchen Ospina, Columbia Heights, MN*

PREP: 20 min. + marinating
GRILL: 15 min. + standing
MAKES: 4 servings

1 large red onion, sliced
1 cup minced fresh cilantro
¼ cup white wine vinegar
¼ cup Key lime juice
3 Tbsp. extra virgin olive oil, divided
6 Key limes, halved
1 beef flank steak (1 lb.)
1 tsp. kosher salt
⅛ tsp. pepper

1. In a small bowl, combine the onion, cilantro, vinegar, lime juice and 2 Tbsp. oil until blended. Pour 1 cup marinade into a large bowl or shallow dish. Add lime halves. Rub steak with remaining 1 Tbsp. oil; sprinkle with salt and pepper. Add to bowl; turn to coat. Refrigerate 8 hours or overnight. Cover and refrigerate the remaining marinade.
2. Drain steak, discarding the marinade and limes in bowl. Place reserved marinade in a food processor; process until chopped.
3. Grill steak, covered, over medium heat or broil 4 in. from heat until meat reaches desired doneness (for medium-rare, a thermometer should read 135°; medium, 140°; medium-well; 145°), 6-8 minutes per side. Baste occasionally with the reserved marinade. Let stand 10 minutes before thinly slicing steak across the grain. If desired, serve with additional limes, onions and cilantro.
3 OZ. COOKED STEAK 271 cal., 16g fat (5g sat. fat), 54mg chol., 431mg sod., 12g carb. (3g sugars, 3g fiber), 23g pro **DIABETIC EXCHANGES** 3 lean meat, 1½ fat.

MOLASSES STEAK SANDWICHES

The classic combination of steak and Swiss gets an added down-home sweetness thanks to a molasses-based marinade. This familiar yet distinctive sandwich is special enough to serve at any get-together.
—Taste of Home *Test Kitchen*

PREP: 15 min. + marinating
GRILL: 15 min. • **MAKES:** 4 servings

¼ cup molasses
2 Tbsp. brown sugar
2 Tbsp. olive oil, divided
1 Tbsp. Dijon mustard
4 beef tenderloin steaks (1 in. thick and 4 oz. each)
2 large portobello mushrooms, stems removed
4 kaiser rolls, split
4 slices Swiss cheese

1. In a shallow dish, mix the molasses, brown sugar, 1 Tbsp. oil and mustard. Add steaks and turn to coat. Cover; refrigerate up to 2 hours.
2. Drain beef, discarding the marinade. Brush mushrooms with the remaining 1 Tbsp. oil. Grill steaks, covered, over medium heat 5-7 minutes on each side or until meat reaches desired doneness (for medium-rare, a thermometer should read 135°; medium, 140°; medium-well, 145°). Meanwhile, grill mushrooms, covered, 8-10 minutes or until tender, turning occasionally. Remove steaks and mushrooms from grill; let stand 5 minutes.
3. Grill rolls, cut side down, until lightly toasted, 2-3 minutes. Cut mushrooms and steaks into slices. Serve in rolls with cheese.
1 SANDWICH 452 cal., 17g fat (5g sat. fat), 59mg chol., 367mg sod., 40g carb. (9g sugars, 2g fiber), 34g pro.

2. Preheat smoker to 225°. Add wood chips or pellets to smoker according to manufacturer's directions. Place brisket in smoker fat side up, point facing toward heat source. Smoke until a thermometer inserted in beef reads 165° and a dark bark has formed, about 8 hours.

3. Wrap the brisket securely in unwaxed butcher paper; smoke until a thermometer inserted in beef reads 202° and meat is very tender, 4-5 more hours.

4. Let wrapped beef stand at room temperature 1 hour before slicing; cut diagonally across the grain into thin slices.

4 OZ. COOKED BEEF 193 cal., 7g fat (2g sat. fat), 64mg chol., 384mg sod., 0 carb. (0 sugars, 0 fiber), 31g pro. **DIABETIC EXCHANGES** 4 lean meat.

GRILLED BURGERS

Sour cream makes these burgers delightfully moist, and thyme and black pepper give them zip. They're a terrific taste of summer.
—*Jesse and Anne Foust, Bluefield, WV*

TAKES: 20 min. • **MAKES:** 10 servings

- ¼ cup sour cream
- 2 tsp. dried parsley flakes
- 1 tsp. dried thyme
- 1 tsp. salt
- ½ tsp. pepper
- 2½ lbs. ground beef
- 10 hamburger buns, split
  Optional: Cheese, lettuce leaves, sliced tomato, pickles, sliced onion, ketchup and mayonnaise

1. Combine first 5 ingredients; add beef and mix lightly but thoroughly. Shape into 10 patties.

2. Grill, uncovered, over medium heat for 4-5 minutes on each side or until meat is no longer pink. Serve on buns with desired toppings.

1 BURGER 358 cal., 17g fat (7g sat. fat), 79mg chol., 534mg sod., 22g carb. (3g sugars, 1g fiber), 26g pro.

SMOKED WHOLE BRISKET

Barbecue enthusiasts will love bringing the smoker out to cook up this tender and juicy beef brisket. This recipe is the perfect starting base with its light yellow mustard, salt, pepper and onion powder seasoning. Flavor it up with your favorite seasonings, or keep it as it is and use it in a dish like tacos or sandwiches.
—*Taste of Home Test Kitchen*

PREP: 20 min. + standing
COOK: 12 hours • **MAKES:** 36 servings

- 1 fresh whole beef brisket (12 to 14 lbs.)
- 3 Tbsp. yellow mustard or olive oil
- 2 Tbsp. kosher salt
- 2 Tbsp. coarsely ground pepper
- 2 tsp. onion powder, optional

1. Place brisket on a cutting board, fat side down. Trim silver skin and fat from top. Turn brisket over. Trim fat to ¼-in.-thickness. Brush mustard over both sides of beef. Combine salt, pepper and, if desired, onion powder; rub over both sides of beef. Let stand at room temperature for 1 hour.

ITALIAN MEATBALL KABOBS

When the temperature climbs, these deliciously different kabobs are so fun to throw on the grill. Add a green salad and rustic bread to make a complete meal.

—*Marie Rizzio, Interlochen, MI*

PREP: 30 min. • **GRILL:** 10 min.
MAKES: 12 kabobs

- 2 large eggs, lightly beaten
- ⅔ cup seasoned bread crumbs
- ½ cup grated Parmesan cheese
- ¼ cup minced fresh parsley
- 4 tsp. Italian seasoning
- ½ tsp. salt
- ½ tsp. garlic powder
- 2½ lbs. ground beef
- 1 medium onion, cut into 1-in. pieces
- 1 medium sweet red pepper, cut into 1-in. pieces
- 1 medium zucchini, cut into 1-in. pieces
- ½ small eggplant, cut into 1-in. pieces
- ½ cup balsamic vinegar
- ½ cup olive oil

1. Combine the first 7 ingredients. Crumble beef over mixture. Mix lightly but thoroughly. Shape into 1½-in. balls.
2. On 12 metal or soaked wooden skewers, alternately thread meatballs and vegetables. In a small bowl, combine vinegar and oil.
3. Grill kabobs, covered, over medium heat for 8-10 minutes or until meatballs are no longer pink and vegetables are tender, basting frequently with vinegar mixture and turning occasionally.

1 KABOB 325 cal., 22g fat (6g sat. fat), 97mg chol., 315mg sod., 10g carb. (4g sugars, 2g fiber), 21g pro.

ITALIAN PATTIES

While trying to think of a new way to fix hamburgers with the same old ground beef, I came up with an Italian twist. They're perfect with a side salad or fresh green beans.

—*Rebekah Beyer, Sabetha, KS*

TAKES: 20 min. • **MAKES:** 4 servings

- 1 cup shredded part-skim mozzarella cheese, divided
- 1 tsp. Worcestershire sauce
- ¼ tsp. Italian seasoning
- ⅛ tsp. salt
- ⅛ tsp. pepper
- 1 lb. ground beef
  Marinara or spaghetti sauce, warmed

1. In a large bowl, combine ½ cup cheese and seasonings. Add beef; mix lightly but thoroughly. Shape into four ½-in.-thick patties.
2. Grill burgers, covered, over medium heat or broil 4 in. from heat until a thermometer reads 160°, 4-5 minutes on each side. Sprinkle with remaining cheese; grill, covered, until cheese is melted, 1-2 minutes longer. Serve with marinara sauce.

1 BURGER 279 cal., 18g fat (8g sat. fat), 86mg chol., 282mg sod., 1g carb. (1g sugars, 0 fiber), 27g pro.

GRILLED GREATS: CHICKEN

4 green onions, chopped
6 apricots, quartered
1 large sweet red pepper, cut into 1½-in. pieces

1. In a shallow dish, combine 1 cup yogurt, 2 Tbsp. orange juice, garlic, orange zest, salt and curry powder. Add chicken; turn to coat. Cover and refrigerate 1 hour.
2. Meanwhile, whisk remaining ⅓ cup yogurt, 2 Tbsp. orange juice, feta and mint. Cover and refrigerate until serving.
3. In a small saucepan, combine 1¼ cups water and remaining ¾ cup orange juice; bring to a boil. Stir in couscous. Sprinkle green onions over couscous. Remove from the heat; let stand, covered, until liquid is absorbed, 5-10 minutes. Fluff with a fork.
4. Drain chicken, discarding marinade. On 6 metal or soaked wooden skewers, alternately thread chicken, apricots and sweet red peppers. Grill on an oiled rack, covered, over medium-high heat until chicken is no longer pink, 6-8 minutes, turning occasionally. Serve with couscous and yogurt sauce.
1 SKEWER WITH ½ CUP COUSCOUS AND 5 TSP. YOGURT SAUCE 312 cal., 5g fat (2g sat. fat), 50mg chol., 266mg sod., 44g carb. (11g sugars, 7g fiber), 25g pro
DIABETIC EXCHANGES 3 starch, 3 lean meat.

ORANGE APRICOT COUSCOUS CHICKEN

I love the bright flavors in this recipe. The orange juice, curry powder, feta and mint really jazz up the rest of the ingredients! Once the ingredients are assembled, this recipe comes together in no time. If you like, you can use large cubed peaches or nectarines instead of apricots.
—*Margee Berry, White Salmon, WA*

PREP: 30 min. + marinating
GRILL: 10 min. • **MAKES:** 6 servings

1⅓ cups plain yogurt, divided
1 cup orange juice, divided
2 garlic cloves, minced
1 tsp. grated orange zest
½ tsp. salt
½ tsp. curry powder
1 lb. boneless skinless chicken breasts, cut into 1½-in. pieces
⅓ cup crumbled feta cheese
2 Tbsp. chopped fresh mint
1¼ cups water
1¼ cups uncooked whole wheat or plain couscous

FAVORITE BARBECUED CHICKEN

Is there a better place than Texas to find a fantastic barbecue sauce? That's where this one is from—it's my father-in-law's own recipe. We have served it at many family reunions and think it's the best!
—*Bobbie Morgan, Woodstock, GA*

PREP: 15 min. • **GRILL:** 40 min.
MAKES: 12 servings

2 broiler/fryer chickens (3 to 4 lbs. each), cut into 8 pieces each
   Salt and pepper
BARBECUE SAUCE
2 Tbsp. canola oil
2 small onions, finely chopped
2 cups ketchup
¼ cup lemon juice
2 Tbsp. brown sugar
2 Tbsp. water
1 tsp. ground mustard
½ tsp. garlic powder
¼ tsp. pepper
⅛ tsp. salt
⅛ tsp. hot pepper sauce

1. Sprinkle chicken pieces with salt and pepper. Grill, skin side down, uncovered, on a greased rack over medium heat for 20 minutes.
2. Meanwhile, in a small saucepan, make barbecue sauce by heating oil over medium heat. Add onions; saute until tender. Stir in remaining sauce ingredients and bring to a boil. Reduce heat; simmer, uncovered, 10 minutes.
3. Turn chicken; brush with barbecue sauce. Grill for 15-25 minutes longer, brushing frequently with sauce, until a thermometer reads 165° when inserted in breast and 170°-175° in thigh.
4 OZ. COOKED CHICKEN 370 cal., 19g fat (5g sat. fat), 104mg chol., 622mg sod., 15g carb. (14g sugars, 0 fiber), 33g pro.

5i GRILLED BUTTERMILK CHICKEN

I created this recipe years ago after one of our farmers market customers, a chef, shared the idea of marinating chicken in buttermilk. The chicken is easy to prepare and always turns out moist and delicious! I bruise the thyme sprigs by twisting them before adding them to the buttermilk mixture; this releases the oils in the leaves and gives the chicken more flavor.
—*Sue Gronholz, Beaver Dam, WI*

PREP: 10 min. + marinating
GRILL: 10 min. • **MAKES:** 12 servings

1½ cups buttermilk
4 fresh thyme sprigs
4 garlic cloves, halved
½ tsp. salt
12 boneless skinless chicken breast halves (about 4½ lbs.)

1. Place buttermilk, thyme, garlic and salt in a large bowl or shallow dish. Add chicken; turn to coat. Refrigerate 8 hours or overnight, turning occasionally.
2. Drain chicken, discarding marinade. Grill, covered, over medium heat until a thermometer reads 165°, 5-7 minutes per side.
1 CHICKEN BREAST HALF 189 cal., 4g fat (1g sat. fat), 95mg chol., 168mg sod., 1g carb. (1g sugars, 0 fiber), 35g pro.
DIABETIC EXCHANGES 5 lean meat.

GRILLED GREEK LEMON CHICKEN

This chicken recipe is so full of flavor! The lemon and oregano flavors shine in this simple dish. It pairs perfectly with roasted vegetables or a side salad.
—*Courtney Stultz, Weir, KS*

PREP: 15min. + marinating
GRILL: 15 min. • **MAKES:** 4 servings

2   medium lemons, zested and juiced
½   cup olive oil
2   garlic cloves, minced
2   tsp. dried oregano
1   tsp. paprika
½   tsp. ground coriander
½   tsp. salt
½   tsp. coarsely ground pepper
2   lbs. bone-in chicken thighs
    Optional: Crumbled feta cheese, minced parsley and sliced lemon

1. In a small bowl, whisk the first 8 ingredients until blended. Reserve ⅓ cup marinade. Pour the remaining marinade into a shallow dish. Add chicken; turn to coat. Refrigerate, covered, for 30 minutes. Cover and refrigerate remaining marinade.
2. Drain chicken, discarding marinade in dish. Place chicken on grill rack, skin side down. Grill, covered, over medium heat for 6-8 minutes. Turn; grill until a thermometer reads 170°-175°, 6-8 minutes longer.
3. Remove chicken to a serving platter; drizzle with reserved ⅓ cup marinade. If desired, top with feta cheese, parsley and lemon slices.
1 CHICKEN THIGH 359 cal., 26g fat (6g sat. fat), 107mg chol., 165mg sod., 1g carb. (0 sugars, 0 fiber), 30g pro.

GRILLED COCONUT CURRY WINGS

Everyone loves grilled wings and this is such a nice change from the usual version we see all summer long.
—*Carla Mendres, Winnipeg, MB*

PREP: 15 min. + marinating
GRILL: 15 min. • **MAKES:** 20 pieces

1   can (13.66 oz.) coconut milk
3   Tbsp. curry powder
4   garlic cloves, crushed
1   Tbsp. minced fresh gingerroot
2   lbs. chicken wingettes
½   tsp. salt
¼   tsp. pepper
2   Tbsp. honey, optional
    Thinly sliced green onions and lime wedges

1. In a large bowl or shallow dish, combine coconut milk, curry powder, garlic and ginger. Add chicken; turn to coat. Cover and refrigerate 8 hours or overnight.
2. Drain chicken, discarding marinade. Sprinkle chicken with salt and pepper. Grill, covered, over medium heat until juices run clear, 15-18 minutes, turning occasionally. If desired, drizzle with honey. Serve with green onions and lime wedges.
1 PIECE 82 cal., 5g fat (2g sat. fat), 36mg chol., 236mg sod., 0 carb. (0 sugars, 0 fiber), 9g pro.

CHICKEN WITH PEACH-AVOCADO SALSA

This super-fresh dinner is pure summer—juicy peaches, creamy avocado, grilled chicken and a kick of hot sauce and lime. To get it on the table even quicker, make the salsa ahead of time.
—*Shannon Norris, Cudahy, WI*

TAKES: 30 min. • **MAKES:** 4 servings

- 1 medium peach, peeled and chopped
- 1 medium ripe avocado, peeled and cubed
- ½ cup chopped sweet red pepper
- 3 Tbsp. finely chopped red onion
- 1 Tbsp. minced fresh basil
- 1 Tbsp. lime juice
- 1 tsp. hot pepper sauce
- ½ tsp. grated lime zest
- ¾ tsp. salt, divided
- ½ tsp. pepper, divided
- 4 boneless skinless chicken breast halves (6 oz. each)

1. For salsa, in a small bowl, combine peach, avocado, red pepper, onion, basil, lime juice, hot pepper sauce, lime zest, ¼ tsp. salt and ¼ tsp. pepper.
2. Sprinkle chicken with the remaining ½ tsp. salt and ¼ tsp. pepper. On a lightly greased grill rack, grill chicken, covered, over medium heat for 5 minutes. Turn; grill until a thermometer reads 165°, 7-9 minutes longer. Serve with salsa.
1 CHICKEN BREAST HALF WITH ½ CUP SALSA 265 cal., 9g fat (2g sat. fat), 94mg chol., 536mg sod., 9g carb. (4g sugars, 3g fiber), 36g pro. **DIABETIC EXCHANGES** 5 lean meat, 1 fat, ½ starch.

SUMMER TURKEY KABOBS

These kabobs let you enjoy Thanksgiving flavors at any time of the year! We enjoy grilling them in the summer.
—*Angela Mathews, Fayetteville, NY*

TAKES: 30 min. • **MAKES:** 6 kabobs

- 2 small yellow summer squash
- 2 small zucchini
- 1 can (about 15 oz.) whole potatoes, drained
- 2 Tbsp. olive oil
- 1 pkg. (20 oz.) turkey breast tenderloins
- ½ tsp. pepper
- ¼ tsp. salt
- 1 pkg. (5 oz.) torn mixed salad greens
- 1 cup salad croutons
- ½ cup red wine vinaigrette

1. Trim ends of squash and zucchini; cut crosswise into 1-in. slices. Place slices in a large bowl; add potatoes. Pour oil over mixture, tossing to coat.
2. Cut turkey into 24 cubes; add to vegetables. Sprinkle with pepper and salt; toss again.
3. On 6 metal or soaked wooden skewers, alternately thread turkey cubes, squash, zucchini and potatoes. Grill, covered, over medium heat, turning occasionally, until turkey is no longer pink and vegetables are crisp-tender, 12-15 minutes. Serve on greens with croutons. Drizzle with vinaigrette.

1 KABOB 274 cal., 13g fat (1g sat. fat), 38mg chol., 720mg sod., 15g carb. (3g sugars, 2g fiber), 26g pro. **DIABETIC EXCHANGES** 2 lean meat, 1 vegetable, 1 fat, ½ starch.

CHILI SAUCE CHICKEN

Chili sauce, with plenty of garlic and basil, flavors these moist chicken thighs. We enjoy this tender grilled chicken not just in the summer, but throughout the year.
—*Marilyn Waltz, Idyllwild, CA*

PREP: 15 min. + marinating
GRILL: 25 min. • **MAKES:** 8 servings

- 1 bottle (12 oz.) chili sauce
- ⅓ cup white wine or chicken broth
- ¼ cup olive oil
- 10 to 12 garlic cloves, minced
- 4½ tsp. dried basil
- ½ tsp. salt
- ⅛ tsp. pepper
- 8 bone-in chicken thighs (about 3 lbs.)

1. In a large bowl, whisk the first 7 ingredients until blended. Pour 1½ cups marinade into a shallow dish. Add chicken and turn to coat. Refrigerate for 8 hours or overnight. Cover and refrigerate remaining marinade.
2. Drain chicken, discarding the marinade in dish. Place chicken on a greased grill rack, skin side down. Grill, covered, over medium heat or broil 4 in. from heat for 15 minutes. Turn; grill for 10-15 minutes longer or until a thermometer reads 170°-175°, basting occasionally with reserved marinade.

FREEZE OPTION Freeze chicken with 1½ cups marinade in an airtight container. Freeze reserved marinade in a freezer container. To use, thaw chicken with marinade and reserved marinade in refrigerator overnight. Drain chicken, discarding marinade. Grill as directed, basting with reserved marinade.

1 CHICKEN THIGH 268 cal., 17g fat (4g sat. fat), 81mg chol., 352mg sod., 5g carb. (3g sugars, 0 fiber), 23g pro.

GRILLED CHERRY-GLAZED CHICKEN WINGS

When I take these grilled wings to events, there are never any leftovers! Friends and family love them.
—*Ashley Gable, Atlanta, GA*

PREP: 20 min. • **GRILL:** 15 min.
MAKES: 2 dozen

- 12 chicken wings (about 3 lbs.)
- 3 Tbsp. canola oil, divided
- 1 garlic clove, minced
- 1 cup ketchup
- ½ cup cider vinegar
- ½ cup cherry preserves
- 2 Tbsp. Louisiana-style hot sauce
- 1 Tbsp. Worcestershire sauce
- 3 tsp. coarse salt, divided
- 1 tsp. coarsely ground pepper, divided

1. Cut through 2 wing joints; discard wing tips. In a small saucepan, heat 1 Tbsp. oil over medium heat. Add garlic; cook and stir 1 minute. Stir in ketchup, vinegar, cherry preserves, hot sauce, Worcestershire sauce, 1 tsp. salt and ½ tsp. pepper. Cook and stir until heated through. Brush wings with remaining 2 Tbsp. oil; sprinkle with remaining 2 tsp. salt and ½ tsp. pepper.
2. Grill, covered, over medium heat until juices run clear, 15-18 minutes, turning occasionally and brushing with glaze during last 5 minutes of grilling. Serve with remaining glaze.
1 PIECE 107 cal., 6g fat (1g sat. fat), 18mg chol., 439mg sod., 7g carb. (7g sugars, 0 fiber), 6g pro.

BRUSCHETTA CHICKEN WRAPS

As an Italian-American, I love, love, love garlic, tomatoes and basil, all of which are musts for good bruschetta. This recipe was created in celebration of the first tomatoes to come out of our home garden this year.
—*Gina Rine, Canfield, OH*

TAKES: 30 min. • **MAKES:** 4 servings

- 2 plum tomatoes, finely chopped (about 1 cup)
- 1 cup fresh baby spinach, coarsely chopped
- ¼ cup finely chopped red onion
- 1 Tbsp. shredded Parmesan or Romano cheese
- 1 Tbsp. minced fresh basil
- 1 tsp. olive oil
- 1 tsp. balsamic vinegar
- ⅛ tsp. plus ¼ tsp. pepper, divided Dash garlic powder
- 4 boneless skinless chicken breast halves (4 oz. each)
- ½ tsp. salt
- 2 oz. fresh mozzarella cheese, cut into 4 slices
- 4 whole wheat tortillas (8 in.)

1. In a small bowl, mix tomatoes, spinach, onion, cheese, basil, oil, vinegar, ⅛ tsp. pepper and garlic powder.
2. Sprinkle chicken with salt and remaining ¼ tsp. pepper; place on lightly oiled grill rack. Grill, covered, over medium heat for 4-6 minutes on each side or until a thermometer reads 165°.
3. Top each chicken breast with 1 cheese slice; cover and grill until cheese is melted, 1-2 minutes longer. Grill tortillas over medium heat until heated through, 20-30 seconds.
4. Place chicken on center of each tortilla; top with about ¼ cup tomato mixture. Fold bottom of tortilla over filling; fold both sides to close.
1 WRAP 330 cal., 10g fat (3g sat. fat), 75mg chol., 569mg sod., 25g carb. (3g sugars, 3g fiber), 31g pro. **DIABETIC EXCHANGES** 3 lean meat, 2 starch, 1 fat.

SMOKED TURKEY

Mouths will water when you bring this flavorful smoked turkey to the table. Add sprigs of your favorite herbs like thyme, sage or rosemary to the brine for extra flavor.
—Taste of Home *Test Kitchen*

PREP: 40 min+ brining
COOK: 3 hours + standing
MAKES: 12 servings

BRINE
2 qt. water
1 medium tart apple, sliced into ¼-in.-thick rounds
1 cup kosher salt
1 cup maple syrup
4 bay leaves
1 Tbsp. cider vinegar
2 tsp. whole peppercorns
3 qt. ice water

TURKEY
1 turkey (10 to 12 lbs.)
1 large sweet onion, cut into wedges
1 large apple, cut into wedges
1 Tbsp. kosher salt
1 Tbsp. brown sugar
1 Tbsp. paprika
1 tsp. onion powder
1 tsp. garlic powder
3 cups soaked apple wood chips

1. To make brine, in a large kettle, combine first 7 ingredients. Bring to a boil; cook and stir until salt is dissolved. Remove from heat. Add ice water to cool brine to room temperature.

2. Place a turkey-sized oven roasting bag inside a second roasting bag; add turkey. Carefully pour cooled brine into the inner bag. Squeeze out as much air as possible; seal bags and turn to coat. Place in a roasting pan or other large container. Refrigerate for 8-12 hours, turning occasionally.

3. Prepare grill for indirect heat, using a drip pan. Add wood chips to the grill according to manufacturer's directions. Drain turkey, discarding brine. Rinse turkey under cold water; pat dry. Add onion and apple wedges to cavity. Tie drumsticks together.

4. In a small bowl, combine kosher salt, brown sugar, paprika, onion powder and garlic powder; rub over outside of turkey. Place turkey breast side up in 2 nested foil roasting pans (stack pans together for sturdiness). Grill, covered, over indirect medium heat for 3-3½ hours, rotating halfway, or until a thermometer inserted in thickest part of thigh reads 170°-175°. Cover and let stand 15 minutes before carving.

8 OZ. COOKED TURKEY 450 cal., 20g fat (6g sat. fat), 205mg chol., 702mg sod., 2g carb. (2g sugars, 0 fiber), 60g pro.

TEST KITCHEN TIP

See p. 84 for more tips on how to turn your grill into a smoker.

GRILLED THIGHS & DRUMSTICKS

This chicken is juicy, has great barbecue flavor and makes a big batch, so it's perfect for summer picnics and family reunions.
—*Brenda Beachy, Belvidere, TN*

PREP: 10 min. + marinating
GRILL: 30 min. • **MAKES:** 18 servings

- 2½ cups packed brown sugar
- 2 cups water
- 2 cups cider vinegar
- 2 cups ketchup
- 1 cup canola oil
- 4 Tbsp. salt
- 3 Tbsp. prepared mustard
- 4½ tsp. Worcestershire sauce
- 1 Tbsp. reduced-sodium soy sauce
- 1 tsp. pepper
- 1 tsp. Liquid Smoke, optional
- 10 lbs. bone-in chicken thighs and chicken drumsticks
- ½ tsp. seasoned salt

1. In a large bowl, combine the first 10 ingredients. If desired, add Liquid Smoke. Pour into 2 large shallow dishes; add equal amounts of chicken to each dish; turn to coat. Cover and refrigerate overnight.
2. Drain and discard marinade. Sprinkle chicken with seasoned salt. Grill chicken, covered, over indirect medium heat for 15-20 minutes on each side until a thermometer reads 170°-175°.
5 OZ. COOKED CHICKEN 384 cal., 19g fat (4g sat. fat), 128mg chol., 970mg sod., 16g carb. (15g sugars, 0 fiber), 36g pro.

TEST KITCHEN TIP

If your cookout gets rained out, you can easily prepare this recipe by broiling or baking the chicken instead.

GRILLED CHICKEN BURGERS

These chicken burgers get a delicious hint of sweetness with tart apples mixed right into the patties. The cranberry-mayo spread elevates it even further.
—*Debbie Gauthier, Timmins, ON*

TAKES: 30 min. • **MAKES:** 4 servings

- 1 medium tart apple, peeled and finely chopped
- 1 small onion, finely chopped
- 1 celery rib, finely chopped
- ¼ tsp. salt
- ¼ tsp. poultry seasoning
  Dash pepper
- 1 lb. ground chicken
- ¼ cup whole-berry cranberry sauce
- 1 Tbsp. mayonnaise
- 4 hamburger buns, split
  Bibb lettuce leaves, optional

1. In a large bowl, combine the first 6 ingredients. Crumble chicken over mixture and mix lightly but thoroughly. Shape into 4 patties.
2. Cook on a grill 10-12 minutes or until a thermometer reads 165°.
3. In a small bowl, combine cranberry sauce and mayonnaise. Serve burgers on buns with cranberry spread and, if desired, lettuce.
1 BURGER 345 cal., 14g fat (3g sat. fat), 76mg chol., 450mg sod., 34g carb. (11g sugars, 2g fiber), 22g pro.

CHICKEN OLE FOIL SUPPER

These Mexi-style chicken packets can be assembled ahead of time and frozen if you like. Just thaw them overnight in the fridge, then grill as directed. I like to serve them with warm tortillas and fresh fruit on the side.
—*Mary Peck, Salina, KS*

TAKES: 30 min. • **MAKES:** 4 servings

- 1 can (15 oz.) black beans, rinsed and drained
- 2 cups fresh or frozen corn (about 10 oz.), thawed
- 1 cup salsa
- 4 boneless skinless chicken breast halves (4 oz. each)
- ¼ tsp. garlic powder
- ¼ tsp. pepper
- ⅛ tsp. salt
- 1 cup shredded cheddar cheese
- 2 green onions, chopped

1. Mix beans, corn and salsa; divide among four 18x12-in. pieces of heavy-duty foil. Top with chicken. Mix the seasonings; sprinkle over chicken. Fold foil over chicken, sealing tightly.
2. Grill packets, covered, over medium heat until a thermometer inserted in chicken reads 165°, 15-20 minutes. Open foil carefully to allow steam to escape. Sprinkle with cheese and green onions.
1 SERVING 405 cal., 13g fat (6g sat. fat), 91mg chol., 766mg sod., 34g carb. (8g sugars, 6g fiber), 37g pro. **DIABETIC EXCHANGES** 4 lean meat, 2 starch, 1 fat.

GRILLED HULI HULI CHICKEN

When I lived in Hawaii, I got this recipe for chicken marinated in a ginger-soy sauce from a friend. *Huli* means "turn" in Hawaiian and refers to turning the meat on the grill.
—*Sharon Boling, San Diego, CA*

PREP: 15 min. + marinating
GRILL: 15 min. • **MAKES:** 12 servings

- 1 cup packed brown sugar
- ¾ cup ketchup
- ¾ cup reduced-sodium soy sauce
- ⅓ cup sherry or chicken broth
- 2½ tsp. minced fresh gingerroot
- 1½ tsp. minced garlic
- 24 boneless skinless chicken thighs (about 6 lbs.)

1. In a small bowl, combine the first 6 ingredients. Reserve 1⅓ cups for basting; cover and refrigerate. Divide remaining marinade between 2 large shallow dishes. Add 12 chicken thighs to each; turn to coat. Refrigerate, covered, for 8 hours or overnight.

2. Drain chicken, discarding marinade. Grill chicken, covered, on an oiled rack over medium heat for 6-8 minutes on each side or until a thermometer inserted into the chicken reads 170°; baste occasionally with the reserved marinade during the last 5 minutes.

2 CHICKEN THIGHS 391 cal., 16g fat (5g sat. fat), 151mg chol., 651mg sod., 15g carb. (14g sugars, 0 fiber), 43g pro.

CHICKEN YAKITORI

I grew up in Tokyo, and some of my favorite memories include eating street food like this yakitori with my friends. Though we now live thousands of miles apart, my friends and I still reminisce about our nights of sharing secrets and bonding over delicious meals. This one is easy to re-create at home, which makes it perfect for when I'm feeling homesick. I like to serve it with rice.
—*Lindsay Howerton-Hastings, Greenville, SC*

TAKES: 30 min. • **MAKES:** 6 servings

- ½ cup mirin (sweet rice wine)
- ½ cup sake
- ½ cup soy sauce
- 1 Tbsp. sugar
- 2 large sweet red peppers, cut into 2-in. pieces
- 2 lbs. boneless skinless chicken thighs, cut into 1½-in. pieces
- 1 bunch green onions

1. In a small saucepan, combine the first 4 ingredients. Bring to a boil over medium-high heat. Remove from heat; set aside half the mixture for serving.
2. Thread red peppers onto 2 metal or soaked wooden skewers. Thread chicken onto 6 metal or soaked wooden skewers. Grill chicken, covered, over medium heat until the meat is cooked through, 10-12 minutes, turning occasionally and basting frequently with soy sauce mixture during the last 3 minutes. Grill red peppers, covered, until tender, 4-5 minutes, turning occasionally. Grill onions, covered, until lightly charred, 1-2 minutes, turning occasionally. Serve chicken and vegetables with reserved sauce for dipping.
4 OZ. COOKED CHICKEN 332 cal., 11g fat (3g sat. fat), 101mg chol., 1316mg sod., 14g carb. (11g sugars, 1g fiber), 32g pro.

TEST KITCHEN TIP

In Japan, you'll find all parts of the chicken used in yakitori, from thighs, breasts and tenders to the skin, tail and heart. For a basic homemade recipe, boneless, skinless chicken thighs are your best bet.

SMOKED CHICKEN WINGS

When you want chicken with deep, rich flavor, there's no better way to achieve it than by bringing out the smoker! The chicken remains juicy and tender while the coating is crispy and full of simple seasonings. Toss it in some barbecue sauce for the perfect tangy flavor.
—*Margaret Knoebel, Milwaukee, WI*

PREP: 15 min. + standing
COOK: 2 hours • **MAKES:** 2 dozen

- 1   Tbsp. baking powder
- 1   tsp. garlic powder
- 1   tsp. salt
- ½   tsp. coarsely ground pepper
- 2½ lbs. whole chicken wings
      Optional: 1 cup wing sauce
      or barbecue sauce, and
      ranch dressing

1. Preheat smoker to 250°. Add wood chips or pellets to smoker according to manufacturer's directions.
2. In a large bowl, combine baking powder, garlic powder, salt and pepper.
3. Using a sharp knife, cut through 2 wing joints; discard wing tips. Place remaining wing pieces in spice mixture, toss to coat. Let stand 30 minutes.
4. Place on greased smoke rack, and smoke until tender and juices run clear, 2-2¼ hours. For extra crispy wings, place on rack in broiler pan. Broil 3-4 in. from heat until crisp, 2-3 minutes. If desired, toss in wing sauce and serve with ranch dressing.
1 PIECE 53 cal., 4g fat (1g sat. fat), 15mg chol., 173mg sod., 0 carb. (0 sugars, 0 fiber), 5g pro.

STUFFED GRILLED CHICKEN

As a single, working mom with two kids, I look for recipes that are fast and simple. My family loves this one and it gets dinner on the table fast.
—*Candi VanMeveren, Lamberton, MN*

TAKES: 30 min. • **MAKES:** 4 servings

- 5   Tbsp. butter, divided
- ½   cup chopped onion
- ½   tsp. minced garlic
- ¾   cup seasoned bread crumbs
- 4   boneless skinless chicken breast
      halves (6 oz. each)
- 1   tsp. grated lemon zest

1. In a small skillet, melt 3 Tbsp. butter over medium heat. Add onion; cook and stir until almost tender, 3-5 minutes. Add garlic; cook and stir 1 minute longer. Remove from heat; stir in bread crumbs. Carefully cut a pocket in each chicken breast half. Fill with bread crumb mixture; secure with toothpicks.
2. In a small microwave-safe bowl, melt remaining 2 Tbsp. butter; stir in lemon zest.
3. Grill chicken, covered, over medium heat or broil 4 in. from heat until juices run clear, 6-8 minutes on each side, basting frequently with lemon butter.
1 STUFFED CHICKEN BREAST HALF 393 cal., 19g fat (10g sat. fat), 132mg chol., 512mg sod., 16g carb. (2g sugars, 1g fiber), 38g pro.

TEST KITCHEN TIP

To save on time, make the stuffing and prepare the stuffed chicken breasts in advance. Then you'll be ready to throw them on the grill when the party starts!

TEST KITCHEN TIP

If you don't have a smoker, don't worry! Learn how to turn your grill into a smoker, p. 84.

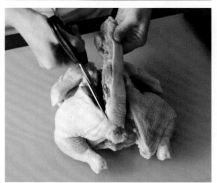

GLAZED SPATCHCOCKED CHICKEN

A few pantry items, such as mustard and preserves, inspired this recipe. Since then it has been the successful centerpiece for both small weeknight meals and big parties.

—*James Schend, Pleasant Prairie, WI*

PREP: 15 min.
GRILL: 40 minutes + standing
MAKES: 6 servings

- 1 cup white wine or chicken broth
- 1 cup apricot preserves or quince jelly
- 1 Tbsp. stone-ground mustard
- 1 broiler/fryer chicken (3 to 4 lbs.)
- ¾ tsp. salt
- ½ tsp. pepper

1. In a small saucepan, bring wine to a boil; cook 3-4 minutes or until wine is reduced by half. Stir in preserves and mustard. Reserve half the glaze for basting.

2. Cut chicken along each side of the backbone with shears. Remove the backbone. Turn chicken breast side up, and press to flatten. Sprinkle with salt and pepper.

3. Prepare the grill for indirect medium heat. Place chicken on greased grill grate, skin side down, covered, over direct heat for 10-15 minutes or until nicely browned. Turn chicken and place over indirect heat until a thermometer in thickest part of thigh reads 170°-175°, brushing occasionally with reserved glaze mixture, about 30 minutes.

4. Remove chicken from grill. Let stand 15 minutes before carving; serve with remaining glaze.

5 OZ. COOKED CHICKEN 437 cal., 17g fat (5g sat. fat), 104mg chol., 458mg sod., 35g carb. (23g sugars, 0 fiber), 34g pro.

READER REVIEW

"I was surprised at how easy it was to [prepare] the chicken. I used the backbone to make some broth and used that to cook some rice for another meal. We will make this again."

—ANNR, TASTEOFHOME.COM

SPICY LEMON CHICKEN KABOBS

When I see Meyer lemons in the store, I know it must be spring. I like using them for these easy chicken kabobs, but regular grilled lemons still add the signature smoky tang.
—*Terri Crandall, Gardnerville, NV*

PREP: 15 min. + marinating
GRILL: 10 min. • **MAKES:** 6 servings

- ¼ cup lemon juice
- 4 Tbsp. olive oil, divided
- 3 Tbsp. white wine
- 1½ tsp. crushed red pepper flakes
- 1 tsp. minced fresh rosemary or ¼ tsp. dried rosemary, crushed
- 1½ lbs. boneless skinless chicken breasts, cut into 1-in. cubes
- 2 medium lemons, halved
  Minced chives

1. In a large shallow dish, combine lemon juice, 3 Tbsp. oil, wine, red pepper flakes and rosemary. Add chicken and turn to coat. Refrigerate up to 3 hours.
2. Drain chicken, discarding marinade. Thread chicken onto 6 metal or soaked wooden skewers. Grill, covered, over medium heat until meat is no longer pink, turning once, 10-12 minutes.
3. Meanwhile, place lemons on grill, cut side down. Grill until lightly browned, 8-10 minutes. Squeeze lemon halves over chicken. Drizzle with remaining 1 Tbsp. oil; sprinkle with chives.
1 KABOB 182 cal., 8g fat (2g sat. fat), 63mg chol., 55mg sod., 2g carb. (1g sugars, 1g fiber), 23g pro. **DIABETIC EXCHANGES** 3 lean meat, 1 fat.

SWEET TEA BARBECUED CHICKEN

Marinades sometimes use coffee or espresso, and that inspired me to try tea and apple juice to perk up this sauce.
—*Kelly Williams, Forked River, NJ*

PREP: 15 min. • **COOK:** 1 hour
MAKES: 8 servings

- 1 cup unsweetened apple juice
- 1 cup water
- 2 tsp. seafood seasoning
- 1 tsp. paprika
- 1 tsp. garlic powder
- 1 tsp. coarsely ground pepper
- 1 chicken (4 to 5 lbs.), cut up
- 1 cup barbecue sauce
- ½ cup sweet tea

1. Preheat oven to 350°. Pour apple juice and water into a large shallow roasting pan. Mix seafood seasoning, paprika, garlic powder and pepper; rub over chicken. Place chicken in roasting pan.
2. Bake, covered, until juices run clear and a thermometer reads 170° to 175°, 50-60 minutes. Transfer chicken to a foil-lined 15x10x1-in. baking pan. Whisk barbecue sauce and sweet tea; brush some mixture over chicken.
3. Place chicken on greased grill rack; grill over medium heat for 3-4 minutes per side, brushing occasionally with remaining sauce.
1 PIECE 374 cal., 17g fat (5g sat. fat), 104mg chol., 608mg sod., 19g carb. (16g sugars, 1g fiber), 33g pro.

GRILLED GREATS: PORK

COUNTRY-STYLE GRILLED RIBS

A sweet and tangy barbecue sauce, sprinkled with celery seed, coats these tender ribs. Chili powder and hot pepper sauce contribute to the zesty flavor.
—*Marilyn Beerman, Worthington, OH*

PREP: 1½ hours + standing
GRILL: 10 min. • **MAKES:** 6 servings

- 4 lbs. bone-in country-style pork ribs
- 1 cup water
- 1 cup ketchup
- ¼ cup packed brown sugar
- ¼ cup cider vinegar
- ¼ cup Worcestershire sauce
- 1 Tbsp. celery seed
- 1 tsp. chili powder
- ⅛ tsp. hot pepper sauce
  Dash pepper

1. Preheat oven to 325°. Place ribs in a shallow roasting pan. Bake, covered, 1½-2 hours or until meat is tender. Meanwhile, in a small saucepan, combine the remaining ingredients. Bring to a boil. Reduce the heat; simmer, uncovered, 5 minutes, stirring occasionally. Pour 1 cup sauce over ribs; turn to coat. Let stand 15 minutes.
2. Drain and discard sauce from ribs. Grill ribs, uncovered, over medium heat 10-12 minutes or until browned, basting with 1 cup sauce and turning occasionally. Serve with remaining sauce.
1 SERVING 409 cal., 18g fat (7g sat. fat), 114mg chol., 463mg sod., 24g carb. (23g sugars, 0 fiber), 35g pro.

⑤ⁱ MOLASSES-GLAZED PORK CHOPS

How can you go wrong with these savory chops that call for only a few ingredients? Best of all, they're impressive enough to serve to guests!
—*Angela Spengler, Niceville, FL*

TAKES: 30 min. • **MAKES:** 4 servings

- ¼ cup molasses
- 1 Tbsp. Worcestershire sauce
- 1½ tsp. brown sugar
- 4 boneless pork loin chops
  (¾ in. thick and 5 oz. each)

1. In a small bowl, combine molasses, Worcestershire sauce and brown sugar. Reserve 3 Tbsp. sauce for serving.
2. Grill pork, covered, over medium heat or broil 4 in. from heat 4-5 minutes on each side or until a thermometer reads 145°, brushing with remaining sauce during the last 3 minutes of cooking. Let stand 5 minutes before serving. Serve with the reserved sauce.
1 PORK CHOP WITH ABOUT 2 TSP. SAUCE
256 cal., 8g fat (3g sat. fat), 68mg chol., 89mg sod., 17g carb. (13g sugars, 0 fiber), 27g pro. **DIABETIC EXCHANGES** 4 lean meat, 1 starch.

CHORIZO BURGERS

A chorizo burger? You bet! Pickled veggie toppers complement the spicy patties especially well.
—*Robert Johnson, Chino Valley, AZ*

PREP: 20 min. + standing
GRILL: 15 min. • **MAKES:** 2 servings

- ⅓ cup sugar
- ⅓ cup water
- ⅓ cup cider vinegar
- ½ large red onion, halved and thinly sliced
- 1 jalapeno pepper, seeded and sliced
- 6 oz. ground beef or bison
- ¼ lb. fresh chorizo or bulk spicy pork sausage
- ¼ tsp. salt
- ¼ tsp. pepper
- 2 sesame seed hamburger buns, split
- ½ cup fresh baby spinach
- 2 Tbsp. peeled and grated horseradish

1. In a large bowl, whisk the sugar, water and vinegar together until the sugar is dissolved. Add red onion and jalapeno; let stand at least 1 hour.
2. Combine the beef and chorizo; shape into two ¾-in.-thick patties. Sprinkle with salt and pepper.
3. Grill burgers, covered, over medium heat until a thermometer reads 160°, 6-8 minutes on each side. Grill buns over medium heat, cut side down, until toasted, 30-60 seconds.
4. Drain the pickled vegetables. Serve burgers on buns with spinach, pickled vegetables and horseradish.
NOTE Wear disposable gloves when cutting hot peppers; the oils can burn skin. Avoid touching your face.
1 BURGER 555 cal., 30g fat (11g sat. fat), 103mg chol., 1264mg sod., 36g carb. (10g sugars, 5g fiber), 34g pro.

GRILLED HAM STEAK

Here's a quick and impressive ham dish. Its smoky grill flavor tastes terrific with the tangy sauce.
—*Sharon Mensing, Greenfield, IA*

TAKES: 30 min. • **MAKES:** 6 servings

- ¼ cup apricot or plum preserves
- 1 Tbsp. prepared mustard
- 1 tsp. lemon juice
- ⅛ tsp. ground cinnamon
- 1 fully cooked bone-in ham steak (about 2 lbs. and 1 in. thick)

1. In a small saucepan, combine the preserves, mustard, lemon juice and cinnamon. Cook and stir over low heat for 2-3 minutes. Set glaze aside. Score edges of ham.
2. Grill, uncovered, over medium heat until a thermometer reads 140°, 5-7 minutes on each side, brushing with glaze during the last few minutes of grilling.
3 OZ. COOKED HAM 175 cal., 7g fat (2g sat. fat), 58mg chol., 1111mg sod., 10g carb. (7g sugars, 0 fiber), 18g pro.
HONEY-MUSTARD GLAZED HAM STEAK
Omit first 4 ingredients. Combine 3 Tbsp. spicy brown mustard, 2 Tbsp. honey and ½ tsp. orange zest. Grill and glaze ham as recipe directs.

BANH MI BABY BACK RIBS

This creative entree has all the flavors of the beloved Vietnamese sandwich— sans bread. Sprinkle the pork with roasted peanuts and sesame seeds, in addition to the other garnishes, for a fun crunch.
—Bonnie Geavaras-Bootz, Chandler, AZ

PREP: 3 hours • **GRILL:** 15 min.
MAKES: 4 servings

- 4   lbs. pork baby back ribs
- 2   whole garlic bulbs
- 1   large navel orange, quartered
- 1   cup Korean barbecue sauce, divided
- ¾   cup rice vinegar
- ½   cup sugar
- ⅓   cup water
- ½   cup shredded carrots
- ½   cup shredded daikon radish
- ½   cup thinly sliced green onions
      Toppings: Thinly sliced cucumber, sliced fresh jalapeno pepper, cilantro leaves and lime wedges

1. Preheat oven to 325°. Place ribs in a large roasting pan. Remove papery outer skin from garlic bulbs, but do not peel or separate the cloves. Cut off top of garlic bulbs, exposing individual cloves; add to roasting pan. Add orange; cover the pan with heavy-duty foil and seal tightly. Bake until tender, 2-2½ hours, brushing with ½ cup barbecue sauce halfway through cooking.
2. Meanwhile, in a small saucepan, combine vinegar, sugar and water. Bring the mixture to a boil over high heat; cook until sugar is dissolved, about 2 minutes. Let cool completely. Place the carrots, radish and green onion in a bowl; add brine. Refrigerate until serving.
3. Prepare grill for medium direct heat. Carefully remove ribs from roasting pan; discard garlic and orange. Place ribs on grill rack; brush with some of the remaining ½ cup barbecue sauce. Grill, covered, over medium heat until browned, 15-20 minutes, occasionally turning and brushing with sauce. Cut into serving-sized portions. Serve with pickled vegetables, toppings and the remaining sauce.
1 SERVING 718 cal., 50g fat (16g sat. fat), 163mg chol., 1499mg sod., 23g carb. (17g sugars, 1g fiber), 45g pro.

GRILLED PORK & POBLANO PEPPERS

My husband and I entertain a lot in summer, and this has quickly become the most-requested dish at our parties. I usually serve it with Mexican rice and a tossed salad.
—Donna Gay Harris, Springdale, AR

TAKES: 30 min. • **MAKES:** 6 servings

- 3   large poblano peppers
- 1½ cups shredded Monterey Jack cheese
- 4½ tsp. chili powder
- 1½ tsp. onion powder
- 1½ tsp. ground cumin
- ½   tsp. garlic powder
- ¼   tsp. salt
- ⅛   tsp. aniseed, ground
- ⅛   tsp. cayenne pepper
- 2   pork tenderloins (about 1 lb. each)

1. Cut each pepper in half and remove the seeds. Stuff peppers with cheese; set aside.
2. Combine the seasonings; rub over pork. Grill, covered, over medium-hot heat until a thermometer reads 145°, about 15 minutes. Place peppers over indirect heat; cook until the peppers are tender and the cheese is melted, 8-10 minutes.
NOTE Wear disposable gloves when cutting hot peppers; the oils can burn skin. Avoid touching your face.
3 OZ. COOKED PORK WITH ½ PEPPER
304 cal., 14g fat (7g sat. fat), 110mg chol., 389mg sod., 5g carb. (2g sugars, 2g fiber), 38g pro.

GRILLED PORK BURGERS

We live on a working hog farm and love this savory burger. Everyone will love these burgers—even if your pork comes from the grocery store!
—Dawnita Phillips, Drexel, MO

TAKES: 25 min. • **MAKES:** 6 servings

- 1   large egg, lightly beaten
- ¾   cup soft bread crumbs
- ¾   cup grated Parmesan cheese
- 1   Tbsp. dried parsley flakes
- 2   tsp. dried basil
- ½   tsp. salt
- ½   tsp. garlic powder
- ¼   tsp. pepper
- 2   lbs. ground pork
- 6   hamburger buns, split
      Optional: Lettuce leaves, sliced tomato and sweet onion

1. Combine the first 8 ingredients. Crumble pork over mixture and mix well. Shape into 6 patties.
2. Grill burgers, covered, over medium heat for 4-5 minutes on each side or until a thermometer reads 160°.
3. Serve on buns; top with lettuce, tomato and onion if desired.
1 BURGER 522 cal., 28g fat (11g sat. fat), 145mg chol., 690mg sod., 28g carb. (4g sugars, 2g fiber), 38g pro.

GRILLED SAUSAGE-BASIL PIZZAS

These easy little pizzas are a wonderful change of pace from the classic cookout menu. Let everybody go crazy with the toppings.
—*Lisa Speer, Palm Beach, FL*

TAKES: 30 min. • **MAKES:** 4 servings

- 4 Italian sausage links (4 oz. each)
- 4 naan flatbreads or whole pita breads
- ¼ cup olive oil
- 1 cup tomato basil pasta sauce
- 2 cups shredded part-skim mozzarella cheese
- ½ cup grated Parmesan cheese
- ½ cup thinly sliced fresh basil

1. Grill sausages, covered, over medium heat until a thermometer reads 160°, 10-12 minutes, turning occasionally. Cut into ¼-in. slices.
2. Brush both sides of flatbreads with oil. Grill flatbreads, covered, over medium heat until bottoms are lightly browned, 2-3 minutes.
3. Remove from grill. Layer grilled sides with sauce, sausage, cheeses and basil. Return to grill; cook, covered, until cheese is melted, 2-3 minutes longer.
1 PIZZA 808 cal., 56g fat (19g sat. fat), 112mg chol., 1996mg sod., 41g carb. (9g sugars, 3g fiber), 34g pro.

TERIYAKI-ORANGE GRILLED HAM STEAK

I love me a good grilled ham steak, so one day I decided to create my own with ingredients that I had on hand. The grilled crispiness on the outside combined with a tangy orange marinade make it perfect for any meal.
—*Cyndy Gerken, Naples, FL*

PREP: 10 min. + marinating
GRILL: 10 min. • **MAKES:** 4 servings

- ¼ cup butter
- 2 Tbsp. dark brown sugar
- 2 Tbsp. honey
- 2 Tbsp. Dijon mustard
- 1 medium orange, zested and juiced
- 2 garlic cloves, minced
- 2 tsp. teriyaki sauce
- 1½ lbs. fully cooked bone-in ham steak

1. In a small saucepan, melt butter over medium-low heat. Stir in brown sugar, honey, mustard, orange juice, orange zest, garlic and teriyaki sauce. Cook and stir until sugar is dissolved. Pour into a large shallow dish. Cool to room temperature. Add the ham steak. Let stand for 20 minutes, turning once.
2. Remove ham from dish, reserving the remaining marinade. Grill the ham, covered, over medium heat until heated through and lightly browned, about 10 minutes, brushing with marinade and turning once.
3 OZ. COOKED HAM 340 cal., 20g fat (10g sat. fat), 96mg chol., 1588mg sod., 20g carb. (19g sugars, 0 fiber), 21g pro.

DRY-RUB PORK CHOPS OVER CANNELLINI BEANS & GREENS

My family was not a huge fan of pork until I tried this recipe. Feel free to incorporate your favorite herbs into the dry rub. You can use the rub on boneless skinless chicken breast or other meats too.
—*Michael Cirlincione, Stockton, NJ*

PREP: 20 min. • **COOK:** 25 min.
MAKES: 4 servings

- 1 Tbsp. olive oil
- 1 medium onion, chopped
- 2 garlic cloves, minced
- 1 can (15 oz.) cannellini beans, rinsed and drained
- 1 cup water-packed artichoke hearts, drained and chopped
- ¾ cup pitted Greek olives, chopped
- ¼ cup chicken broth
- ¼ cup dry white wine or additional chicken broth
- ¼ tsp. salt
- ¼ tsp. smoked paprika
- ¼ tsp. pepper
- 4 bone-in pork loin chops (8 oz. each)
- 2 tsp. Greek seasoning or seasoning of your choice
- 5 oz. fresh baby spinach (about 6 cups)

1. In a large skillet, heat oil over medium-high heat. Add onion; cook and stir until tender, 4-5 minutes. Add the garlic; cook 1 minute longer. Stir in beans, artichokes, olives, broth, wine, salt, paprika and pepper. Bring to a boil; reduce the heat. Simmer until liquid is almost evaporated, 12-15 minutes.

2. Meanwhile, sprinkle pork chops with Greek seasoning. Grill over medium heat until a thermometer reads 145°, 6-8 minutes on each side. Let stand 5 minutes before serving.

3. Stir spinach into the bean mixture; cook and stir until spinach is wilted, 2-3 minutes. Serve with pork.

1 SERVING 530 cal., 29g fat (8g sat. fat), 111mg chol., 1345mg sod., 22g carb. (1g sugars, 6g fiber), 42g pro.

GRILLED PORK CHOPS WITH SPICY FENNEL RELISH

Pork chops are terrific for grilling! If you have time, marinate the pork chops for several hours or overnight before grilling for even more flavor. You could also add lemon juice and zest to the marinade to add a bright citrus note to the pork.
—*Gilda Lester, Millsboro, DE*

PREP: 20 min. • **GRILL:** 15 min.
MAKES: 4 servings

½   cup lemon juice, divided
½   cup extra virgin olive oil, divided
2   garlic cloves, minced
1½ tsp. salt, divided
1   tsp. ground cumin
4   bone-in pork loin chops
     (1 in. thick and 8 oz. each)
1   medium sweet red pepper, halved
½   large onion, cut into ½-in. slices
½   medium fennel bulb, cut into
     ½-in. slices
¼   cup coarsely chopped pitted
     green olives
2   Tbsp. chopped fresh basil
⅛   tsp. crushed red pepper flakes

1. In a shallow dish, combine ¼ cup lemon juice, ¼ cup oil, garlic, 1 tsp. salt and cumin. Add the pork; turn to coat. Let stand while preparing vegetables.
2. Place red peppers, onion and fennel in grill basket; brush with 2 Tbsp. oil. Grill, covered, over medium-high heat until lightly charred, 4-5 minutes. Remove to a cutting board and finely chop. In a large bowl, combine vegetables, olives, basil, remaining ¼ cup lemon juice, remaining 2 Tbsp. oil, remaining ½ tsp. salt and red pepper flakes.
3. Drain and discard marinade from pork. Grill pork, covered, over medium-high heat until a thermometer reads 145°, 6-8 minutes on each side. Let stand 5 minutes before serving with relish.
1 PORK CHOP WITH ½ CUP RELISH
487 cal., 34g fat (9g sat. fat), 111mg chol., 864mg sod., 8g carb. (4g sugars, 2g fiber), 37g pro.

GRILLED ITALIAN SAUSAGE SANDWICHES

Try these sausage sandwiches for a casual but hearty meal. Full of traditional Italian flavor, they're a snap to make.
—*Mike Yaeger, Brookings, SD*

PREP: 30 min. • **GRILL:** 10 min.
MAKES: 20 servings

4   large green peppers, thinly sliced
½   cup chopped onion
2   Tbsp. olive oil
4   garlic cloves, minced
1   can (15 oz.) tomato sauce
1   can (12 oz.) tomato paste
1   cup water
1   Tbsp. sugar
2   tsp. dried basil
1   tsp. salt
1   tsp. dried oregano
20   uncooked Italian sausage links
20   sandwich buns
     Shredded part-skim mozzarella
     cheese, optional

1. In a large saucepan, saute peppers and onion in oil until crisp-tender. Add garlic; cook 1 minute longer. Drain. Stir in tomato sauce, tomato paste, water, sugar, basil, salt and oregano. Bring to a boil. Reduce heat; cover and simmer for 30 minutes or until heated through.
2. Meanwhile, grill sausages, covered, over medium heat for 10-16 minutes or until a thermometer reads 160°, turning occasionally. Serve on buns with sauce and cheese if desired.
1 SANDWICH 525 cal., 28g fat (10g sat. fat), 60mg chol., 1327mg sod., 45g carb. (10g sugars, 2g fiber), 25g pro.

GRILLED PORK TENDERLOINS

We do a lot of grilling during the summer months, and this recipe is one my family asks for again and again.
—*Betsy Carrington, Lawrenceburg, TN*

PREP: 10 min. + marinating
GRILL: 20 min. • **MAKES:** 8 servings

- ⅓ cup honey
- ⅓ cup reduced-sodium soy sauce
- ⅓ cup teriyaki sauce
- 3 Tbsp. brown sugar
- 1 Tbsp. minced fresh gingerroot
- 3 garlic cloves, minced
- 4 tsp. ketchup
- ½ tsp. onion powder
- ½ tsp. ground cinnamon
- ¼ tsp. cayenne pepper
- 2 pork tenderloins (about 1 lb. each)
  Hot cooked rice

1. In a large bowl, combine the first 10 ingredients. Pour half the marinade into a bowl or shallow dish; add the tenderloins and turn to coat. Cover and refrigerate 8 hours or overnight, turning pork occasionally. Cover and refrigerate the remaining marinade.

2. Drain pork, discarding marinade in the bowl. Grill, covered, over indirect medium-hot heat for 20-35 minutes or until a thermometer reads 145°, turning occasionally and basting with reserved marinade. Let stand 5 minutes before slicing. Serve with rice.

FREEZE OPTION Freeze uncooked pork in a freezer container with the marinade. Transfer reserved marinade to a freezer container; freeze separately. To use, completely thaw tenderloins and marinade in refrigerator. Grill as directed.

3 OZ. COOKED PORK 196 cal., 4g fat (1g sat. fat), 64mg chol., 671mg sod., 15g carb. (14g sugars, 0 fiber), 24g pro **DIABETIC EXCHANGES** 3 lean meat, 1 starch.

TEST KITCHEN TIP

Keep in mind that for pork, pink does not mean raw, so avoid the impulse to overcook it. Once the meat's internal temperature hits 145°, you can stop cooking.

BALSAMIC-GLAZED FIG & PORK TENDERLOIN

I have a huge fig tree that produces an abundance of figs. One year I tried drying some and developed this sweet and smoky recipe as a result. Now it's a regular at family gatherings.
—*Greg Fontenot, The Woodlands, TX*

PREP: 35 min. • **GRILL:** 10 min.
MAKES: 12 kabobs

- 1½ lbs. pork tenderloin, trimmed
- 1 Tbsp. smoked paprika
- 1 tsp. salt
- 1 tsp. pepper
- 1 tsp. onion powder
- ½ tsp. garlic powder
- ½ tsp. white pepper
- ¼ tsp. cayenne pepper
- ¼ cup balsamic vinegar
- 3 Tbsp. honey
- 1 Tbsp. Dijon mustard
- 2 tsp. olive oil
- 12 dried figs, halved
- 12 cherry tomatoes
- ½ cup crumbled blue cheese
- 4 fresh basil leaves, thinly sliced
  Hot cooked rice, optional

1. Cut pork into 1-in. cubes. Combine the next 7 ingredients; rub over pork. Refrigerate, covered, until ready to grill. Meanwhile, make the glaze by whisking together vinegar, honey, mustard and oil. Set aside.
2. On water-soaked wooden skewers, thread pork cubes and fig halves. Grill, covered, on a greased rack over medium-high direct heat, turning occasionally, until a thermometer reads 145°, 8-10 minutes. During last half of grilling, brush cooked surfaces frequently with glaze.
3. Let skewers stand for 5 minutes; add a tomato to each. Transfer to a serving platter and sprinkle lightly with blue cheese and basil. If desired, serve with rice.
1 KABOB 139 cal., 4g fat (2g sat. fat), 35mg chol., 306mg sod., 13g carb. (10g sugars, 1g fiber), 13g pro.

ZESTY GRILLED HAM

If it's ham, my kids will eat it, and they like this kicked-up recipe best of all. Even the small ones eat adult-sized portions, so be sure to make plenty!
—*Mary Ann Lien, Tyler, TX*

TAKES: 15 min. • **MAKES:** 4 servings

- ⅓ cup packed brown sugar
- 2 Tbsp. prepared horseradish
- 4 tsp. lemon juice
- 1 fully cooked bone-in ham steak (1 lb.)

1. Place brown sugar, horseradish and lemon juice in a small saucepan; bring to a boil, stirring constantly. Brush over both sides of the ham.
2. Place ham on an oiled grill rack over medium heat. Grill, covered, until glazed and heated through, 7-10 minutes, turning occasionally.
1 SERVING 180 cal., 5g fat (2g sat. fat), 44mg chol., 845mg sod., 20g carb. (19g sugars, 0 fiber), 14g pro.

HERB-STUFFED PORK LOIN

This stunning pork roast is one of my favorite recipes when I'm entertaining company. It's especially good with garden-fresh herbs, but dried ones work nicely as well.
—*Michele Montgomery, Lethbridge, AB*

PREP: 20 min.
BAKE: 1 hour 20 min. + standing
MAKES: 12 servings

- 1   boneless pork loin roast (3 lbs.)
- ¼   cup Dijon mustard
- 4   garlic cloves, minced
- ⅓   cup minced chives
- ¼   cup minced fresh sage or
     4 tsp. rubbed sage
- 2   Tbsp. minced fresh thyme or
     2 tsp. dried thyme
- 1   Tbsp. minced fresh rosemary or
     1 tsp. dried rosemary, crushed
- 2¾ tsp. pepper, divided
- 1   tsp. salt, divided
- 1   Tbsp. olive oil

1. Starting about a third of the way in from 1 side, make a lengthwise slit down the roast to within ½ in. of the bottom. Turn the roast over and make another lengthwise slit, starting about a third of the way in from the opposite side. Open the roast so it lies flat; cover with plastic wrap. Flatten to ¾-in. thickness; remove plastic wrap.
2. Combine the mustard and garlic; rub two-thirds of the mixture over roast. Combine chives, sage, thyme, rosemary, ¾ tsp. pepper and ½ tsp. salt. Sprinkle two-thirds of herb mixture over roast. Roll up roast jelly-roll style, starting with a long side; tie several times with kitchen string. Rub oil over roast; sprinkle with the remaining ½ tsp. salt and pepper.
3. Lightly oil grill rack and prepare grill for indirect heat using a drip pan. Place roast over drip pan and grill, covered, over indirect medium heat (or bake, uncovered, at 350°) for 1 hour.
4. Brush remaining mustard mixture over roast; sprinkle with remaining

herb mixture. Grill (or bake) until a thermometer reads 160°, 20-25 minutes longer. Let stand 10 minutes before slicing.
3 OZ. COOKED PORK 199 cal., 10g fat (3g sat. fat), 69mg chol., 372mg sod., 2g carb., 1g fiber), 25g pro. **DIABETIC EXCHANGES** 3 lean meat.

FAVORITE GRILLED PORK CHOPS

I start preparing this entree the night before I plan to grill it. The fabulous marinade officially convinced my family to eat pork chops.
—*Erica Svejda, Janesville, WI*

PREP: 5 min. + marinating
GRILL: 20 min. • **MAKES:** 4 servings

- ½   cup Worcestershire sauce
- ¼   cup minced fresh parsley
- ¼   cup balsamic vinegar
- ¼   cup soy sauce
- 2   Tbsp. olive oil
- 1   tsp. minced garlic
- ½   tsp. pepper
- ¼   tsp. cayenne pepper
- 4   boneless pork loin chops
     (8 oz. each and 1 in. thick)

1. In a large bowl, combine the first 8 ingredients. Add pork chops; turn to coat. Refrigerate 8 hours or overnight.
2. Drain and discard marinade. Grill pork chops, covered, over medium heat for 10-15 minutes on each side or until a thermometer reads 145°. Let the meat stand for 5 minutes before serving.
1 PORK CHOP 328 cal., 14g fat (5g sat. fat), 109mg chol., 358mg sod., 3g carb. (2g sugars, 0 fiber), 44g pro.

READER REVIEW

"Oh my stars, these are delicious! The pork grills up juicy and the flavor hits all the right notes."
—EBRAMKAMP, TASTEOFHOME.COM

TEST KITCHEN TIP

When cooking ribs on the grill, always place them directly over the grill's heat source for the last 8-10 minutes. They'll get a gorgeous caramelization and a nice sear that helps lock in the juices.

PEACHY PORK RIBS

These meaty ribs are a wonderful picnic fare. Bake them first to make them tender, then simply finish them off on the grill with a fruity basting sauce.
—*Tom Arnold, Milwaukee, WI*

PREP: 20 min. • **COOK:** 2 hours 10 min.
MAKES: 4 servings

- 2 racks pork baby back ribs (4 lbs.), cut into serving-size pieces
- ½ cup water
- 3 medium ripe peaches, peeled and cubed
- 2 Tbsp. chopped onion
- 2 Tbsp. butter
- 1 garlic clove, minced
- 3 Tbsp. lemon juice
- 2 Tbsp. orange juice concentrate
- 1 Tbsp. brown sugar
- 2 tsp. soy sauce
- ½ tsp. ground mustard
- ¼ tsp. salt
- ¼ tsp. pepper

1. Place ribs in a shallow roasting pan; add water. Cover and bake at 325° for 2 hours.

2. Meanwhile, for sauce, place peaches in a blender; cover and process until blended. In a small saucepan, saute onion in butter until tender. Add garlic; cook 1 minute longer. Stir in lemon juice, orange juice concentrate, brown sugar, soy sauce, mustard, salt, pepper and peach puree; heat through.

3. Drain ribs. Spoon some of the sauce over ribs. Grill ribs on a lightly oiled rack, covered, over medium heat until browned, 8-10 minutes, turning occasionally and brushing with sauce.

1 SERVING 884 cal., 67g fat (26g sat. fat), 260mg chol., 553mg sod., 16g carb. (13g sugars, 1g fiber), 52g pro.

VIETNAMESE PORK CHOPS

Serve these tender chops with rice and sliced cucumbers. In addition to grilling or broiling, they can also be cooked in a skillet.
—Taste of Home *Test Kitchen*

PREP: 20 min. + chilling
COOK: 10 min. • **MAKES:** 6 servings

- 2 lemongrass stalks, chopped
- 2 shallot, chopped
- ¼ cup soy sauce
- ¼ cup fish sauce or additional soy sauce
- 3 Tbsp. brown sugar
- 2 Tbsp. canola oil
- 3 garlic cloves, minced
- 1½ lbs. thin-cut boneless pork loin chops

DIPPING SAUCE

- ½ cup hot water
- 3 Tbsp. sugar
- 3 Tbsp. lime juice
- 2 Tbsp. fish sauce or soy sauce
- 1 garlic cloves, minced
- ¼ tsp. red chili pepper (like bird's eye chili), optional

1. In a shallow dish, combine the first 7 ingredients. Add pork; turn to coat. Refrigerate 4 hours or overnight.
2. In a small bowl, whisk the dipping sauce ingredients until the sugar is dissolved. Cover and refrigerate until serving.
3. Drain pork, discarding marinade. Grill pork, covered, over medium heat or broil 4 in. from heat until a thermometer reads 145°, 5-6 minutes on each side. Let stand 5 minutes before serving. Serve with dipping sauce.

1 PORK CHOP 227 cal., 9g fat (3g sat. fat), 55mg chol., 1368mg sod., 11g carb. (10g sugars, 0 fiber), 24g pro.

GRILLED HAM BURGERS

My family loves my ham loaf, so I decided to make my ham loaf mixture into patties and grill them—it was an instant hit. Adding arugula gives these burgers a peppery bite and honey mustard dressing adds just the right sweet and sour flavor.
—Susan Bickta, Kutztown, PA

PREP: 20 min. + chilling • **GRILL:** 10 min.
MAKES: 8 servings

- 1½ lbs. fully cooked boneless ham
- ¾ lb. ground pork
- 2 large eggs
- ⅔ cup graham cracker crumbs
- ⅓ cup packed brown sugar
- ⅓ cup unsweetened crushed pineapple plus 3 Tbsp. juice
- 1 Tbsp. spicy brown mustard
- ¼ tsp. ground cloves
- 8 slices Swiss cheese (1 oz. each)
- 8 kaiser rolls, split
- 2 large tomatoes, cut in sixteen ¼-in. slices
- ½ cup honey mustard salad dressing
- 1½ cups fresh baby arugula, packed
  Additional honey mustard salad dressing, optional

1. Pulse the ham in food processor until finely ground. Combine with pork, eggs, cracker crumbs, brown sugar, pineapple and juice, mustard and cloves. Mix lightly but thoroughly. Shape into 8 patties. Using fingertips, make a shallow indentation in center of each patty so it remains flat while grilling. Refrigerate for 1 hour.
2. Grill burgers, covered, on a greased rack over medium-high direct heat for 5-6 minutes; turn and grill another 3-4 minutes. Add 1 slice cheese to each burger; grill, covered, until cheese melts, 1-2 minutes more. Remove from heat when a thermometer reads 160°.
3. Place a burger on the bottom half of each roll; add 2 tomato slices. Drizzle with 1 Tbsp. honey mustard dressing. Divide arugula evenly among rolls; top each burger with a few sprigs. Replace top half of roll. If desired, serve with additional dressing.
1 BURGER 632 cal., 28g fat (9g sat. fat), 149mg chol., 1430mg sod., 55g carb. (18g sugars, 2g fiber), 40g pro.

BIG JOHN'S CHILI-RUBBED RIBS

When my family thinks of summer grilling, it's ribs all the way. Our Asian-inspired recipe is a welcome change from the usual barbecue-sauce versions.
—Ginger Sullivan, Cutler Bay, FL

PREP: 20 min. + chilling
GRILL: 1½ hours • **MAKES:** 10 servings

- 3 Tbsp. packed brown sugar
- 2 Tbsp. paprika
- 2 Tbsp. chili powder
- 3 tsp. ground cumin
- 2 tsp. garlic powder
- 1 tsp. salt
- 6 lbs. pork baby back ribs

GLAZE
- 1 cup reduced-sodium soy sauce
- 1 cup packed brown sugar
- ⅔ cup ketchup
- ⅓ cup lemon juice
- 1½ tsp. minced fresh gingerroot
  Chopped fresh parsley, optional

1. Mix the first 6 ingredients; rub over ribs. Refrigerate, covered, 30 minutes.
2. Wrap the rib racks in large pieces of heavy-duty foil; seal tightly. Grill, covered, over indirect medium heat until tender, 1-1½ hours.
3. In a large saucepan, combine glaze ingredients; cook, uncovered, over medium heat until heated through and the sugar is dissolved, 6-8 minutes, stirring occasionally.
4. Carefully remove ribs from foil. Place ribs over direct heat; brush with some of the glaze. Grill, covered, over medium heat until browned, 25-30 minutes, turning and brushing ribs occasionally with the remaining glaze. If desired, sprinkle with parsley just before serving.
1 SERVING 486 cal., 26g fat (9g sat. fat), 98mg chol., 1543mg sod., 34g carb. (30g sugars, 1g fiber), 29g pro.

GRILLED GREATS: SEAFOOD & MORE

GRILLED CAPRESE QUESADILLAS

This is a quick and healthy summer recipe with ingredients right from the garden. Feta or mozzarella cheese can be substituted for the goat cheese, or try it with grilled chicken.
—*Amy Mongiovi, Lititz, PA*

TAKES: 20 min. • **MAKES:** 2 servings

- 4 whole wheat tortillas (8 in.)
- 6 oz. fresh mozzarella cheese, sliced
- 2 medium tomatoes, sliced and patted dry
- ⅓ cup julienned fresh basil
- ¼ cup pitted Greek olives, chopped
  Freshly ground pepper to taste

1. Layer half of each tortilla with cheese and tomatoes; sprinkle with basil, olives and pepper to taste. Fold tortillas to close.
2. Grill, covered, over medium-high heat until tortillas are lightly browned and cheese is melted, 2-3 minutes per side.
1 QUESADILLA 535 cal., 25g fat (13g sat. fat), 67mg chol., 665mg sod., 52g carb. (5g sugars, 8g fiber), 25g pro.

CEDAR PLANK SALMON WITH BLACKBERRY SAUCE

Here's my favorite entree for a warm-weather cookout. The salmon has a rich grilled taste that's enhanced by the savory blackberry sauce. It's a nice balance of sweet, smoky and spicy.
—*Stephanie Matthews, Tempe, AZ*

PREP: 20 min. + soaking • **GRILL:** 15 min.
MAKES: 6 servings (¾ cup sauce)

- 2 cedar grilling planks
- 2 cups fresh blackberries
- 2 Tbsp. white wine
- 1 Tbsp. brown sugar
- 1½ tsp. honey
- 1½ tsp. chipotle hot pepper sauce
- ¼ tsp. salt, divided
- ¼ tsp. pepper, divided
- ¼ cup finely chopped shallots
- 1 garlic clove, minced
- 6 salmon fillets (5 oz. each)

1. Soak grilling planks in water for at least 1 hour.
2. In a food processor, combine the blackberries, wine, brown sugar, honey, hot pepper sauce, ⅛ tsp. salt and ⅛ tsp. pepper; cover and process until blended. Strain and discard seeds. Stir shallots and garlic into the sauce; set aside.
3. Place planks on grill over medium-high heat. Cover and heat until planks create a light to medium smoke and begin to crackle, about 3 minutes (this indicates planks are ready). Turn planks over.
4. Sprinkle salmon with the remaining ⅛ tsp. salt and ⅛ tsp. pepper. Place on planks. Grill, covered, over medium heat 12-15 minutes or until fish flakes easily with a fork. Serve with sauce.
1 FILLET WITH 2 TBSP. SAUCE 304 cal., 16g fat (3g sat. fat), 84mg chol., 186mg sod., 10g carb. (6g sugars, 3g fiber), 29g pro. **DIABETIC EXCHANGES** 4 lean meat, ½ starch.

SKILLET-GRILLED CATFISH

You can use this recipe with any thick fish fillet, but I suggest catfish or haddock. The Cajun flavor is great.
—*Traci Wynne, Denver, PA*

TAKES: 25 min. • **MAKES:** 4 servings

- ¼ cup all-purpose flour
- ¼ cup cornmeal
- 1 tsp. onion powder
- 1 tsp. dried basil
- ½ tsp. garlic salt
- ½ tsp. dried thyme
- ¼ to ½ tsp. white pepper
- ¼ to ½ tsp. cayenne pepper
- ¼ to ½ tsp. pepper
- 4 catfish fillets (6 oz. each)
- ¼ cup butter
    Optional: Lemon wedges and minced fresh parsley

1. In a large shallow dish, combine the first 9 ingredients. Add catfish, 1 fillet at a time, turning to coat.
2. Place a large cast-iron skillet on a grill rack over medium-high heat. Melt butter in the skillet; add catfish in batches, if necessary. Grill, covered, until fish just begins to flake easily with a fork, 5-10 minutes on each side. If desired, serve with lemon wedges and fresh parsley.
1 FILLET 222 cal., 15g fat (8g sat. fat), 51mg chol., 366mg sod., 14g carb. (0 sugars, 1g fiber), 8g pro.

GRILLED EGGPLANT WITH FIG, FETA & WALNUTS

My recipe checks all the flavor boxes: sweet, savory, spicy, salty, acidic and nutty. It can be a vegetarian main dish or a side dish for any type of grilled Mediterranean meal. Add small pieces of prosciutto or a sprinkle of parsley for even more flavor.
—*Kevin French, Dawsonville, GA*

PREP: 15 min. + standing • **GRILL:** 10 min.
MAKES: 4 servings

- 1 large eggplant, cut into ½-in. slices
- ¾ tsp. salt
- ¼ cup olive oil
- ¾ tsp. ground chipotle pepper
- ½ cup fig preserves, warmed
- 1 small lemon, halved
- ½ cup crumbled feta cheese
- ¼ cup chopped walnuts

1. Place eggplant in a colander over a plate; sprinkle with salt and toss. Let stand 30 minutes. Rinse and drain well; blot dry with paper towels.
2. Brush the eggplant slices with oil. Sprinkle with chipotle pepper. Grill eggplant, covered, over medium heat for 3 minutes. Spread with ¼ cup preserves. Turn and brush with the remaining ¼ cup preserves. Grill until tender, 3-4 minutes longer. Remove to a serving platter.
3. Squeeze juice from lemon halves over eggplant. Sprinkle with feta and walnuts. Serve warm.
1 SERVING 352 cal., 21g fat (4g sat. fat), 8mg chol., 362mg sod., 39g carb. (30g sugars, 6g fiber), 6g pro.

GRILLED BEAN BURGERS

These juicy veggie patties have major flavor with cumin, garlic and a little chili powder. They can hold their own against any veggie burger from the supermarket.
—*Marguerite Shaeffer, Sewell, NJ*

PREP: 25 min. • **GRILL:** 10 min.
MAKES: 8 servings

- 1 Tbsp. olive oil
- 1 large onion, finely chopped
- 4 garlic cloves, minced
- 1 medium carrot, shredded
- 1 to 2 tsp. chili powder
- 1 tsp. ground cumin
- ¼ tsp. pepper
- 1 can (15 oz.) pinto beans, rinsed and drained
- 1 can (15 oz.) black beans, rinsed and drained
- 2 Tbsp. Dijon mustard
- 2 Tbsp. reduced-sodium soy sauce
- 1 Tbsp. ketchup
- 1½ cups quick-cooking oats
- 8 whole wheat hamburger buns, split
- 8 lettuce leaves
- ½ cup salsa

1. In a large nonstick skillet, heat oil over medium-high heat; saute onion 2 minutes. Add garlic; cook and stir 1 minute. Stir in carrot, chili powder, cumin and pepper; cook and stir until carrot is tender, 2-3 minutes. Remove from heat.
2. In a large bowl, mash pinto and black beans using a potato masher. Stir in mustard, soy sauce, ketchup and the carrot mixture. Add oats, mixing well. Shape into eight 3½-in. patties.
3. Place burgers on an oiled grill rack over medium heat or on a greased rack of a broiler pan. Grill, covered, or broil 4 in. from heat until lightly browned and heated through, 4-5 minutes per side. Serve on buns with lettuce and salsa.
1 BURGER 305 cal., 5g fat (1g sat. fat), 0 chol., 736mg sod., 54g carb. (8g sugars, 10g fiber), 12g pro. **DIABETIC EXCHANGES** 3½ starch, 1 lean meat.

CAJUN BOIL ON THE GRILL

I came up with these everything-in-one seafood packets for a family reunion, since the recipe easily can be increased to feed a bunch. The packets steam up inside, so open them carefully.
—*Allison Brooks, Fort Collins, CO*

TAKES: 30 min. • **MAKES:** 4 servings

- 1 pkg. (20 oz.) refrigerated red potato wedges
- 2 salmon fillets (6 oz. each), halved
- ¾ lb. uncooked shrimp (31-40 per lb.), peeled and deveined
- ½ lb. summer sausage, cubed
- 2 medium ears sweet corn, halved
- 2 Tbsp. olive oil
- 1 tsp. seafood seasoning
- ½ tsp. salt
- ¼ tsp. pepper
- 1 medium lemon, cut into 4 wedges

1. Divide the potatoes, salmon, shrimp, sausage and corn among 4 pieces of heavy-duty foil (18x12-in. each). Drizzle with oil; sprinkle with seasoning, salt and pepper. Squeeze lemon juice over top; place 1 squeezed wedge in each packet. Fold foil around mixture, sealing tightly.
2. Grill, covered, over medium heat until the fish just begins to flake easily with a fork, shrimp turn pink and potatoes are tender, 12-15 minutes. Open foil carefully to allow steam to escape.
1 PACKET 509 cal., 30g fat (7g sat. fat), 181mg chol., 1302mg sod., 21g carb. (5g sugars, 3g fiber), 40g pro.

BUTTERY GRILLED SHRIMP

This is easy and delicious! These shrimp are great with steak. For a special occasion, you can also brush the sauce on lobster tails and grill them.
—Sheryl Shenberger, Albuquerque, NM

TAKES: 25 min. • **MAKES:** 8 servings

- ½ cup butter, melted
- 3 Tbsp. lemon juice
- 2 tsp. chili powder
- 1 tsp. ground ginger
- ¼ tsp. salt
- 2 lbs. uncooked shrimp (16-20 per lb.), peeled and deveined

1. In a small bowl, combine the first 5 ingredients; set aside ¼ cup mixture. Thread shrimp onto 8 metal or soaked wooden skewers.
2. Grill shrimp, covered, over medium heat 3-5 minutes per side or until shrimp turn pink, basting occasionally with butter mixture. Remove from grill; brush with reserved ¼ cup butter mixture.
1 SKEWER 201 cal., 13g fat (8g sat. fat), 168mg chol., 295mg sod., 2g carb. (0 sugars, 0 fiber), 19g pro.

BUTTERY GRILLED SHRIMP TIPS

Can I use frozen uncooked shrimp? Yes! But be sure to defrost, peel and devein them before using.

What should I do with the leftovers? Store leftovers in an airtight container in the fridge for up to 3 days. Use them cold in your favorite salad or, to reheat them, cook for a just few seconds in a medium-hot skillet.

PEPPERED TUNA KABOBS

When we barbecue, we like to wow our guests with these perfectly easy tuna skewers topped with salsa. My kids like to help me put them together.
—Jennifer Ingersoll, Herndon, VA

TAKES: 30 min. • **MAKES:** 4 servings

- ½ cup frozen corn, thawed
- 4 green onions, chopped
- 1 jalapeno pepper, seeded and chopped
- 2 Tbsp. coarsely chopped fresh parsley
- 2 Tbsp. lime juice
- 1 lb. tuna steaks, cut into 1-in. cubes
- 1 tsp. coarsely ground pepper
- 2 large sweet red peppers, cut into 2x1-in. pieces
- 1 medium mango, peeled and cut into 1-in. cubes

1. For salsa, in a small bowl, combine the first 5 ingredients; set aside.
2. Rub tuna with pepper. On 4 metal or soaked wooden skewers, alternately thread red peppers, tuna and mango.
3. Place skewers on a greased grill rack. Cook, covered, over medium heat, turning occasionally, until tuna is slightly pink in center (medium-rare) and peppers are tender, 10-12 minutes. Serve with salsa.
NOTE Wear disposable gloves when cutting hot peppers; the oils can burn skin. Avoid touching your face.
1 KABOB 205 cal., 2g fat (0 sat. fat), 51mg chol., 50mg sod., 20g carb. (12g sugars, 4g fiber), 29g pro. **DIABETIC EXCHANGES** 3 lean meat, 1 starch.

GINGER-GLAZED GRILLED HONEYDEW

If you've never grilled fruit like this before, you're in for a real treat! I love the idea of cooking everything from appetizers to desserts on the grill. This makes a sweet, light treat for summer.
—Jacqueline Correa, Landing, NJ

TAKES: 25 min. • **MAKES:** 6 servings

- ¼ cup peach preserves
- 1 Tbsp. lemon juice
- 1 Tbsp. finely chopped crystallized ginger
- 2 tsp. grated lemon zest
- ⅛ tsp. ground cloves
- 1 medium honeydew melon, cut into 2-in. cubes

1. For the glaze, combine the first 5 ingredients. Thread honeydew onto 6 metal or soaked wooden skewers; brush with half the glaze.
2. On a lightly oiled rack, grill honeydew, covered, over medium-high heat or broil 4 in. from the heat just until the melon begins to soften and brown, 4-6 minutes, turning and basting frequently with remaining glaze.
1 SKEWER 101 cal., 0 fat (0 sat. fat), 0 chol., 18mg sod., 26g carb. (23g sugars, 1g fiber), 1g pro. **DIABETIC EXCHANGES** 1 fruit, ½ starch.

GRILLED MAHI MAHI

Instead of grilling the usual hamburgers or chicken breasts, prepare this grilled mahi mahi and reel in raves!
—Taste of Home *Test Kitchen*

PREP: 20 min. + marinating
GRILL: 10 min. • **MAKES:** 8 servings

- ¾ cup reduced-sodium teriyaki sauce
- 2 Tbsp. sherry or pineapple juice
- 2 garlic cloves
- 8 mahi mahi fillets (6 oz. each)

TROPICAL FRUIT SALSA
- 1 medium mango, peeled and diced
- 1 cup chopped seeded peeled papaya
- ¾ cup chopped green pepper
- ½ cup cubed fresh pineapple
- ½ medium red onion, chopped
- ¼ cup minced fresh cilantro
- ¼ cup minced fresh mint
- 1 Tbsp. chopped seeded jalapeno pepper
- 1 Tbsp. lime juice
- 1 Tbsp. lemon juice
- ½ tsp. crushed red pepper flakes

1. In a shallow dish, combine the teriyaki sauce, sherry and garlic; add mahi mahi. Turn to coat; cover and refrigerate for 30 minutes.
2. Meanwhile, in a large bowl, combine salsa ingredients. Cover and refrigerate until serving.
3. Drain fillets, discarding the marinade. Place mahi mahi on an oiled grill rack. Grill, covered, over medium heat or broil 4 in. from the heat for 4-5 minutes on each side until fish flakes easily with a fork. Serve with salsa.

NOTE Wear disposable gloves when cutting hot peppers; the oils can burn skin. Avoid touching your face.

1 FILLET WITH ¼ CUP SALSA 195 cal., 2g fat (0 sat. fat), 124mg chol., 204mg sod., 12g carb. (9g sugars, 2g fiber), 32g pro. **DIABETIC EXCHANGES** 5 lean meat, 1 fruit.

FIRECRACKER SHRIMP

These delightful sizzling shrimp skewers are coated in a sweet and spicy glaze that comes together in moments.
—Mary Tallman, Arbor Vitae, WI

TAKES: 20 min. • **MAKES:** 2½ dozen

- ½ cup apricot preserves
- 1 tsp. canola oil
- 1 tsp. soy sauce
- ½ tsp. crushed red pepper flakes
- 1 lb. uncooked large shrimp, peeled and deveined

1. In a small bowl, combine the apricot preserves, oil, soy sauce and pepper flakes. Thread shrimp onto metal or soaked wooden skewers.
2. Grill, uncovered, over medium heat or broil 4 in. from the heat until shrimp turn pink, 2-3 minutes on each side, basting frequently with apricot mixture.

1 SHRIMP 27 cal., 0 fat (0 sat. fat), 18mg chol., 30mg sod., 4g carb. (2g sugars, 0 fiber), 3g pro.

SALMON GRILLED IN FOIL

This tender salmon steams up in foil packets, meaning easy cleanup later.
—*Merideth Berkovich, The Dalles, OR*

TAKES: 20 min. • **MAKES:** 4 servings

- 4 salmon fillets (4 oz. each)
- 1 tsp. garlic powder
- 1 tsp. lemon-pepper seasoning
- 1 tsp. curry powder
- ½ tsp. salt
- 1 small onion, cut into rings
- 2 medium tomatoes, seeded and chopped

1. Place each salmon fillet, skin side down, on a double thickness of heavy-duty foil (about 18x12 in.). Combine the garlic powder, lemon-pepper seasoning, curry powder and salt; sprinkle over salmon. Top with onion and tomatoes. Fold foil over fish and seal tightly.

2. Grill, covered, over medium heat for 10-15 minutes or until fish flakes easily with a fork. Open foil carefully to allow steam to escape.

1 PACKET 199 cal., 11g fat (2g sat. fat), 57mg chol., 436mg sod., 5g carb. (2g sugars, 1g fiber), 20g pro. **DIABETIC EXCHANGES** 3 lean meat.

TEST KITCHEN TIP

Checking the internal temperature is the easiest way to tell if your salmon is cooked just right—the salmon needs to reach 140°F.

51 GRILLED LOBSTER TAILS

I had never made lobster at home until I tried this convenient and deliciously different grilled recipe. It turned out amazing, and has left me with little reason to ever order lobster at a restaurant again.
—*Katie Rush, Kansas City, MO*

PREP: 15 min. + marinating
GRILL: 10 min. • **MAKES:** 6 servings

- 6 frozen lobster tails (8 to 10 oz. each), thawed
- ¾ cup olive oil
- 3 Tbsp. minced fresh chives
- 3 garlic cloves, minced
- ½ tsp. salt
- ½ tsp. pepper

1. Using scissors, cut 3-4 lengthwise slits in the underside of the tail to loosen shell slightly. Cut the top of the lobster shell lengthwise down the center with scissors, leaving the tail fin intact. Cut shell at an angle away from the center of the tail at base of tail fin. Loosen meat from shell, keeping the fin end attached; lift meat and lay over shell.
2. In a small bowl, combine remaining ingredients; spoon over lobster meat. Cover and refrigerate for 20 minutes.
3. Place lobster tails, meat side up, on grill rack. Grill, covered, over medium heat until meat is opaque, 10-12 minutes.
1 LOBSTER TAIL 446 cal., 29g fat (4g sat. fat), 215mg chol., 869mg sod., 2g carb. (0 sugars, 0 fiber), 43g pro.
BAKED LOBSTER TAILS Prepare lobster tails as recipe directs. Preheat oven to 375°. Place on a baking sheet. Bake, uncovered, 15-20 minutes or until meat is firm and opaque.

TILAPIA FLORENTINE FOIL PACKETS

I love fish and serving healthy food to my family. This ticks both boxes—plus it's absolutely delicious, making it a winner in my house!
—*Shanna Belz, Prineville, OR*

PREP: 30 min. • **GRILL:** 15 min.
MAKES: 4 servings

12 cups fresh baby spinach
1   Tbsp. butter
1   Tbsp. extra virgin olive oil, divided
4   tilapia fillets (6 oz. each)
½   tsp. salt
¼   tsp. pepper
½   large sweet or red onion, thinly
    sliced
2   Tbsp. fresh lemon juice
2   garlic cloves, minced
    Lemon wedges, optional

1. Prepare grill for medium-high heat or preheat oven to 475°. In a large skillet, cook spinach in butter and 1 tsp. olive oil over medium-high heat until spinach is wilted, 2-3 minutes.
2. Divide spinach among four 18x12-in. pieces of heavy-duty nonstick foil, placing food on dull side of foil. Place tilapia fillets on top of spinach; sprinkle with salt and pepper. Top with onion, lemon juice, garlic and the remaining 2 tsp. olive oil. Fold foil around mixture, sealing tightly.
3. Place packets on grill or on a baking pan in oven. Cook until fish just begins to flake easily with a fork, 12-15 minutes. Open packets carefully to allow steam to escape. Serve with lemon wedges if desired.

1 PACKET 233 cal., 8g fat (3g sat. fat), 90mg chol., 453mg sod., 8g carb. (3g sugars, 2g fiber), 35g pro. **DIABETIC EXCHANGES** 5 lean meat, 1 vegetable, 1 fat.

HALIBUT SOFT TACOS

This warm-weather favorite is quick, colorful and full of nutrients. I sometimes serve the fish wrapped in lettuce instead of tortillas. Either way, the salsa tastes amazing with the grilled halibut.
—*Kristin Kossak, Bozeman, MT*

TAKES: 30 min. • **MAKES:** 4 servings

1   medium mango, peeled and cubed
½   cup cubed avocado
¼   cup chopped red onion
2   Tbsp. chopped seeded jalapeno
    pepper
1   Tbsp. minced fresh cilantro
3   tsp. olive oil, divided
1   tsp. lemon juice
1   tsp. honey
1   lb. halibut steaks (¾ in. thick)
½   tsp. salt
¼   tsp. pepper
4   Bibb lettuce leaves
4   flour tortillas (6 in.), warmed
4   tsp. sweet Thai chili sauce

1. In a small bowl, combine the mango, avocado, onion, jalapeno, cilantro, 2 tsp. oil, lemon juice and honey; set aside. Brush halibut with remaining 1 tsp. oil; sprinkle with salt and pepper.
2. Grill halibut on a greased rack, covered, over high heat or broil 3-4 in. from the heat until fish flakes easily with a fork, 3-5 minutes on each side.
3. Place lettuce leaves on tortillas; top with fish and mango salsa. Drizzle with chili sauce.
NOTE Wear disposable gloves when cutting hot peppers; the oils can burn skin. Avoid touching your face.
1 TACO WITH ⅓ CUP MANGO SALSA 330 cal., 12g fat (1g sat. fat), 36mg chol., 648mg sod., 28g carb. (12g sugars, 2g fiber), 28g pro. **DIABETIC EXCHANGES** 3 lean meat, 2 starch, 1 fat.

⑤ᵢ SMOKED DEVILED EGGS

Give all those leftover Easter eggs a flavor upgrade. The grilling step gives these deviled eggs a distinctive smoky taste that will have everyone talking.
—*Catherine Woods, Lexington, MO*

PREP: 20 min. • **GRILL:** 10 min. + chilling
MAKES: 2 dozen

- ½ cup soaked hickory wood chips
- 12 hard-cooked large eggs, peeled
- ½ cup Miracle Whip
- 1 tsp. prepared mustard
- ¼ tsp. salt
- ⅛ tsp. pepper
- ⅛ tsp. paprika
  Minced fresh parsley, optional

1. Add wood chips to grill according to manufacturer's directions. Place eggs on grill rack. Grill, covered, over indirect medium heat until golden brown, 7-10 minutes. Cool slightly.
2. Cut eggs lengthwise in half. Remove yolks, reserving whites. In a small bowl, mash yolks. Stir in Miracle Whip, mustard, salt, pepper and paprika. Spoon or pipe into egg whites. Top with additional paprika and, if desired, chopped parsley. Refrigerate, covered, until serving.

1 STUFFED EGG HALF 52 cal., 4g fat (1g sat. fat), 95mg chol., 91mg sod., 1g carb. (1g sugars, 0 fiber), 3g pro.

TEST KITCHEN TIP

The eggs take on a mild smoky flavor from the hickory chips and turn a light amber color. The idea isn't to further cook the eggs on the grill, just to add smoke flavor. So be sure to place them over indirect heat, not over the coals.

GRILLED SHRIMP & WATERMELON SLIDERS

These fun little sliders combine seafood and my favorite Mexican flavors into a handheld treat. They make such a fresh summer meal!
—*Jeanette Decker, Corpus Christi, TX*

PREP: 40 min. + marinating
GRILL: 5 min. • **MAKES:** 10 sliders

- ¾ cup minced fresh cilantro
- 1 small onion, chopped
- ¼ cup olive oil
- 2 Tbsp. lemon juice
- 1 envelope Goya sazon with coriander and annatto
- 2 tsp. reduced-sodium soy sauce
- 1 garlic clove, minced
- ½ tsp. pepper
- ¾ lb. uncooked shrimp (26-30 per lb.), peeled and deveined

GUACAMOLE
- 2 medium ripe avocados, peeled and cubed
- 1 medium tomato, chopped
- 1 small onion, chopped
- 3 Tbsp. lemon juice
- 1 Tbsp. minced fresh cilantro
- ½ tsp. salt
- ½ tsp. pepper

SLIDERS
- 1 cup seeded watermelon, finely chopped
- 2 Tbsp. finely chopped seeded jalapeno pepper
- 2 Tbsp. minced fresh cilantro
- 10 slider buns or dinner rolls, split
- ½ cup chopped lettuce

1. Place the first 8 ingredients in a blender; process until blended. Transfer to a bowl or shallow dish. Add shrimp and turn to coat. Cover and refrigerate for 30 minutes.

2. In a small bowl, mash avocados with a fork. Stir in tomato, onion, lemon juice, cilantro, salt and pepper. Refrigerate until serving.

3. Drain shrimp, discarding marinade. Arrange shrimp on a grilling grid; place grid on grill rack. Grill, covered, over medium heat for 2-3 minutes on each side or until shrimp turn pink.

4. Chop shrimp; transfer to a small bowl. Stir in watermelon, jalapeno and cilantro. Spread guacamole over bun tops and bottoms. Top bun bottoms with lettuce and shrimp mixture; replace tops.

NOTE Wear disposable gloves when cutting hot peppers; the oils can burn skin. Avoid touching your face.

2 SLIDERS 416 cal., 18g fat (2g sat. fat), 118mg chol., 782mg sod., 48g carb. (8g sugars, 8g fiber), 20g pro.

FARMERS MARKET STREET TACOS

No matter what I bring home from the local farmers market, I always end up stuffing it into a taco for a fresh veggie-filled treat. You really can't go wrong.
—*Ralph Jones, San Diego, CA*

TAKES: 30 min. • **MAKES:** 4 servings

- 2 bunches bok choy, halved
- 1 medium zucchini, cut into 3-in. sticks
- ½ lb. fresh asparagus spears
- 2 medium ripe avocados, peeled and quartered
- 1 bunch green onions
- 2 jalapeno peppers, halved and seeded
- 2 Tbsp. olive oil
- ½ tsp. kosher salt
- ½ tsp. pepper
- 8 mini corn tortillas
  Fresh cilantro leaves
  Optional: Pickled red onions, lime wedges, sliced radishes and salsa verde

1. Prepare grill for medium-high heat. Brush bok choy, zucchini, asparagus, avocados, green onions and jalapenos with olive oil; sprinkle with salt and pepper. Transfer to a greased grill rack.
2. Grill, covered, or broil 4 in. from heat until vegetables are crisp-tender and slightly charred, 4-5 minutes, turning occasionally. Grill tortillas until warmed and slightly charred, 30-45 seconds per side.
3. Cut vegetables to desired sizes; serve in tortillas with cilantro and toppings of your choice.
NOTE Wear disposable gloves when cutting hot peppers; the oils can burn skin. Avoid touching your face.
2 TACOS 319 cal., 19g fat (3g sat. fat), 0 chol., 536mg sod., 33g carb. (9g sugars, 13g fiber), 11g pro.

GARLIC-HERB SALMON SLIDERS

These patties make great appetizers, but I'll often I serve them as full-size burgers on kaiser rolls too. The fresh flavors of the salmon and herbs are just unbeatable.
—*Margee Berry, White Salmon, WA*

PREP: 25 min. • **GRILL:** 10 min.
MAKES: 8 sliders

- ⅓ cup panko bread crumbs
- 4 tsp. finely chopped shallot
- 2 tsp. snipped fresh dill
- 1 Tbsp. prepared horseradish
- 1 large egg, beaten
- ¼ tsp. salt
- ⅛ tsp. pepper
- 1 lb. salmon fillet, skin removed, cut into 1-in. cubes
- 8 whole wheat dinner rolls, split and toasted
- ¼ cup reduced-fat garlic-herb spreadable cheese
- 8 small lettuce leaves
- 8 slices red onion

1. In a large bowl, combine the first 7 ingredients. Place salmon in a food processor; pulse until coarsely chopped, and add to bread crumb mixture. Mix lightly but thoroughly. Shape into eight ½-in.-thick patties.
2. On a lightly greased grill rack, grill burgers, covered, over medium heat or broil 4 in. from heat until a thermometer reads 160°, 3-4 minutes on each side. Serve on rolls with spreadable cheese, lettuce and onion.
2 SLIDERS 446 cal., 17g fat (5g sat. fat), 112mg chol., 719mg sod., 43g carb. (7g sugars, 6g fiber), 30g pro. **DIABETIC EXCHANGES** 3 starch, 3 lean meat, 1 fat.

GRILLED ELOTE
FLATBREAD P. 157

PARTY
PIZZAS

ARUGULA PIZZA

This pizza is great served as an appetizer when family or friends get together. My girlfriends and I love it because it has that sophisticated gourmet touch, and it's healthy too! This also serves four for a main course.
—*Annette Riva, Naperville, IL*

TAKES: 20 min. • **MAKES:** 8 servings

- ½ cup pizza sauce
- 1 prebaked 12-in. pizza crust (14 oz.)
- 1 cup shaved Parmesan cheese
- 3 oz. thinly sliced prosciutto
- 2 cups fresh arugula
  Additional fresh arugula, optional

Preheat oven to 425°. Spread sauce over pizza crust. Layer with ½ cup Parmesan cheese, prosciutto and arugula; top with remaining ½ cup cheese. Bake directly on oven rack until the edge is lightly browned, 10-12 minutes. Cut into small squares. If desired, top with additional arugula.
2 PIECES 204 cal., 7g fat (3g sat. fat), 17mg chol., 689mg sod., 23g carb. (2g sugars, 1g fiber), 12g pro.

TEST KITCHEN TIP

Like other pizza recipes, you can store arugula pizza in the fridge in an airtight bag or wrap each slice individually in foil. Your slices should last for 3 to 4 days when stored this way.

NEW HAVEN CLAM PIZZA

With rich toppings and plenty of garlic, clam pizza isn't well known outside of New England, which is a shame! This is a perfect appetizer for any meal. It's always a hit with my family and friends!
—*Susan Seymour, Valatie, NY*

PREP: 20 min. + rising • **BAKE:** 20 min.
MAKES: 8 servings

- 1 pkg. (¼ oz.) active dry yeast
- 1 cup warm water (110° to 115°)
- 1 tsp. sugar
- 2½ cups all-purpose flour
- 1 tsp. salt
- 2 Tbsp. canola oil
- 2 cans (6½ oz. each) chopped clams, drained
- 4 bacon strips, cooked and crumbled
- 3 garlic cloves, minced
- 2 Tbsp. grated Parmesan cheese
- 1 tsp. dried oregano
- 1 cup shredded mozzarella cheese

1. In a large bowl, dissolve yeast in water. Add sugar; let stand for 5 minutes. Add the flour, salt and oil; beat until smooth. Cover and let rise in a warm place until doubled, about 15-20 minutes.
2. Punch dough down. Press onto the bottom and up the sides of a greased 14-in. pizza pan; build up edge slightly. Prick dough several times with a fork.
3. Bake at 425° for 6-8 minutes. Sprinkle remaining ingredients over crust in the order listed. Bake 13-15 minutes or until crust is golden and cheese is melted. Cut into wedges.
1 PIECE 268 cal., 9g fat (3g sat. fat), 33mg chol., 716mg sod., 33g carb. (1g sugars, 1g fiber), 13g pro.

ABOUT OUTDOOR PIZZA OVENS

Where should I put my oven? Pizza ovens require ventilation and space. Place your oven several feet away from your home or any flammable items like patio furniture, and far enough away from guests so they're not inhaling smoke and ash.

Can I leave it outside? Brick ovens or stone-encased models can stay outside indefinitely—just clean it before use. Portable ovens should be covered for protection from the elements or brought inside during the off-season. Treat these similarly to your favorite grill or BBQ setup.

Gas, electric, wood or charcoal—which should I choose? For occasional use, you may want to start with a grill attachment. If you're used to grilling, a gas or charcoal model would be an easy transition. If you find you truly love cooking pizza outdoors, look into investing in a larger wood-fired oven. Think about your space. If you have a big backyard and you entertain regularly, a brick oven might be worth the cost. If you have a small patio or deck, a smaller electric unit might be perfect.

CHICKEN PARMESAN PIZZA

This tasty pizza is quick and easy to make and a sure winner with picky eaters. It's a handy option for a family dinner on a busy night or for the center of the table at a kids' party.
—*Karen Wittmeier, Parkland, FL*

PREP: 25 min. • **BAKE:** 15 min.
MAKES: 6 pieces

- 8 frozen breaded chicken tenders
- 1 loaf (1 lb.) frozen pizza dough, thawed
- ½ cup marinara sauce
- ¼ tsp. garlic powder
- 2 cups shredded part-skim mozzarella cheese
- ¼ cup shredded Parmesan cheese
- 2 Tbsp. thinly sliced fresh basil
   Additional warmed marinara sauce

1. Bake chicken tenders according to the package directions. Remove from oven; increase oven setting to 450°.
2. Meanwhile, grease a 12-in. pizza pan. Roll out dough to fit pan. In a small bowl, mix marinara sauce and garlic powder; spread over dough.
3. Cut chicken into 1-in. pieces. Top pizza with the chicken and mozzarella cheese. Bake on a lower oven rack until crust is golden brown and cheese is melted, 12-15 minutes. Sprinkle with Parmesan cheese and basil. Serve with additional marinara.
1 PIECE 440 cal., 18g fat (6g sat. fat), 38mg chol., 807mg sod., 47g carb. (4g sugars, 3g fiber), 23g pro.

PIZZA ON A STICK

My daughter and her friends had fun turning sausage, pepperoni, veggies and pizza dough into these cute kabobs.
—*Charlene Woods, Norfolk, VA*

TAKES: 30 min. • **MAKES:** 5 servings

- 8 oz. Italian turkey sausage links
- 2 cups whole fresh mushrooms
- 2 cups cherry tomatoes
- 1 medium onion, cut into 1-in. pieces
- 1 large green pepper, cut into 1-in. pieces
- 30 slices turkey pepperoni (2 oz.)
- 1 tube (13.8 oz.) refrigerated pizza crust
- 1½ cups shredded part-skim mozzarella cheese
- 1¼ cups pizza sauce, warmed

1. Preheat oven to 400°. In a large nonstick skillet, cook sausage over medium heat until no longer pink; drain. When cool enough to handle, cut sausage into 20 pieces. On 10 metal or wooden skewers, alternately thread sausage, vegetables and pepperoni.

2. Unroll pizza dough onto a lightly floured surface; cut widthwise into 1-in.-wide strips. Starting at the pointed end of a prepared skewer, pierce skewer through 1 end of dough strip. Spiral-wrap dough strip around skewer, allowing vegetables and meats to peek through. Wrap remaining end of dough strip around skewer above first ingredient. Repeat with remaining dough strips and skewers.

3. Arrange kabobs on a baking sheet coated with cooking spray. Bake until the vegetables are tender and the pizza crust is golden, 10-12 minutes. Immediately sprinkle with cheese. Serve with pizza sauce.

2 KABOBS WITH ¼ CUP SAUCE 429 cal., 15g fat (6g sat. fat), 52mg chol., 1337mg sod., 52g carb. (13g sugars, 3g fiber), 26g pro.

THE BEST SAUSAGE PIZZAS

What makes this recipe unique is the slow overnight fermentation of the dough. The flour has time to hydrate and relax, which makes the dough so much easier to roll out!
—*Josh Rink, Milwaukee, WI*

PREP: 30 min. • **BAKE:** 15 min.
MAKES: 2 pizzas (8 pieces each)

- 1 batch The Best Pizza Dough (p. 158)
- 1 lb. bulk Italian sausage
- 1 cup pizza sauce
- 4 cups shredded part-skim mozzarella cheese
- 1 medium red onion, sliced
- 1 medium green pepper, chopped
- 2 cups sliced fresh mushrooms
  Optional: Grated Parmesan cheese, crushed red pepper flakes and fresh oregano leaves

1. Divide the dough in half. With greased fingers, pat each half onto an ungreased 12-in. pizza pan. Prick dough thoroughly with a fork. Bake at 400° until lightly browned, 10-12 minutes. In a large skillet, cook and crumble sausage over medium heat until no longer pink; drain.
2. Spread the pizza sauce over crusts. Top with cheese, onion, green pepper, mushrooms and sausage. Bake until golden brown and cheese is bubbling, 12-15 minutes. If desired, top with grated Parmesan cheese, crushed red pepper flakes and fresh oregano leaves.
FREEZE OPTION Wrap unbaked pizzas and freeze for up to 2 months. To use, unwrap and place on pizza pans; thaw in the refrigerator. Bake at 400° until crust is golden brown, 18-22 minutes.
1 PIECE 311 cal., 17g fat (6g sat. fat), 33mg chol., 565mg sod., 26g carb. (2g sugars, 2g fiber), 14g pro.

GRILLED ELOTE FLATBREAD
(PICTURED ON P. 151)

Here's a fun twist on a classic Mexican dish! Keep your kitchen cooled down during the summer by grilling this fresh flatbread outdoors.
—*Amanda Phillips, Portland, OR*

PREP: 20 min. • **GRILL:** 15 min.
MAKES: 12 servings

- 2 medium ears sweet corn, husked
- 3 Tbsp. olive oil, divided
- 1 lb. fresh or frozen pizza dough, thawed
- ½ cup mayonnaise
- ⅓ cup crumbled Cotija cheese, divided
- ⅓ cup chopped fresh cilantro, divided
- 1 Tbsp. lime juice
- ½ tsp. chili powder
- ⅛ tsp. pepper

1. Brush corn with 1 Tbsp. oil. Grill corn, covered, over medium heat until lightly browned and tender, 10-12 minutes, turning occasionally. Cool slightly. Cut corn from cobs; transfer to a large bowl.
2. On a lightly floured surface, roll or press dough into a 15x10-in. oval (about ¼ in. thick); place on a greased sheet of foil. Brush top with 1 Tbsp. oil.
3. Carefully invert crust onto grill rack, removing foil. Brush top with remaining 1 Tbsp. oil. Grill, covered, over medium heat until golden brown, 2-3 minutes on each side. Remove from grill; cool slightly.
4. Add mayonnaise, 3 Tbsp. cheese, 3 Tbsp. cilantro, lime juice, chili powder and pepper to corn; stir to combine. Spread over warm crust. Sprinkle with the remaining cheese and cilantro.
1 PIECE 211 cal., 13g fat (2g sat. fat), 4mg chol., 195mg sod., 20g carb. (2g sugars, 1g fiber), 5g pro.

GARLIC PIZZA WEDGES

Our pastor made this for a get-together, and my husband and I just couldn't stay away from the hors d'oeuvres table! The cheesy slices taste terrific served warm, but they're still wonderful when they've cooled slightly.
—*Krysten Johnson, Simi Valley, CA*

TAKES: 25 min. • **MAKES:** 2 dozen

- 1 prebaked 12-in. pizza crust
- 1 cup grated Parmesan cheese
- 1 cup mayonnaise
- 1 small red onion, chopped
- 3½ tsp. minced garlic
- 1 Tbsp. dried oregano
  Alfredo sauce, optional

Place crust on an ungreased 14-in. pizza pan. In a small bowl, combine Parmesan cheese, mayonnaise, onion, garlic and oregano; spread over crust. Bake at 450° until the edge is lightly browned, 8-10 minutes. Cut into wedges. If desired, serve with Alfredo sauce.
1 PIECE 119 cal., 8g fat (2g sat. fat), 4mg chol., 193mg sod., 8g carb. (0 sugars, 0 fiber), 3g pro.

5i
THE BEST PIZZA DOUGH

This easy dough is the key to making an extraordinary homemade pizza. All-purpose flour does just fine here, but if you're lucky enough to live near an Italian market or willing to purchase double zero flour online, it will take your crust to the next level. You can also customize your crust by adding dried basil or oregano and by substituting garlic or onion salt for the sea salt. Use this dough to make The Best Sausage Pizzas (p. 157) or any other pizza recipe that calls for unbaked dough!
—*Josh Rink, Milwaukee, WI*

PREP: 30 min. + chilling
MAKES: 2 crusts (8 servings each)

1¼ cups warm water (110° to 115°)
2 tsp. sugar, divided
1 pkg. (¼ oz.) active dry yeast
3½ to 4 cups all-purpose or 00 flour
1 tsp. sea salt
1 tsp. each dried basil, oregano and marjoram, optional
⅓ cup canola or olive oil

1. In a small bowl, mix warm water and 1 tsp. sugar; add yeast and whisk until dissolved. Let stand until bubbles form on surface. In a large bowl, whisk 3 cups flour, salt, remaining 1 tsp. sugar and, if desired, dried herbs. Make a well in center; add yeast mixture and oil. Stir until smooth. Add enough remaining flour to form a soft dough.

2. Turn dough onto a floured surface; knead, adding more flour to surface as needed until no longer sticky and dough is smooth and elastic, 6-8 minutes. Place in a large greased bowl; turn once to grease top. Cover and let rise in a warm place for 30 minutes

3. Transfer bowl to refrigerator and chill overnight. Allow dough to come to room temperature, about 30 minutes, before rolling out.

1 PIECE 144 cal., 5g fat (1g sat. fat), 0 chol., 121mg sod., 22g carb. (1g sugars, 1g fiber), 3g pro.

PEPPERONI PIZZA POCKETS

Stuffed with a pizza-style filling, these special sandwiches surprise you with a burst of flavor in every bite. They were popular at our son's birthday party, but you can be sure adults will love them too!
—*Robin Werner, Brush Prairie, WA*

PREP: 1 hour • **BAKE:** 20 min.
MAKES: 16 pockets

- 2   pkg. (¼ oz. each) active dry yeast
- 2   cups warm water (110° to 115°)
- 2   Tbsp. sugar
- 2   Tbsp. butter, melted
- 2   tsp. salt
- 6   to 6½ cups all-purpose flour
- 1   can (8 oz.) pizza sauce, divided
- 96 slices turkey pepperoni
- 4   cups shredded part-skim mozzarella cheese
- 1   large egg, lightly beaten
- 8   tsp. grated Parmesan cheese
- 2   tsp. Italian seasoning

1. Preheat oven to 400°. In a large bowl, dissolve yeast in warm water. Add sugar, butter, salt and 4½ cups flour. Beat until smooth. Stir in enough of the remaining flour to form a soft dough.
2. Turn onto a floured surface; knead until smooth and elastic, 6-8 minutes. Divide into 16 pieces. On a lightly floured surface, roll each piece into a 6-in. circle. Place 2 tsp. pizza sauce, 6 slices pepperoni and ¼ cup mozzarella on each circle. Lightly brush the edge of 1 circle with egg. Bring dough over filling; press firmly, then crimp seam to seal. Repeat to fill and seal remaining circles.
3. Place on greased or parchment-lined baking sheets. Brush with egg; sprinkle with Parmesan and Italian seasoning. Bake until golden brown, 18-20 minutes. Warm remaining pizza sauce; serve with pizza pockets.
1 POCKET 316 cal., 9g fat (5g sat. fat), 47mg chol., 751mg sod., 41g carb. (3g sugars, 2g fiber), 16g pro.

⏱ 5i
SPEEDY SHRIMP FLATBREADS

My husband and I are hooked on flatbread pizzas. I make at least one a week just to have something tasty around as a snack. This one came together easily because I already had all the ingredients on hand.
—*Cheryl Woodson, Liberty, MO*

TAKES: 15 min. • **MAKES:** 2 servings

- 2   naan flatbreads or whole pita breads
- 1   pkg. (5.2 oz.) garlic-herb spreadable cheese
- ½   lb. peeled and deveined cooked shrimp (31-40 per lb.)
- ½   cup chopped oil-packed sun-dried tomatoes
- ¼   cup fresh basil leaves
     Lemon wedges, optional

Preheat oven to 400°. Place flatbreads on a baking sheet. Spread with cheese; top with shrimp and tomatoes. Bake until heated through, 4-6 minutes. Sprinkle with basil. If desired, serve with lemon wedges.
1 FLATBREAD 634 cal., 41g fat (24g sat. fat), 263mg chol., 1163mg sod., 38g carb. (3g sugars, 3g fiber), 33g pro.

PIZZA CAPRESE

One of my favorite pizzas is incredibly easy to make and comes together quickly. Pizza Caprese is simply an heirloom tomato, fresh mozzarella and really good extra virgin olive oil. I could have this every day!
—*Beth Berlin, Oak Creek, WI*

TAKES: 30 min. • **MAKES:** 6 servings

- 1 pkg. (6½ oz.) pizza crust mix
- 2 Tbsp. extra virgin olive oil, divided
- 2 garlic cloves, thinly sliced
- 1 large tomato, thinly sliced
- 4 oz. fresh mozzarella cheese, sliced
- ⅓ cup loosely packed basil leaves

1. Preheat oven to 425°. Prepare pizza dough according to package directions. With floured hands, press dough onto a greased 12-in. pizza pan.
2. Drizzle 1 Tbsp. olive oil over dough; sprinkle with sliced garlic. Bake until crust is lightly browned, 10-12 minutes.

Top with tomato and fresh mozzarella; bake until cheese is melted, 5-7 minutes longer. Drizzle with the remaining 1 Tbsp. olive oil and top with fresh basil. Serve immediately.
1 PIECE 208 cal., 9g fat (3g sat. fat), 15mg chol., 196mg sod., 23g carb. (3g sugars, 1g fiber), 7g pro.

TEST KITCHEN TIP

You can substitute a homemade pizza dough for this pizza without changing the recipe at all. You can also start with a precooked crust, French bread or a soft flatbread, such as naan—just skip the prebaking step and start by adding the toppings.

NEW YORK-STYLE PIZZA

This is a no-nonsense pizza. Since the crust is pliable, cut the pie into larger pieces if you want to eat your slices in the traditional New York way—folded! Who says pizza isn't portable?
—*Mariam Ishaq, Buffalo, NY*

PREP: 1 hour + rising • **BAKE:** 15 min.
MAKES: 8 servings

- 1 tsp. active dry yeast
- ⅔ cup warm water (110° to 115°)
- 2 Tbsp. olive oil
- 1 tsp. salt
- 1¾ to 2¼ cups all-purpose flour
- 1 can (8 oz.) tomato sauce
- 2 cups shredded mozzarella cheese
- ½ cup grated Romano cheese
  Optional: Chopped fresh basil, dried oregano and crushed red pepper flakes

1. In a small bowl, dissolve yeast in warm water. In a large bowl, combine oil, salt, yeast mixture and 1 cup flour; beat on medium speed until smooth. Stir in enough of the remaining flour to form a soft dough (dough will be sticky). Turn dough onto a floured surface; knead until smooth and elastic, 6-8 minutes. Place in a greased bowl, turning once to grease the top. Cover and let rise in a warm place until doubled, about 1 hour.
2. Preheat oven to 475°. Grease a 14-in. pizza pan. Roll out dough to fit pan. Pinch edge to form a rim. Cover and let rest 10 minutes.
3. Spread dough with tomato sauce; top with cheeses. If desired, sprinkle with basil, oregano and pepper flakes. Bake on a lower oven rack until crust is lightly browned and cheese is melted, 15-20 minutes. Let stand 5 minutes before slicing.
1 PIECE 254 cal., 12g fat (6g sat. fat), 24mg chol., 714mg sod., 23g carb. (1g sugars, 2g fiber), 13g pro.

TRIPLE TOMATO FLATBREAD

Tomatoes are the reason I have a vegetable garden, and I developed this recipe as a way to show off my garden's plum, sun-dried and cherry tomatoes. The dish is easy and will impress.
—*Rachel Kimbrow, Portland, OR*

TAKES: 20 min. • **MAKES:** 8 pieces

- 1 tube (13.8 oz.) refrigerated pizza crust
  Cooking spray
- 3 plum tomatoes, finely chopped (about 2 cups)
- ½ cup soft sun-dried tomato halves (not packed in oil), julienned
- 2 Tbsp. olive oil
- 1 Tbsp. dried basil
- ¼ tsp. salt
- ¼ tsp. pepper
- 1 cup shredded Asiago cheese
- 2 cups yellow and/or red cherry tomatoes, halved

1. Unroll crust and press into a 15x10-in. rectangle. Transfer to an 18x12-in. piece of heavy-duty foil coated with cooking spray; spritz crust with cooking spray. In a large bowl, toss plum tomatoes and sun-dried tomatoes with oil and seasonings.
2. Carefully invert crust onto grill rack; remove foil. Grill, covered, over medium heat for 2-3 minutes or until bottom is golden brown. Turn; grill until second side begins to brown, 1-2 minutes longer.
3. Remove crust from grill. Spoon plum tomato mixture over crust; top with cheese and cherry tomatoes. Return flatbread to grill. Grill, covered, until crust is golden brown and cheese is melted, 2-4 minutes.
1 PIECE 235 cal., 9g fat (3g sat. fat), 12mg chol., 476mg sod., 29g carb. (7g sugars, 3g fiber), 8g pro. **DIABETIC EXCHANGES** 1½ starch, 1½ fat, 1 vegetable.

OLD-FASHIONED
CONEY HOT DOG
SAUCE P. 172

CAMPFIRE COOKING

S'MORE TO LOVE

Pair your roasted marshmallow with a slew of sweet goodies to craft the ultimate campfire confection.

Cover your bases
Graham crackers are a classic, but consider using chocolate chip cookies or Oreo cookies as your s'more base.

Add a spread
Try smearing a dollop of Nutella or creamy peanut butter over your base of choice.

Choose a chocolate
You can't go wrong with milk chocolate pieces, but white chocolate squares and peanut butter cups help you customize your campfire treat.

Be playful!
Unexpected additions such as white chocolate-covered pretzels add extra crunch, while strawberry slices lend fruity sweetness.

More 'mallows
We do love plain marshmallows, but look for flavored varieties such as chocolate or caramel to make your s'more stand out.

LEMON-DILL SALMON PACKETS

Grilling in foil is an easy technique with foods that cook quickly, such as fish, shrimp, bite-sized meats and fresh veggies. The options are endless—and the cleanup is easy.
—A.J. Weinhold, McArthur, CA

TAKES: 25 min. • **MAKES:** 4 servings

- 1   Tbsp. butter, softened
- 4   salmon fillets (6 oz. each)
- ½   tsp. salt
- ¼   tsp. pepper
- ½   medium onion, sliced
- 4   garlic cloves, sliced
- 4   fresh dill sprigs
- 1   Tbsp. minced fresh basil
- 1   medium lemon, sliced

1. Prepare campfire or grill for medium heat. Ready 4 pieces of a double thickness of foil (about 12 in. square).

Spread butter in the center of each. Place 1 salmon fillet in the center of each; sprinkle with salt and pepper. Top with onion, garlic, dill, basil and lemon. Fold foil around fillets; seal.
2. Place packets on a grill grate over a campfire or grill. Cook 8-10 minutes or until fish just begins to flake easily with a fork. Open carefully to allow the steam to escape.
1 FILLET 305 cal., 19g fat (5g sat. fat), 93mg chol., 405mg sod., 4g carb. (1g sugars, 1g fiber), 29g pro. **DIABETIC EXCHANGES** 5 lean meat, 1 fat.

TEST KITCHEN TIP

To make this recipe at home, place the packets, evenly spaced on a baking sheet and pop them into a 350° oven.

CHERRY-CHOCOLATE PUDGY PIE

Here's an ooey-gooey treat that's just right for campfires and cookouts.
—Josh Carter, Birmingham, AL

TAKES: 10 min. • **MAKES:** 1 serving

- 2   slices white bread
- 3   Tbsp. cherry pie filling
- 1   Tbsp. chopped almonds
- 1   Tbsp. semisweet chocolate chips

1. Place 1 slice of bread in a greased sandwich iron. Spread with pie filling; top with almonds, chocolate chips and remaining bread slice. Close iron.
2. Cook over a hot campfire until golden brown and heated through, 3-6 minutes, turning occasionally.
1 SANDWICH 309 cal., 9g fat (3g sat. fat), 0 chol., 294mg sod., 51g carb. (9g sugars, 3g fiber), 7g pro.

CAMPFIRE CINNAMON TWISTS

Cinnamon rolls get the toasty treatment when wrapped around skewers and warmed over a fire. Brush with butter, then sprinkle with sugar and spice.
—*Lauren McAnelly, Des Moines, IA*

TAKES: 25 min. • **MAKES:** 16 servings

- ¼ cup sugar
- 2 tsp. ground cinnamon
- 1 tube (12.4 oz.) refrigerated cinnamon rolls with icing
- 2 Tbsp. butter, melted

1. Mix sugar and cinnamon. Remove icing from cinnamon rolls; transfer to a resealable plastic bag for drizzling.
2. Separate rolls; cut each in half. Roll halves into 6-in. ropes. Wrap each rope tightly around a long metal skewer, beginning ½ in. from pointed end; pinch each end to secure.
3. Cook rolls over a hot campfire until golden brown, about 5 minutes, turning occasionally. Brush with butter; sprinkle with sugar mixture. Cut a small hole in 1 corner of the icing bag. Drizzle icing over twists.

1 TWIST 98 cal., 4g fat (2g sat. fat), 4mg chol., 183mg sod., 15g carb. (8g sugars, 0 fiber), 1g pro.

CAMPFIRE CHEESE HASH BROWN PACKETS

This easy packet of potatoes, bacon and cheese makes a terrific hash that works as dinner or breakfast. We like to serve it with eggs and fresh pico de gallo.
—*Gina Nistico, Denver, CO*

TAKES: 30 min. • **MAKES:** 4 servings

- 1 pkg. (28 oz.) frozen O'Brien potatoes, thawed
- 1¼ cups shredded cheddar cheese, divided
- 8 bacon strips, cooked and chopped
- ½ tsp. salt
- ¼ tsp. pepper
  Optional: Hard-boiled large eggs and pico de gallo

1. Prepare campfire or grill for medium-high heat. Toss potatoes with ¾ cup cheese, bacon, salt and pepper.
2. Divide mixture among four 18x12-in. pieces of heavy-duty nonstick foil, placing food on dull side of foil. Fold foil around potato mixture, sealing tightly.
3. Place packets over campfire or grill; cook 6-9 minutes on each side or until potatoes are tender. Open packets carefully to allow steam to escape; sprinkle with the remaining ¾ cup cheese. If desired, serve with eggs and pico de gallo.

1 SERVING 329 cal., 15g fat (9g sat. fat), 37mg chol., 708mg sod., 31g carb. (3g sugars, 5g fiber), 14g pro.

CAMPFIRE PEACH COBBLER

Peach cobbler has been a family classic for 60 years. We prefer peaches, but fresh cherries and berries are fun too. Almost any fruit would work—why not mix and match?
—*Jackie Wilson, Wellsville, UT*

PREP: 25 min. • **COOK:** 30 min. + standing
MAKES: 8 servings

- 2 cups all-purpose flour
- 1 cup sugar
- 4 tsp. baking powder
- ½ tsp. salt
- 1 cup 2% milk
- ½ cup butter, melted
FILLING
- 2 cans (15¼ oz. each) sliced peaches
- ¼ cup sugar
- ½ tsp. ground cinnamon, optional

1. Prepare campfire or grill for low heat, using 32-40 charcoal briquettes.
2. Line the inside of a 10-in. Dutch oven with heavy-duty foil. In a large bowl, whisk together first 4 ingredients. Add milk and melted butter, stirring just until moistened. Pour into prepared pot.
3. Drain peaches, reserving 1 cup syrup. Arrange peaches over batter; sprinkle with sugar and, if desired, cinnamon. Pour reserved syrup over fruit. Place lid on Dutch oven.
4. When briquettes are covered with white ash, place Dutch oven directly on half of the briquettes. Using long-handled tongs, place remaining briquettes on top of pot lid. Cook 30-40 minutes or until cobbler is set and beginning to brown, using tongs to lift lid carefully when checking. If necessary, cook 5 minutes longer. Remove from heat; let stand, uncovered, 15 minutes before serving.
1 SERVING 455 cal., 12g fat (8g sat. fat), 33mg chol., 505mg sod., 82g carb. (57g sugars, 2g fiber), 4g pro.

CAMPERS' FAVORITE DIP

Our family craves this cheesy chili dip so much we make two batches—one just for the guys. If you're not grilling out, make it in the oven or the microwave.
—*Valorie Ebie, Bel Aire, KS*

TAKES: 15 min. • **MAKES:** 3½ cups

- 1 pkg. (8 oz.) reduced-fat cream cheese
- 1 can (15 oz.) chili with beans
- 2 cups shredded cheddar cheese
- 2 thinly sliced green onions, optional
  Tortilla chip scoops

1. Prepare campfire or grill for medium-low heat. Spread cream cheese in the bottom of a 9-in. disposable foil pie pan. Top with chili; sprinkle with cheese.
2. Place pan on a grill grate over a campfire or on grill until cheese is melted, 5-8 minutes. If desired, sprinkle with green onion. Serve with chips.
¼ CUP 250 cal., 17g fat (7g sat. fat), 32mg chol., 403mg sod., 15g carb. (2g sugars, 2g fiber), 9g pro.

MICROWAVE DIRECTIONS

Spread the cream cheese in the bottom of a 9-in. microwave-safe pie plate. Top with chili; sprinkle with cheese. Microwave on high for 3-4 minutes or until cheese is mostly melted. Let stand in microwave 2 minutes before serving. Serve with tortilla chips.

APPLE-CINNAMON PUDGY PIE

I remember the first time I tasted a pie-iron pie. My sister buttered the bread while I peeled the apple. She sliced the apple thin, arranged it the bread, and poured white sugar and cinnamon over top. I couldn't believe the magic that came out of that fire! We made them with raspberry jam too. *Mmm!*
—*Monica Kronemeyer DeRegt, Abbotsford, BC*

TAKES: 10 min. • **MAKES:** 1 serving

- 1 Tbsp. butter, softened
- 2 slices white bread
- 1 small McIntosh apple, thinly sliced
- 2 to 3 tsp. cinnamon sugar

1. Spread butter over bread slices; place 1 slice in a greased sandwich iron, buttered side down. Top with sliced apples, cinnamon sugar and remaining slice, buttered side up. Close iron.
2. Cook over a hot campfire until golden brown, turning occasionally, 5-7 minutes.
1 SANDWICH 341 cal., 14g fat (8g sat. fat), 31mg chol., 377mg sod., 51g carb. (22g sugars, 4g fiber), 6g pro.

5i
ECLAIRS ON THE GRILL

My best camping treat is an easy eclair on a stick. This is the one that makes people watch what you're doing and beg to be included.
—*Bonnie Hawkins, Elkhorn, WI*

PREP: 5 min. • **GRILL:** 5 min./batch
MAKES: 6 servings

Stick or wooden dowel (⅝-in. diameter and 24 in. long)
1 tube (8 oz.) refrigerated seamless crescent dough sheet
3 snack-size cups (3¼ oz. each) vanilla or chocolate pudding
½ cup chocolate frosting
Whipped cream in a can, optional

1. Prepare campfire or grill for high heat. Wrap 1 end of a stick or wooden dowel with foil. Unroll crescent dough and cut into six 4-in. squares. Wrap 1 piece of dough around prepared stick, covering 1 end; pinch end and seam to seal.
2. Cook over campfire or grill until golden brown, 5-7 minutes, turning occasionally. When dough is cool enough to handle, remove from stick. Cool completely. Repeat with the remaining dough.
3. Place pudding in a resealable plastic bag; cut a small hole in 1 corner. Squeeze the bag to press mixture into each shell. Spread with frosting; top with whipped cream if desired.

1 ECLAIR 293 cal., 12g fat (4g sat. fat), 0 chol., 418mg sod., 43g carb. (27g sugars, 0 fiber), 4g pro.

READER REVIEW

"I am camping right now and am going to try your pudding addition immediately. Thank you for sharing this new twist on our old favorite!"
—MTGIRLKRISSY, TASTEOFHOME.COM

LEMON BASIL SALMON

My husband came up with this easy foil-packet recipe for flaky, fork-tender salmon. This one is a winner.
—*Marianne Bauman, Modesto, CA*

TAKES: 20 min. • **MAKES:** 2 servings

- 2 salmon fillets (5 oz. each)
- 1 Tbsp. butter, melted
- 1 Tbsp. minced fresh basil
- 1 Tbsp. lemon juice
- ⅛ tsp. salt
- ⅛ tsp. pepper
   Lemon wedges, optional

1. Prepare campfire or grill for medium heat. Place each fillet skin side down on a piece of heavy-duty foil (about 12 in. square). Mix melted butter, basil, lemon juice, salt and pepper; spoon over the salmon. Fold foil around fish, sealing tightly.

2. Cook on campfire or in covered grill until fish just begins to flake easily with a fork, 10-15 minutes. Open foil carefully to allow steam to escape. If desired, serve with lemon wedges.

1 FILLET 274 cal., 19g fat (6g sat. fat), 86mg chol., 264mg sod., 1g carb. (0 sugars, 0 fiber), 24g pro. **DIABETIC EXCHANGES** 4 lean meat, 1½ fat.

PIZZA MOUNTAIN PIES

We liked this pudgy pie recipe so much, I started making them for my daughter on our stove at home!
—*Pam Weik, West Lawn, PA*

TAKES: 10 min. • **MAKES:** 1 serving

- 1 Tbsp. butter, softened
- 2 slices white bread
- 1 Tbsp. pizza sauce
- 4 Tbsp. shredded part-skim mozzarella cheese, divided
- 4 slices pepperoni
- 1 Tbsp. chopped green pepper, optional

1. Spread butter over bread slices. Place 1 slice in a sandwich iron, buttered side down. Spread with pizza sauce; sprinkle with 2 Tbsp. cheese, pepperoni and, if desired, green pepper. Top with the remaining 2 Tbsp. cheese and bread slice, buttered side up. Close iron.

2. Cook over a hot campfire until golden brown and cheese is melted, 3-6 minutes, turning occasionally.

1 SANDWICH 388 cal., 23g fat (12g sat. fat), 56mg chol., 745mg sod., 32g carb. (4g sugars, 2g fiber), 14g pro.

OLD-FASHIONED CONEY HOT DOG SAUCE

Camping and hot dogs go hand in hand. Roast some up over the fire, then top them with this irresistible one-pot sauce.
—*Loriann Cargill Bustos, Phoenix, AZ*

PREP: 10 min. • **COOK:** 30 min.
MAKES: 2 cups

- 1 lb. lean ground beef (90% lean)
- 1 cup beef stock
- 2 Tbsp. tomato paste
- 1 Tbsp. chili powder
- 1 Tbsp. Worcestershire sauce
- ½ tsp. salt
- ½ tsp. onion powder
- ½ tsp. garlic powder
- ½ tsp. celery salt
- ½ tsp. ground cumin
- ¼ tsp. pepper

Prepare campfire or grill for medium-high heat. In a Dutch oven, cook beef over campfire 8-10 minutes or until no longer pink, breaking into crumbles. Stir in the remaining ingredients; bring to a boil. Move pot to indirect heat. Cook, uncovered, 20-25 minutes or until thickened, stirring occasionally.

¼ CUP 103 cal., 5g fat (2g sat. fat), 35mg chol., 355mg sod., 2g carb. (1g sugars, 1g fiber), 12g pro.

TEST KITCHEN TIP

This meaty sauce freezes well in airtight freezer containers. To use, partially thaw overnight in the refrigerator, then heat through in a saucepan. Tuck a container of the frozen sauce into your cooler bag for your next camping trip.

5i

CHEESE-TOPPED POTATOES IN FOIL

Whenever we go camping, these cheesy potato packets are a must. They just may remind you of scalloped potatoes. In the winter, I bake them in the oven.
—*Denise Wheeler, Newaygo, MI*

PREP: 15 min. • **COOK:** 35 min.
MAKES: 8 servings

- 2½ lbs. potatoes (about 3 large), peeled and cut into ¼-in. slices
- 1 medium onion, finely chopped
- 5 bacon strips, cooked and crumbled
- ¼ cup butter, melted
- ½ tsp. salt
- ¼ tsp. pepper
- 6 slices American cheese
  Sour cream, optional

1. Prepare campfire or grill for medium heat. In a large bowl, toss potatoes with onion, bacon, butter, salt and pepper. Place on a large piece of greased heavy-duty foil (about 36x12-in. rectangle). Fold foil around potatoes, sealing tightly.

2. Cook on campfire or in covered grill until the potatoes are tender, about 15 minutes per side. Open foil carefully to allow steam to escape; place cheese over potatoes. Cook until the cheese is melted, 1-2 minutes. If desired, serve with sour cream.

NOTE For single-serve packets, prepare as directed, dividing mixture among 8 smaller pieces of foil. Cook as directed, decreasing time to 10-14 minutes per side and increasing cheese to 8 slices.

¾ CUP 217 cal., 11g fat (7g sat. fat), 24mg chol., 454mg sod., 21g carb. (3g sugars, 2g fiber), 7g pro.

SUGAR COOKIE S'MORES

Change up traditional s'mores by using sugar cookies and candy bars in place of the expected ingredients. This fun twist on the campfire classic will delight everyone!
—Taste of Home *Test Kitchen*

TAKES: 15 min. • **MAKES:** 4 servings

- 8   fun-size Milky Way candy bars
- 8   sugar cookies (3 in.)
- 4   large marshmallows

1. Place 2 candy bars on each of 4 cookies; place on grill rack. Grill, uncovered, over medium-high heat until bottoms of cookies are browned, 1-1½ minutes.
2. Meanwhile, using a long-handled fork, toast marshmallows 6 in. from the heat until golden brown, turning occasionally. Remove marshmallows from fork and place over candy bars; top with the remaining cookies. Serve immediately.
1 COOKIE S'MORE 271 cal., 10g fat (5g sat. fat), 13mg chol., 123mg sod., 43g carb. (31g sugars, 1g fiber), 3g pro.

ROOT BEER APPLE BAKED BEANS

All the men in our family love roughing it outdoors. My beans with bacon and apples is a must to keep their outdoor energy going.
—*Nancy Heishman, Las Vegas, NV*

PREP: 20 min. • **COOK:** 45 min.
MAKES: 12 servings

- 6   thick-sliced bacon strips, chopped
- 4   cans (16 oz. each) baked beans
- 1   can (21 oz.) apple pie filling
- 1   can (12 oz.) root beer
- 1   tsp. ground ancho chile pepper, optional
- 1   cup shredded smoked cheddar cheese, optional

1. Prepare campfire or grill for medium heat, using 32-36 charcoal briquettes or large wood chips.
2. In a 10-in. Dutch oven, cook bacon over campfire until crisp. Remove; discard drippings. Return bacon to pot; stir in baked beans, pie filling, root beer and, if desired, ancho chili pepper
3. Cover Dutch oven. When briquettes or wood chips are covered with ash, place Dutch oven on top of 16-18 briquettes. Place 16-18 briquettes on pan cover.
4. Cook 30-40 minutes to allow flavors to blend. If desired, sprinkle individual servings with cheese.
¾ CUP 255 cal., 5g fat (2g sat. fat), 16mg chol., 778mg sod., 47g carb. (11g sugars, 9g fiber), 10g pro.

MILKY WAY PUDGY PIE

My favorite pudgy pies have Milky Way candy bars, graham cracker crumbs and marshmallows. So irresistible! And buttered bread is a must.
—*Susan Hein, Burlington, WI*

TAKES: 10 min. • **MAKES:** 1 serving

- 1 Tbsp. butter, softened
- 2 slices white bread
- 1 Tbsp. graham cracker crumbs
- 1 fun-size Milky Way candy bar, chopped
- 2 Tbsp. miniature marshmallows

1. Spread butter over bread slices. Place 1 slice in a sandwich iron, buttered side down. Top with cracker crumbs, chopped candy, marshmallows and remaining bread slice, buttered side up. Close iron.
2. Cook over a hot campfire until golden brown and marshmallows are melted, 3-6 minutes, turning occasionally.
1 SANDWICH 380 cal., 17g fat (10g sat. fat), 32mg chol., 438mg sod., 51g carb. (19g sugars, 2g fiber), 6g pro.

READER REVIEW

"You can use all sorts of candy bars ... [or] use marshmallow creme instead of marshmallows. These are so great to make on campouts."
—RANDCBRUNS, TASTEOFHOME.COM

⑤ᵢ
CAKE & BERRY CAMPFIRE COBBLER

This warm cobbler is one of our favorite ways to end a busy day of fishing, hiking, swimming or rafting. It's yummy with ice cream—and so easy to make!
—*June Dress, Meridian, ID*

PREP: 10 min. • **GRILL:** 30 min.
MAKES: 12 servings

- 2 cans (21 oz. each) raspberry pie filling
- 1 pkg. yellow cake mix (regular size)
- 1¼ cups water
- ½ cup canola oil
  Vanilla ice cream, optional

1. Prepare grill or campfire for low heat, using 16-20 charcoal briquettes or large wood chips.
2. Line an ovenproof Dutch oven with heavy-duty aluminum foil; add pie filling. In a large bowl, combine the cake mix, water and oil. Spread over pie filling.
3. Cover Dutch oven. When briquettes or wood chips are covered with white ash, place Dutch oven directly on top of 8-10 of them. Using long-handled tongs, place the remaining briquettes on pot lid.
4. Cook until the filling is bubbly and a toothpick inserted in the topping comes out clean, 30-40 minutes. To check for doneness, use the tongs to carefully lift the lid. If desired, serve with ice cream.
1 SERVING 342 cal., 12g fat (2g sat. fat), 0 chol., 322mg sod., 57g carb. (34g sugars, 2g fiber), 1g pro.

SWEET HORSERADISH GLAZED RIBS

If you like to prep ahead of camping, roast these ribs, wrap them and finish with a sweet, savory sauce at your campfire or grill.
—*Ralph Jones, San Diego, CA*

PREP: 10 min. + chilling • **COOK:** 2¼ hours
MAKES: 8 servings

- 3 racks pork baby back ribs (about 8 lbs.)
- 1½ tsp. salt, divided
- 1½ tsp. coarsely ground pepper, divided
- 2 bottles (12 oz. each) beer or 3 cups unsweetened apple juice
- 1 jar (12 oz.) apricot preserves
- ¼ cup prepared horseradish, drained
- 2 Tbsp. honey or maple syrup
- 1 tsp. liquid smoke, optional

1. Preheat oven to 325°. If necessary, remove thin membrane from ribs and discard. Sprinkle 1 tsp. each salt and pepper over ribs. Transfer to a large shallow roasting pan, bone side down; add beer or juice. Bake, covered, until tender, 2-3 hours.
2. Meanwhile, puree the preserves, horseradish, honey, remaining ½ tsp. salt and ½ tsp. pepper and, if desired, liquid smoke in a blender.
3. Drain ribs. Place 1 rib rack on a large piece of aluminum foil. Brush with apricot-horseradish mixture; wrap tightly. Repeat with remaining ribs. Refrigerate up to 2 days.
4. Prepare campfire or grill for medium heat. Remove the ribs from foil; grill until browned, 10-15 minutes, turning occasionally.
1 SERVING 690 cal., 42g fat (15g sat. fat), 163mg chol., 674mg sod., 33g carb. (23g sugars, 0 fiber), 45g pro.

Ⓛ ⑤ᵢ
HAM & JACK PUDGY PIE

Pepper jack cheese spices up these warm, melty sandwiches.
—*Terri McKitrick, Delafield, WI*

TAKES: 10 min. • **MAKES:** 1 serving

- 2 slices sourdough bread
- 2 Tbsp. diced fully cooked ham
- 2 Tbsp. canned sliced mushrooms
- 3 Tbsp. shredded pepper jack cheese
- 1 Tbsp. salsa

1. Place 1 slice bread in a greased sandwich iron. Top with ham, mushrooms, cheese, salsa and the remaining bread slice. Close iron.
2. Cook over a hot campfire until golden brown and cheese is melted, 3-6 minutes, turning occasionally.
1 SANDWICH 268 cal., 9g fat (4g sat. fat), 33mg chol., 823mg sod., 32g carb. (4g sugars, 2g fiber), 15g pro. **DIABETIC EXCHANGES** 2 starch, 2 medium-fat meat.

SCRAMBLED EGG BREAD

We always eat ham, eggs and bread on camping trips, and we often have extras. Combine them and you've got scrambled egg bread. We first made this on a visit to Mount Shasta.
—Shirley Mondeau, Rohnert Park, CA

PREP: 25 min. • **COOK:** 10 min.
MAKES: 4 servings

- 1 loaf (1 lb.) unsliced French bread
- 2 Tbsp. butter, softened, divided

FILLING
- 2 Tbsp. butter, divided
- 1 small onion, chopped
- 1 cup cubed fully cooked ham
- 1 large tomato, chopped
- 6 large eggs
- ⅛ tsp. pepper
- 1½ cups shredded cheddar cheese, divided

1. Prepare campfire or grill for medium heat. Cut bread crosswise in half; cut each piece lengthwise in half. Hollow out 2 pieces, leaving ½-in. shells. Cut removed bread into cubes; reserve 1½ cups (save remaining cubes for another use). Spread 1 Tbsp. softened butter over the bread shells. Spread the remaining 1 Tbsp. softened butter over the remaining bread halves. Set aside.

2. In a small Dutch oven, heat 1 Tbsp. butter over campfire. Add onion; cook and stir 3-4 minutes or until tender. Stir in ham and tomato; remove from pan.

3. In a small bowl, whisk eggs and pepper. In same pan, heat remaining 1 Tbsp. butter. Pour in egg mixture; cook and stir until eggs are thickened and no liquid egg remains. Stir in ham mixture, 1 cup cheese and reserved bread cubes. Spoon filling into bread shells; sprinkle with remaining ½ cup cheese. Transfer to a 13x9-in. disposable foil pan; cover with foil.

4. Place pan over campfire. Cook until heated through and cheese is melted, 8-10 minutes. Cook reserved bread halves, buttered side down, until toasted, 1-2 minutes. Cut each piece of egg bread and toast in half.

1 SERVING 723 cal., 37g fat (19g sat. fat), 372mg chol., 1530mg sod., 60g carb. (7g sugars, 3g fiber), 39g pro.

REUBEN PUDGY PIE

Our favorite pudgy pie is the Reuben: Corned beef, sauerkraut and Swiss cheese! We always use buttered bread.
—Taste of Home *Test Kitchen*

TAKES: 10 min. • **MAKES:** 1 serving

- 1 Tbsp. butter, softened
- 2 slices white bread
- 2 oz. sliced deli corned beef
- 3 to 4 Tbsp. sauerkraut
- 1 to 2 slices Swiss cheese

1. Spread butter over the bread slices; place 1 slice in a greased sandwich iron, buttered side down. Top with corned beef, sauerkraut, cheese and remaining bread slice, buttered side up. Close iron.

2. Cook over a hot campfire until golden brown and cheese has melted, turning occasionally, 5-7 minutes.

1 SANDWICH 358 cal., 19g fat (11g sat. fat), 72mg chol., 1228mg sod., 30g carb. (4g sugars, 2g fiber), 17g pro.

BLUEBERRY-CINNAMON CAMPFIRE BREAD

A neighboring camper made a bread so tempting, I had to ask for the details. Here's my version, best enjoyed with a steaming cup of coffee by the campfire.
—Joan Hallford, North Richland Hills, TX

PREP: 10 min. • **COOK:** 30 min. + standing
MAKES: 8 servings

- 1 loaf (1 lb.) cinnamon-raisin bread, sliced
- 6 large eggs
- 1 cup 2% milk or half-and-half cream
- 2 Tbsp. maple syrup
- 1 tsp. vanilla extract
- ½ cup chopped pecans, toasted
- 2 cups fresh blueberries, divided

1. Prepare campfire or grill for low heat. Arrange the bread slices on a greased double thickness of heavy-duty foil (about 24x18 in.). Bring foil up the sides, leaving the top open. Whisk eggs, milk, syrup and vanilla. Pour over bread; sprinkle with nuts and 1 cup blueberries. Fold edges over top, crimping to seal.
2. Place on a grill grate over campfire or grill until the eggs are cooked through, 30-40 minutes. Remove from heat; let stand 10 minutes. Sprinkle with remaining blueberries; serve with additional maple syrup if desired.
2 PIECES 266 cal., 10g fat (2g sat. fat), 142mg chol., 185mg sod., 36g carb. (14g sugars, 5g fiber), 12g pro. **DIABETIC EXCHANGES** 2 starch, 1 medium-fat meat, ½ fruit, ½ fat.

POT OF S'MORES

This easy Dutch oven version of the popular campout treat is so good and gooey. The hardest part is waiting for it to cool a bit so you can dig in!
—June Dress, Meridian, ID

TAKES: 25 min. • **MAKES:** 12 servings

- 1 pkg. (14½ oz.) graham crackers, crushed
- ½ cup butter, melted
- 1 can (14 oz.) sweetened condensed milk
- 2 cups semisweet chocolate chips
- 1 cup butterscotch chips
- 2 cups miniature marshmallows

1. Prepare grill or campfire for low heat, using 16-18 charcoal briquettes or large wood chips.
2. Line a cast-iron Dutch oven with heavy-duty aluminum foil. Combine cracker crumbs and butter; press into bottom of pot. Pour milk over crust and sprinkle with chocolate and butterscotch chips. Top with marshmallows.
3. Cover Dutch oven. When briquettes or wood chips are covered with white ash, place Dutch oven directly on top of 6 of them. Using long-handled tongs, place remaining briquettes on pot lid.
4. Cook until marshmallows begin to melt, about 15 minutes. To check for doneness, use the tongs to carefully lift the lid.
1 SERVING 584 cal., 28g fat (17g sat. fat), 31mg chol., 326mg sod., 83g carb. (47g sugars, 3g fiber), 8g pro.

EASY STRAWBERRY CHEESECAKE ICE CREAM P. 188

FROSTY
TREATS

INDIAN KULFI ICE CREAM

I grew up near Little India in California, and loved the baked goods and desserts from Indian sweets shops. One of them sold *kulfi*, similar to a sort of spiced and nutty frozen custard in cone molds. Here I use a shortcut method to make kulfi quickly and without any special equipment. The milk can be replaced with mango pulp for mango kulfi.
—*Justine Kmiecik, Crestview, FL*

PREP: 30 min. + freezing
MAKES: 6 servings

- 1 can (14 oz.) sweetened condensed milk
- 1 cup whole milk
- 1 cup heavy whipping cream
- ¼ cup nonfat dry milk powder
- ½ tsp. ground cardamom
- ¼ tsp. sea salt
- 1 pinch saffron threads or ¼ tsp. ground turmeric, optional
- ¼ cup chopped cashews, toasted
- ¼ cup chopped shelled pistachios
- ¼ tsp. almond extract

1. In a large heavy saucepan, whisk milks, cream, milk powder, cardamom, sea salt and, if desired, saffron until blended. Cook over low heat until the mixture thickens slightly, about 15 minutes, stirring constantly. Do not allow mixture to boil. Remove from heat. Strain through a fine-mesh strainer into a small bowl; cool.
2. Stir in the cashews, pistachios and extract. Transfer to six 4-oz. ramekins. Cover and freeze 8 hours or overnight. If desired, sprinkle with additional chopped nuts before serving.
½ CUP 446 cal., 27g fat (14g sat. fat), 72mg chol., 266mg sod., 44g carb. (41g sugars, 1g fiber), 11g pro.

5i
WATERMELON BOMBE DESSERT

When cut, this sherbet dessert looks like actual watermelon slices—complete with mini chips representing seeds. It is fun to eat and refreshing too.
—*Renae Moncur, Burley, ID*

PREP: 20 min. + freezing
MAKES: 8 servings

- About 1 pint lime sherbet
- About 1 pint pineapple sherbet
- About 1½ pints raspberry sherbet
- ¼ cup miniature semisweet chocolate chips

1. Line a 1½-qt. bowl with plastic wrap. Press a thin layer of lime sherbet around the inside of bowl. Freeze, uncovered, until firm. Spread a thin layer of pineapple sherbet evenly over lime sherbet layer. Freeze, uncovered, until firm. Pack raspberry sherbet in center of sherbet-lined bowl. Smooth the top to resemble a cut watermelon.
2. Cover and freeze until firm, about 8 hours. Just before serving, uncover bowl of molded sherbet. Place a serving plate on the bowl and invert. Remove bowl and peel off plastic wrap.
3. Cut the bombe into wedges; press a few chocolate chips into the raspberry section of each wedge to resemble watermelon seeds.
1 PIECE 205 cal., 4g fat (2g sat. fat), 8mg chol., 60mg sod., 43g carb. (35g sugars, 0 fiber), 2g pro.

5i
LEMON SHERBET

Lemon juice provides the snappy flavor in this wonderful ice cream recipe from our Test Kitchen. The light, make-ahead treat looks splendid served in individual boats made from lemon halves.
—Taste of Home *Test Kitchen*

PREP: 10 min. + freezing
MAKES: 2 servings

- 1 cup half-and-half cream
- ⅓ cup sugar
- 3 Tbsp. lemon juice
- 1 tsp. grated lemon zest

1. In a small bowl, stir cream and sugar until sugar is dissolved. Stir in lemon juice and zest (mixture will thicken slightly). Cover and freeze until firm, about 8 hours or overnight.
2. Remove sherbet from the freezer 10 minutes before serving. Spoon into lemon boats or dessert dishes.
¾ CUP 295 cal., 12g fat (8g sat. fat), 60mg chol., 61mg sod., 39g carb. (38g sugars, 0 fiber), 4g pro.

TEST KITCHEN TIP

While both desserts are fruit based, the difference between sherbet and sorbet is simple. Sorbet does not contain dairy—such as milk or cream—and sherbet typically does! Because of this, sorbet usually has a drier, icier consistency, while sherbet has a slight creaminess.

⑤ᵢ FROSTY WATERMELON ICE

For a different way to serve watermelon, try this make-ahead frozen dessert. It's so refreshing on a summer day ... and you don't have to worry about seeds while you're enjoying it!
—*Kaaren Jurack, Manassas, VA*

PREP: 20 min. + freezing
MAKES: 4 servings

- 1   tsp. unflavored gelatin
- 2   Tbsp. water
- 2   Tbsp. lime juice
- 2   Tbsp. honey
- 4   cups cubed seedless watermelon

1. In a microwave-safe bowl, sprinkle gelatin over water; let stand 1 minute.

Microwave on high for 40 seconds. Stir and let stand until gelatin is completely dissolved, 1-2 minutes.
2. Place the lime juice, honey and gelatin mixture in a blender. Add 1 cup watermelon; cover and process until blended. Add the remaining watermelon, 1 cup at a time, processing until smooth after each addition.
3. Transfer to a shallow dish; freeze until almost firm. In a chilled bowl, beat with an electric mixer until mixture is bright pink. Divide among 4 serving dishes; freeze, covered, until firm. Remove from freezer 15-20 minutes before serving.
¾ CUP 81 cal., 0 fat (0 sat. fat), 0 chol., 3mg sod., 21g carb. (18g sugars, 1g fiber), 1g pro. **DIABETIC EXCHANGES** 1 fruit, ½ starch.

⏱ ⑤ᵢ HONEYDEW LIME COOLER

Serve up a frosty glass of this citrusy blend of lime sherbet and honeydew melon for a real thirst-quencher.
—*Mitzi Sentiff, Annapolis, MD*

TAKES: 30 min. • **MAKES:** 5 servings

- 4½ cups cubed honeydew (about 1 small melon)
- 1½ cups lime sherbet
- 2   Tbsp. lime juice
- 5   fresh strawberries

1. Place melon cubes in a 15x10x1-in. baking pan; cover and freeze until firm, about 15 minutes. Set aside five melon cubes.
2. In a food processor, combine sherbet, lime juice and remaining frozen melon; cover and process until smooth. Pour into glasses; garnish with strawberries and reserved melon cubes.
¾ CUP 135 cal., 1g fat (0 sat. fat), 3mg chol., 34mg sod., 32g carb. (28g sugars, 1g fiber), 1g pro. **DIABETIC EXCHANGES** 1 starch, 1 fruit.

ROCKY ROAD FREEZER PIE

Whip up this simple chocolaty pie the day before and you'll feel like a champ when you serve it on party day.
—*Addrenne Roth, Donna, TX*

PREP: 15 min. + freezing
MAKES: 8 servings

- 1½ cups half-and-half cream
- 1 pkg. (3.9 oz.) instant chocolate pudding mix
- 1 carton (8 oz.) frozen whipped topping, thawed
- ⅓ cup semisweet chocolate chips
- ⅓ cup miniature marshmallows
- ⅓ cup chopped pecans
- 1 graham cracker crust (9 in.) Optional: Miniature marshmallows, chopped pecans and chocolate sauce

1. In a large bowl, whisk cream and pudding mix for 2 minutes. Fold in whipped topping. Stir in chocolate chips, marshmallows and pecans. Transfer to pie crust. Freeze until firm, about 6 hours.
2. Remove from freezer 10 minutes before serving. If desired, top with marshmallows, pecans and chocolate sauce.
1 PIECE 184 cal., 10g fat (5g sat. fat), 11mg chol., 175mg sod., 20g carb. (15g sugars, 1g fiber), 2g pro.

READER REVIEW

"Good and easy; great recipe for the camper. Don't skip the chocolate sauce drizzle!"
—GRAMMY DEBBIE, TASTEOFHOME.COM

PEANUT BUTTER & JELLY ICE CREAM

What could be better than peanut butter and jelly ice cream? You'll love the sweet-salty combination. Use your favorite flavor of jelly, and switch to crunchy peanut butter if you like extra texture.
—Taste of Home *Test Kitchen*

PREP: 20 min. + chilling
PROCESS: 20 min. + freezing
MAKES: 5 cups

- 1½ cups whole milk
- ⅔ cup packed brown sugar
- ½ tsp. salt
- 1 large egg, lightly beaten
- ⅔ cup creamy peanut butter
- 2 cups heavy whipping cream
- 2 tsp. vanilla extract
- ½ cup grape jelly or strawberry jelly

1. In a large heavy saucepan, heat the milk, brown sugar and salt until bubbles form around the side of the pan. Whisk a small amount of hot mixture into egg. Return all to pan, whisking constantly.
2. Cook and stir over low heat until mixture is thickened and coats the back of a spoon. Remove from the heat; whisk in peanut butter. Quickly transfer to a bowl; place bowl in ice water and stir for 2 minutes. Stir in cream and vanilla. Press plastic wrap onto surface of custard. Refrigerate several hours or overnight.
3. Fill cylinder of ice cream maker two-thirds full with custard; freeze according to the manufacturer's directions.
4. When ice cream is frozen, spoon into a freezer container, layering with jelly; freeze for 2-4 hours before serving.
NOTE Reduced-fat peanut butter is not recommended for this recipe.
½ CUP 393 cal., 28g fat (14g sat. fat), 77mg chol., 231mg sod., 32g carb. (29g sugars, 1g fiber), 7g pro.

5i QUICK MANGO SORBET

Last summer, I decided to try my hand at making a passion fruit and mango sorbet. But fresh fruits require more prep and are difficult to find ripened at the same time. So I experimented using frozen fruit and juice, and voila! Both are readily available and inexpensive too.
—*Carol Klein, Franklin Square, NY*

TAKES: 5 min. • **MAKES:** 2½ cups

- 1 pkg. (16 oz.) frozen mango chunks, slightly thawed
- ½ cup passion fruit juice
- 2 Tbsp. sugar

Place all ingredients in a blender; cover and process until smooth. Serve immediately. If desired, for a firmer texture, cover and freeze at least 3 hours.
½ CUP 91 cal., 0 fat (0 sat. fat), 0 chol., 2mg sod., 24g carb. (21g sugars, 2g fiber), 1g pro.

EASY STRAWBERRY CHEESECAKE ICE CREAM

When I first got my ice cream maker, a friend shared her dreamy frozen cheesecake recipe to help me break it in.
—Joan Hallford, North Richland Hills, TX

PREP: 15 min.
PROCESS: 25 min. + freezing
MAKES: 1½ qt.

- 1   cup half-and-half cream
- 1   Tbsp. vanilla extract
- 2   tsp. grated lemon zest
- 2   tsp. lemon juice
- 1   cup sugar
- 1   pkg. (8 oz.) cream cheese, cubed and softened
- 1   cup heavy whipping cream
- 1½ cups fresh strawberries
     Optional: Sliced fresh strawberries and crushed graham crackers

1. Place the first 6 ingredients in a blender; cover and process until smooth. Add whipping cream; cover and process until blended. Transfer to a large bowl.
2. Add 1½ cups strawberries to blender; cover and process until pureed. Stir into the cream mixture.
3. Fill cylinder of ice cream maker no more than two-thirds full; freeze according to manufacturer's directions. (Refrigerate any remaining mixture until ready to freeze.)
4. Transfer the ice cream to freezer containers, allowing headspace for expansion. Freeze 4-6 hours or until firm. If desired, serve with sliced strawberries and crushed graham crackers.
½ CUP 234 cal., 16g fat (10g sat. fat), 58mg chol., 87mg sod., 20g carb. (20g sugars, 0 fiber), 2g pro.

CHERRY & CHOCOLATE ICE CREAM PIE

We took cherry pie to a whole new level as a frozen treat. With a luscious layer of chocolate fudge inside, this is one impressive pie.
—*Scarlett Elrod, Newnan, GA*

PREP: 20 min. + freezing
MAKES: 8 servings

- 15 Oreo cookies
- ¼ cup butter, melted
- ¾ cup hot fudge ice cream topping
- 4 cups vanilla ice cream, softened
- 3 cups fresh or frozen dark sweet cherries, pitted and quartered, divided
- ½ cup water
- ¼ cup sugar
- 2 Tbsp. thawed cranberry juice concentrate
- 1 Tbsp. cornstarch
- 1 Tbsp. cherry liqueur, optional

1. Pulse cookies in a food processor until fine crumbs form. Add butter; process until blended. Press mixture onto bottom and up the side of an ungreased 9-in. pie plate. Freeze until firm, about 15 minutes. Carefully spread hot fudge topping over bottom of crust. Freeze until firm, about 30 minutes.

2. Combine ice cream and 1 cup cherries; spread over hot fudge. Freeze until firm, about 8 hours.

3. In a large saucepan, combine water, sugar, cranberry juice concentrate and cornstarch; bring to a boil over medium heat, stirring constantly. Stir in the remaining 2 cups cherries. Reduce heat; simmer, uncovered, until thickened and cherries are soft, about 5 minutes. Remove from heat; stir in liqueur if desired. Cool completely.

4. Remove pie from freezer 10 minutes before cutting. Serve with sauce.

1 PIECE 460 cal., 19g fat (10g sat. fat), 44mg chol., 224mg sod., 69g carb. (47g sugars, 2g fiber), 5g pro.

CREAMY WATERMELON SMOOTHIE

I love this refreshing watermelon smoothie recipe and the bright, summery flavor. The key is to freeze the watermelon cubes just a little. Otherwise it'll be too difficult to blend.
—*Sarah Scott, Murfreesboro, TN*

TAKES: 10 min. • **MAKES:** 4 servings

- 4 cups seeded cubed watermelon, partially frozen
- ½ cup reduced-fat vanilla ice cream
- ½ cup fat-free milk
- 1 Tbsp. sugar
- 6 fresh mint leaves

Place all ingredients in a blender; cover and process until blended.

¾ CUP 100 cal., 1g fat (1g sat. fat), 5mg chol., 29mg sod., 20g carb. (18g sugars, 1g fiber), 3g pro. **DIABETIC EXCHANGES** 1 fruit, ½ starch.

BEST ICE CREAM SANDWICHES

These chilly treats are perfect for hot, sunny days. The gluten-free chocolate cookie is so tasty you could eat it plain ... but you won't want to miss out on the ice cream!
—Taste of Home *Test Kitchen*

PREP: 20 min. • **BAKE:** 10 min. + freezing
MAKES: 6 servings

- ⅓ cup butter, softened
- ½ cup sugar
- ½ tsp. vanilla extract
- 2 Tbsp. beaten large egg
- ⅔ cup white rice flour
- ¼ cup potato starch
- ¼ cup baking cocoa
- 2 Tbsp. tapioca flour
- ½ tsp. baking powder
- ½ tsp. baking soda
- ½ tsp. xanthan gum
- ⅛ tsp. salt
- 1½ cups vanilla ice cream, softened

1. In a small bowl, cream butter, sugar and vanilla. Beat in egg. Combine rice flour, starch, cocoa, tapioca flour, baking powder, baking soda, xanthan gum and salt; add to the creamed mixture and mix well.
2. Drop by rounded tablespoonfuls 2 in. apart onto a baking sheet coated with cooking spray, forming 12 cookies; flatten slightly. Bake at 350° until set, 8-10 minutes. Remove to a wire rack to cool completely.
3. Spread ¼ cup ice cream on bottoms of half the cookies; top with remaining cookies. Wrap each in waxed paper. Freeze until firm, about 3 hours.
NOTE Read all ingredient labels for possible gluten content prior to use. Ingredient formulas can change, and production facilities vary among brands. If you're concerned that your brand may contain gluten, contact the company.
1 SANDWICH 325 cal., 15g fat (9g sat. fat), 60mg chol., 312mg sod., 47g carb. (24g sugars, 2g fiber), 3g pro.

LEMON COCONUT STREUSEL ICE CREAM CAKE

I developed this cool treat because I wanted to find a new use for cream of coconut. The sweet coconut combines beautifully with the tart lemon juice, and the streusel adds a nice crunch. Look for cream of coconut in the cocktail mixer section of your grocery store.
—*Janet Gill, Canton, OH*

PREP: 30 min. + freezing
MAKES: 16 servings

- 1 pkg. (11.2 oz.) shortbread cookies
- ½ cup sweetened shredded coconut, toasted
- ¼ cup macadamia nuts, coarsely chopped and toasted
- 1 tsp. grated lemon zest
- 1 can (15 oz.) cream of coconut
- ½ cup lemon juice
- 1½ qt. vanilla ice cream, softened
- 1 carton (8 oz.) frozen whipped topping, thawed, divided
  Optional: Fresh blueberries, raspberries and strawberries

1. Reserve 10 cookies for decoration. Crush remaining cookies; transfer to a bowl. Stir in the coconut, macadamia nuts and lemon zest. Reserve 2 Tbsp. crumb mixture for topping.
2. In a large bowl, whisk the cream of coconut and lemon juice until combined. Stir in softened ice cream until smooth. Fold in 1 cup whipped topping.
3. Sprinkle 1 cup crumb mixture onto bottom of a greased 9-in. springform pan. Top with half the ice cream mixture. Layer with remaining crumbs and ice cream mixture. Place reserved whole cookies around edge of pan. Top with remaining 2½ cups whipped topping; sprinkle with reserved 2 Tbsp. crumb mixture. Freeze, covered, until firm, at least 8 hours or overnight. Serve with berries if desired.
NOTE To toast nuts and coconut, bake in separate shallow pans in a 350° oven for 5-10 minutes or until golden brown, stirring occasionally.
1 PIECE 384 cal., 21g fat (13g sat. fat), 29mg chol., 149mg sod., 45g carb. (35g sugars, 1g fiber), 4g pro.

MARGARITA ICE CREAM FLOATS

On a hot afternoon, what could be better than a cold margarita? The addition of creamy ice cream takes this treat to the next level.
—*Teri Schloessmann, Tulsa, OK*

TAKES: 5 min. • **MAKES:** 6 servings

Lime wedges
Sugar
2 cups vanilla ice cream
2 cups lime sherbet
6 cups lemon-lime soda, chilled
¾ cup lime juice
9 oz. silver tequila

1. Using lime wedges, moisten the rims of 6 margarita or cocktail glasses. Set aside lime wedges for garnish. Sprinkle sugar on a plate; hold each glass upside down and dip rim into sugar. Set aside. Discard remaining sugar on plate.
2. Scoop the ice cream and sherbet into prepared glasses. Combine soda, lime juice and tequila; pour into the glasses. Garnish with the reserved lime wedges. Serve immediately.

1 MARGARITA 372 cal., 6g fat (4g sat. fat), 20mg chol., 83mg sod., 55g carb. (46g sugars, 1g fiber), 2g pro.

READER REVIEW

"These were a delight—refreshing and easy to make! I had a dinner party of six, and everyone remarked how perfect the floats were after a big dinner and it being summertime."
—LSHAW, TASTEOFHOME.COM

GRASSHOPPER BAKED ALASKA

Can you believe it? This stunning dessert is completely make ahead, including the meringue. All you need to do is bake it for a few minutes in the oven before serving.
—Taste of Home *Test Kitchen*

PREP: 45 min. + freezing • **BAKE:** 5 min.
MAKES: 12 servings

½ cup butter, cubed
2 oz. unsweetened chocolate, chopped
1 cup sugar
1 tsp. vanilla extract
2 large eggs, room temperature
¾ cup all-purpose flour
½ tsp. baking powder
½ tsp. salt
2 qt. vanilla ice cream, softened
1 pkg. (4.67 oz.) mint Andes candies, chopped
2 Tbsp. creme de menthe
1 Tbsp. creme de cacao
Green food coloring, optional

MERINGUE
8 large egg whites
1 cup sugar
1 tsp. cream of tartar

1. In a microwave-safe bowl, melt butter and chocolate; stir until smooth. Stir in sugar. Beat in vanilla and eggs, 1 at a time, beating well after each addition. Combine flour, baking powder and salt; stir into the chocolate mixture.

2. Transfer to a greased 8-in. round baking pan. Bake at 350° for 30-35 minutes or until a toothpick inserted in center comes out with moist crumbs (do not overbake). Cool for 10 minutes before removing from the pan to a wire rack to cool completely.

3. Meanwhile, in a large bowl, combine the ice cream, Andes candies, liqueurs and, if desired, food coloring. Transfer to an 8-in. round bowl (1½ qt.) lined with plastic wrap; freeze until set.

4. For the meringue, in a large heavy saucepan, combine the egg whites, sugar and cream of tartar. With a hand mixer, beat on low speed for 1 minute. Continue beating over low heat until egg mixture reaches 160°, about 8 minutes. Transfer to a bowl; beat until stiff glossy peaks form and sugar is dissolved.

5. Place the brownie on an ungreased foil-lined baking sheet; top with inverted ice cream mold. Remove plastic wrap. Immediately spread meringue over ice cream, sealing it to the edge of the brownie. Freeze until ready to serve, up to 24 hours.

6. Bake at 400° for 2-5 minutes or until meringue is lightly browned. Transfer to a serving plate; serve immediately.

1 PIECE 523 cal., 24g fat (16g sat. fat), 94mg chol., 294mg sod., 70g carb. (57g sugars, 1g fiber), 9g pro.

TEST KITCHEN TIP

The final step is to toast the outer layer of meringue—you can get the same effect by using a kitchen torch, as with creme brulee. Do it at the table and amaze your guests!

CORNFLAKE FRIED ICE CREAM

Yes, you can make this crunchy, creamy Mexican restaurant-style dessert at home—it's easier than you think!
—*Ronda Weirich, Plains, KS*

PREP: 20 min. + freezing • **COOK:** 5 min.
MAKES: 2 servings

- 1 cup vanilla ice cream
- ¼ cup heavy whipping cream, divided
- ¼ tsp. vanilla extract, divided
- ¾ cup crushed frosted cornflakes
- ¼ tsp. ground cinnamon
  Oil for deep-fat frying
  Whipped cream
  Optional: Hot fudge and/or caramel sauce

1. Using a ½-cup ice cream scoop, form 2 balls of ice cream. Cover and freeze 1 hour or until firm. In a small bowl, whisk 2 Tbsp. cream and ⅛ tsp. vanilla. In a shallow bowl, combine cornflakes and cinnamon. Dip ice cream balls into cream mixture; then roll in cornflake mixture. Set aside remaining cornflake mixture. Cover and freeze ice cream balls 1 hour or until firm.

2. In a small bowl, whisk together the remaining 2 Tbsp. cream and ⅛ tsp. vanilla. Dip ice cream balls into cream mixture; roll in reserved cereal mixture. Cover and freeze for 1 hour or until firm.

3. In an electric skillet or deep-fat fryer, heat oil to 375°. Fry each ice cream ball for 5-10 seconds or until golden. Drain on paper towels. Serve immediately with whipped cream; drizzle with hot fudge and caramel sauce if desired.

1 SERVING 323 cal., 22g fat (12g sat. fat), 70mg chol., 138mg sod., 31g carb. (18g sugars, 1g fiber), 3g pro.

⑤i
BLUEBERRY CREAM POPS

Blueberry and cream pops are a fun and surprisingly simple afternoon snack.
—*Cindy Reams, Philipsburg, PA*

PREP: 15 min. + freezing • **MAKES:** 8 pops

- ⅔ cup sugar
- ⅔ cup water
- 2 cups fresh or frozen blueberries, thawed
- ¼ cup heavy whipping cream
- 8 freezer pop molds or 8 paper cups (3 oz. each) and wooden pop sticks

1. In a small saucepan, combine sugar and water; bring to a boil, stirring to dissolve sugar. Cool completely.

2. In a bowl, coarsely mash blueberries; stir in cream and cooled sugar syrup. Spoon into molds or paper cups. Top molds with holders. If using cups, top with foil and insert pop sticks through foil. Freeze until firm. To serve, let pops stand at room temperature 10 minutes before unmolding.

1 POP 112 cal., 3g fat (2g sat. fat), 10mg chol., 3mg sod., 22g carb. (21g sugars, 1g fiber), 0 pro.

5i
STRAWBERRY SORBET

I first made a raspberry sorbet with an abundance of raspberries I had growing, but this simple recipe is amazing with any kind of berry. Strawberry is another of my go-tos.
—*Karen Bailey, Golden, CO*

PREP: 5 min. + freezing
MAKES: 7 servings

¼ cup plus 1½ tsp. fresh lemon juice
3¾ cups fresh or frozen unsweetened chopped strawberries
2¼ cups confectioners' sugar

Place all the ingredients in a blender or food processor; cover and process until smooth. Transfer to a freezer-safe container; freeze until firm.
½ CUP 181 cal., 0 fat (0 sat. fat), 0 chol., 2mg sod., 46g carb. (42g sugars, 2g fiber), 1g pro.

TEST KITCHEN TIP

For a fun flavor twist, try replacing the lemon juice with a different citrus fruit—lime, orange or even grapefruit!

CHERRY ICE CREAM

Cherry lovers will be delighted by this chunky home-churned ice cream. Serve with hot fudge sauce for an extra-special treat.
—Taste of Home *Test Kitchen*

PREP: 20 min. + chilling
PROCESS: 20 min./batch + freezing
MAKES: 2 qt.

- 3 large egg yolks
- ¾ cup sugar
- ⅛ tsp. salt
- 5 cups heavy whipping cream
- 3 tsp. almond extract
- 3 cups fresh dark sweet cherries, pitted, or frozen pitted dark sweet cherries, thawed
- 3 drops red food coloring

1. In a large heavy saucepan, whisk egg yolks, sugar and salt until blended; stir in cream. Cook over low heat until mixture thickens slightly and a thermometer reads at least 160°, stirring constantly.

Do not allow to boil. Remove from heat immediately.

2. Quickly transfer to a large bowl; place bowl in a pan of ice water. Stir gently and occasionally for 2 minutes. Stir in almond extract. Press plastic wrap onto surface of custard. Refrigerate several hours or overnight.

3. Place half the cherries in a food processor; pulse until finely chopped. Stir into custard with red food coloring. Coarsely chop the remaining cherries. Fill cylinder of ice cream maker no more than two-thirds full. Freeze according to manufacturer's directions, adding a portion of the chopped cherries during the last 5 minutes of processing. (Refrigerate any remaining mixture and chopped cherries until ready to freeze.)

4. Transfer ice cream to freezer containers, allowing headspace for expansion. Freeze until firm, 2-4 hours.

½ CUP 323 cal., 28g fat (18g sat. fat), 119mg chol., 40mg sod., 16g carb. (15g sugars, 0 fiber), 3g pro.

CREAMY PINA COLADA PIES

This is a family favorite and super easy to make. Some like the consistency of this pie right out of the freezer and others prefer a softer pie—either way it's delicious!
—Jenny Hales, Arcadia, OK

PREP: 15 min. + chilling
MAKES: 2 pies (8 servings each)

1   carton (8 oz.) frozen whipped topping, thawed
1   can (10 oz.) frozen nonalcoholic pina colada mix, thawed
¾   cup sweetened condensed milk
½   cup sweetened shredded coconut
½   cup macadamia nuts, chopped
1   can (8 oz.) crushed pineapple, well drained
2   graham cracker crusts (9 in.)
    Maraschino cherries, optional

In a large bowl, combine the first 3 ingredients until smooth. Fold in coconut, nuts and pineapple. Divide and pour mixture into prepared crusts. Refrigerate, covered, until firm, at least 4 hours. If desired, serve with additional whipped topping and cherries.
1 PIECE 299 cal., 14g fat (7g sat. fat), 5mg chol., 168mg sod., 41g carb. (36g sugars, 1g fiber), 2g pro.

TEST KITCHEN TIP

If you prefer, you can use fresh pineapple instead of canned. Since this recipe calls for crushed pineapple, we suggest adding the fresh pineapple chunks to your food processor or blender and pulsing for a few seconds at a time until you're left with small, even pieces.

3-INGREDIENT WATERMELON SORBET

No ice cream maker is needed to make this easy 3-ingredient sorbet. My family loves it so much that I can never keep enough watermelon in the house to meet their demand for it!
—Kory Figura, Waverly, IA

PREP: 35 min. + freezing
MAKES: 6 servings

1   cup sugar
1   cup water
8   cups cubed seedless watermelon
2   Tbsp. lemon juice
    Fresh mint leaves, optional

1. In a small saucepan, bring sugar and water to a boil. Cook and stir until sugar is dissolved; set aside.
2. In a blender or food processor, process watermelon in batches until pureed. Transfer to a large bowl; stir in sugar syrup and lemon juice.
3. Pour the mixture into a 13x9-in. dish; cover and freeze 8 hours or until firm.
4. Just before serving, puree watermelon mixture in batches until smooth. Garnish with fresh mint leaves if desired.
1 CUP 184 cal., 0 fat (0 sat. fat), 0 chol., 7mg sod., 52g carb. (49g sugars, 1g fiber), 1g pro.

⑤ ICE CREAM COOKIE DESSERT

Our family loves dessert, and this chocolaty, layered treat is one of Mom's most requested recipes. It's so easy to prepare.
—*Kimberly Laabs, Hartford, WI*

PREP: 15 min. + freezing
MAKES: 12 servings

- 1 pkg. (15½ oz.) Oreo cookies, crushed, divided
- ¼ cup butter, melted
- ½ gallon vanilla ice cream, softened
- 1 jar (16 oz.) hot fudge ice cream topping, warmed
- 1 carton (8 oz.) frozen whipped topping, thawed

1. In a large bowl, combine 3 cups cookie crumbs and butter. Press into a greased 13x9-in. dish. Spread with ice cream; cover and freeze until set.
2. Drizzle the fudge topping over the ice cream; cover and freeze until set. Spread with whipped topping; sprinkle with the remaining cookie crumbs. Cover and freeze 2 hours or until firm. Remove from the freezer 10 minutes before serving.
1 PIECE 573 cal., 27g fat (14g sat. fat), 49mg chol., 353mg sod., 76g carb. (46g sugars, 2g fiber), 6g pro.

TEST KITCHEN TIP

The best way to keep your ice cream cake from melting is to freeze it throughout the assembly process. Popping the cake in the freezer every few minutes or after every step helps to keep it solid. If you're traveling with your cake, pack it in an insulated cooler with multiple ice packs.

CINNAMON-BASIL ICE CREAM

I started experimenting with herbal ice creams when I was teaching herb classes at our local technical college. Not only were the ice creams popular with my students, but my family loved them as well! One of our favorites is made with a variety of basil called cinnamon basil; however, unless you grow it yourself, it can be difficult to find. I decided to try to re-create the flavor with regular basil and a cinnamon stick, and this delicious recipe was the result!
—*Sue Gronholz, Beaver Dam, WI*

PREP: 45 min. + chilling
PROCESS: 10 min. + freezing
MAKES: 2 cups

1¼ cups whole milk
12 fresh basil leaves
1 cinnamon stick (3 in.)
½ cup sugar
4 large egg yolks, lightly beaten
¾ cup heavy whipping cream
¼ tsp. vanilla extract
   Ground cinnamon, optional

1. In a small saucepan, heat milk to 175°. Remove from the heat; add basil and cinnamon stick. Cover and steep for 30 minutes. Strain, discarding basil and cinnamon stick.
2. Return to the heat; stir in sugar until dissolved. Whisk a small amount of the hot mixture into egg yolks. Return all to the pan, whisking constantly. Cook and stir over low heat until the mixture is just thick enough to coat a metal spoon and a thermometer reads at least 160°, stirring constantly. Do not allow to boil. Remove from heat immediately.
3. Quickly transfer to a large bowl; place bowl in a pan of ice water. Stir gently and occasionally until cool, about 5 minutes. Stir in cream and vanilla. Press plastic wrap onto the surface of the custard. Refrigerate several hours or overnight.
4. Fill cylinder of ice cream maker no more than two-thirds full; freeze according to manufacturer's directions. (Refrigerate any remaining mixture until ready to freeze.)
5. Transfer the ice cream to freezer containers, allowing headspace for expansion. Freeze until firm, 2-4 hours.
6. If desired, sprinkle individual servings with ground cinnamon.
½ CUP 353 cal., 23g fat (13g sat. fat), 243mg chol., 53mg sod., 31g carb. (30g sugars, 0 fiber), 6g pro.

STRAWBERRY SHAKES

Full of summer fruit, these thick berry blends are the perfect way to savor hot days. I serve tall glasses with strawberry garnishes.
—*Ruby Williams, Bogalusa, LA*

TAKES: 5 min. • **MAKES:** 4 servings

⅔ cup 2% milk
3 cups strawberry ice cream
1 cup fresh strawberries
2 Tbsp. strawberry syrup

In a blender, combine all ingredients; cover and process until smooth. Pour into chilled glasses. Serve immediately.
1 CUP 253 cal., 10g fat (6g sat. fat), 34mg chol., 81mg sod., 38g carb. (9g sugars, 1g fiber), 5g pro.

CHOCOLATE PEANUT BUTTER SHAKES

These rich chocolate peanut butter shakes will make you feel as if you're sitting in a 1950s soda fountain. Make it modern with an over-the-top garnish such as skewered doughnut holes, chocolate-dipped cookies or fluffernutter sandwich squares.
—Taste of Home *Test Kitchen*

TAKES: 10 min. • **MAKES:** 2 servings

- ¾ cup 2% milk
- 1½ cups chocolate ice cream
- ¼ cup creamy peanut butter
- 2 Tbsp. chocolate syrup
  Optional: Sweetened whipped cream, quartered miniature peanut butter cups and additional chocolate syrup

In a blender, combine the milk, ice cream, peanut butter and syrup; cover and process until smooth. If desired, garnish individual shakes with whipped cream, peanut butter cups and additional chocolate syrup.

1 CUP 501 cal., 29g fat (11g sat. fat), 41mg chol., 262mg sod., 51g carb. (43g sugars, 3g fiber), 14g pro.

READER REVIEW

"Oh my goodness, this is so tasty! Chocolate and peanut butter are two of my favorite flavors. Definitely a shake I will make again!"
—REMENEC, TASTEOFHOME.COM

PINEAPPLE CRUNCH

My crunchy pineapple dessert offers quick refreshment. This recipe was given to me years ago by a co-worker. Every time I take it somewhere, it's a favorite.
—Betty Wiersma, Sherwood Park, AB

PREP: 15 min. • **BAKE:** 10 min. + cooling
MAKES: 9 servings

- 1 cup crushed cornflakes
- 2 Tbsp. sugar
- ⅓ cup butter, melted
- 2 Tbsp. cornstarch
- 2 cans (8 oz. each) crushed pineapple, undrained
- 2 cups vanilla ice cream, softened
- 1 pkg. (3.4 oz.) instant vanilla pudding mix
  Whipped topping, optional

1. Preheat oven to 350°. Combine the cornflake crumbs, sugar and butter. Press mixture into a greased 9-in. square baking dish. Bake 10 minutes. Cool on a wire rack.
2. In a saucepan, combine cornstarch and pineapple until blended. Bring to a boil; cook and stir 2 minutes or until thickened. Cool.
3. In a bowl, beat ice cream and pudding mix on low speed for 2 minutes or until blended and thickened. Spoon over the crust. Top with the pineapple mixture. Refrigerate until serving. Serve with whipped topping and additional corn flakes if desired.

1 PIECE 254 cal., 10g fat (6g sat. fat), 31mg chol., 217mg sod., 40g carb. (27g sugars, 1g fiber), 2g pro.

CANTALOUPE ICE POPS

Your reminders to your kids to eat their fruit will finally stick, once they take a lick of these mmm-melony snacks. A perfect use for overripe cantaloupe, these pops make a light dessert or healthy between-meal refresher.
—Susan Hein, Burlington, WI

PREP: 10 min. + freezing
MAKES: 1 dozen

- 4 cups cubed cantaloupe
- ¼ cup sugar
- 2 Tbsp. lemon juice
- 1 Tbsp. chopped fresh mint or 1 tsp. dried mint
- ½ tsp. grated lemon zest
- 12 plastic cups or ice pop molds (3 oz. each)
- 12 wooden pop sticks

In a blender or food processor, combine the first 5 ingredients; cover and process until smooth. Pour ¼ cup mixture into each cup or mold; insert the pop sticks. Freeze until firm.

1 POP 35 cal., 0 fat (0 sat. fat), 0 chol., 9mg sod., 9g carb. (8g sugars, 0 fiber), 0 pro. **DIABETIC EXCHANGES** ½ starch.

MINT CHIP ICE CREAM

We have a milk cow, so homemade ice cream is a regular dessert in our household. This creamy version has a mild mint flavor.
—*Farrah McGuire, Springdale, WA*

PREP: 15 min. + chilling
PROCESS: 20 min./batch + freezing
MAKES: 1½ qt.

- 1¾ cups whole milk
- ¾ cup sugar
  Pinch salt
- 3 large eggs, lightly beaten
- 1¾ cups heavy whipping cream
- 1 tsp. vanilla extract
- ¼ tsp. peppermint extract
- 4 drops green food coloring, optional
- ½ cup miniature semisweet chocolate chips

1. In a small saucepan, heat the milk to 175°; stir in the sugar and salt until dissolved. Whisk a small amount of the hot mixture into the eggs. Return all to the pan, whisking constantly. Cook and stir over low heat until mixture coats the back of a metal spoon and reaches at least 160°, 2-3 minutes. Remove from the heat.
2. Cool quickly by placing pan in a bowl of ice water; stir for 2 minutes. Stir in whipping cream, extracts and food coloring if desired. Press plastic wrap onto surface of custard. Refrigerate for several hours or overnight.
3. Stir in the chocolate chips. Fill ice cream maker cylinder two-thirds full; freeze according to the manufacturer's directions. Refrigerate remaining mixture until ready to freeze. Transfer the ice cream to a freezer container; freeze for 2-4 hours before serving.
½ CUP 243 cal., 17g fat (10g sat. fat), 90mg chol., 56mg sod., 20g carb. (19g sugars, 0 fiber), 4g pro.

5i
STRAWBERRY LEMONADE FREEZER PIE

Three simple ingredients mixed together and spread into a graham cracker crust make magic while your freezer does all the work. Prep this pie ahead and freeze it overnight or even longer. Feel free to vary the fruit if you'd like!
—*Debbie Glasscock, Conway, AR*

PREP: 15 min. + freezing
MAKES: 8 servings

- 1 container (23.2 oz.) frozen sweetened sliced strawberries, thawed (2½ cups thawed)
- 1 pkg. (3.4 oz.) instant lemon pudding mix
- 1 carton (8 oz.) frozen whipped topping, thawed
- 1 graham cracker crust (9 in.)
  Optional: Additional whipped topping and fresh strawberries

1. In a large bowl, combine strawberries (with juices) and pudding mix; let stand until slightly thickened, about 5 minutes. Fold in whipped topping. Spread into the crust. Freeze for at least 8 hours or overnight.
2. Let stand 5-10 minutes before serving. If desired, serve with additional whipped topping and fresh strawberries.
1 PIECE 306 cal., 10g fat (6g sat. fat), 0 chol., 273mg sod., 51g carb. (45g sugars, 2g fiber), 1g pro.

TEST KITCHEN TIP

This recipe calls for a premade graham cracker crust for convenience, but of course you can make your own and use a regular 9-in. pie plate.

SMOKED WALNUT
PIE P. 211

SUMMER DESSERTS

SOUTHERN BRULEED PEACH TARTS

This is my homage to our beloved southern fresh peach cobbler. It is an upscale presentation with delicious peaches and is very easy to prepare.
—*Mary Louise Lever, Rome, GA*

PREP: 15 min. + standing • **BROIL:** 5 min.
MAKES: 12 servings

    3   medium ripe peaches, peeled and
        thinly sliced
    3   Tbsp. peach preserves
    1   tsp. lemon juice
    ¼   tsp. minced fresh gingerroot
    ¼   tsp. ground cinnamon
    6   English muffins, split and toasted
    1   carton (8 oz.) mascarpone cheese
    ⅓   cup packed light brown sugar
        Fresh mint leaves

1. In a large bowl, combine the first 5 ingredients. Let stand for 15 minutes, stirring occasionally. Spread cut sides of English muffins with mascarpone cheese.
2. Drain peaches, reserving liquid. Arrange peaches over muffins; brush with some of the reserved liquid. Place on a foil-lined baking sheet; sprinkle with brown sugar.
3. Broil tarts 3-4 in. from heat until caramelized and bubbly, 3-4 minutes. Garnish with mint.
1 TART 202 cal., 9g fat (5g sat. fat), 24mg chol., 136mg sod., 27g carb. (13g sugars, 1g fiber), 4g pro.

TEST KITCHEN TIP

For an adult version, use 1 Tbsp. peach schnapps or Grand Marnier instead of the peach preserves.

CREAMY BISCOFF PIE

I tasted Biscoff cookie butter at a grocery store one day, and it was so delicious that I decided to create a no-bake pie with it. You can make it your own by using peanut butter or another kind of spread and matching toppings instead.
—*Katrina Adams, Mount Olive, AL*

PREP: 20 min. + freezing
MAKES: 2 pies (8 servings each)

    1   pkg. (8 oz.) cream cheese, softened
    1   cup Biscoff creamy cookie spread
    ¾   cup confectioners' sugar
    2   cartons (8 oz. each) frozen whipped
        topping, thawed (6 cups total),
        divided
    2   graham cracker crusts (9 in.)
    ¼   cup caramel sundae syrup
    4   Biscoff cookies, crushed

In a large bowl, beat the cream cheese, cookie spread and confectioners' sugar until combined. Fold in 1 carton whipped topping. Divide mixture between crusts. Top with the remaining whipped topping. Drizzle with syrup; sprinkle with cookie crumbs. Freeze, covered, until firm, at least 4 hours.
1 PIECE 367 cal., 21g fat (10g sat. fat), 14mg chol., 187mg sod., 40g carb. (31g sugars, 0 fiber), 3g pro.

SUMMER STRAWBERRY SHORTCAKE SOUP

When folks are longing for something sweet and refreshing, this soup is sure to hit the spot. To serve it as an appetizer, simply omit the sponge cakes.
—*Joan Hallford, North Richland Hills, TX*

PREP: 15 min. + chilling • **MAKES:** 4 cups

- 2 cups fresh or frozen strawberries, hulled
- 1½ cups unsweetened pineapple juice
- ½ cup white grape juice
- ⅓ cup confectioners' sugar
- ½ cup moscato wine or additional white grape juice
- ½ cup sour cream
- 6 individual round sponge cakes
  Whipped cream and additional strawberries

1. Place strawberries in a blender; cover and process until pureed. Add juices and confectioners' sugar; cover and process until smooth. Transfer to a bowl; whisk in wine and sour cream. Refrigerate, covered, until chilled, 1-2 hours. Stir.
2. Serve with sponge cakes topped with whipped cream and sliced strawberries.
¾ CUP 227 cal., 6g fat (3g sat. fat), 32mg chol., 191mg sod., 37g carb. (27g sugars, 1g fiber), 3g pro.

GOLDEN PEACH PIE

Years ago, I entered this pie in the Park County Fair in Livingston. It won a first-place blue ribbon plus a purple ribbon for Best All Around! Family and friends agree with the judges—it's a perfectly peachy pie.
—*Shirley Olson, Polson, MT*

PREP: 20 min. • **BAKE:** 50 min. + cooling
MAKES: 8 servings

- 2 sheets refrigerated pie crust
- 5 cups sliced peeled fresh peaches (about 5 medium)
- 2 tsp. lemon juice
- ½ tsp. grated orange zest
- ⅛ tsp. almond extract
- 1 cup sugar
- ¼ cup cornstarch
- ¼ tsp. ground nutmeg
- ⅛ tsp. salt
- 2 Tbsp. butter
  Optional: Heavy whipping cream and coarse sugar

1. Line a 9-in. pie plate with 1 crust; trim, leaving a 1-in. overhang around the rim of the pie plate. Set aside. In a large bowl, combine the peaches, lemon juice, orange zest and extract. Combine the sugar, cornstarch, nutmeg and salt. Add to the peach mixture; toss gently to coat. Pour into crust; dot with butter.
2. Roll out the remaining crust to a ⅛-in.-thick circle; cut into strips. Arrange over filling in a lattice pattern. Trim and seal strips to bottom crust; fold overhang over top. Lightly press or flute edge. If desired, brush lattice with heavy cream and sprinkle with sugar. Cover the edge loosely with foil.
3. Bake at 400° for 40 minutes. Remove foil; bake until crust is golden brown and filling is bubbly, 10-15 minutes longer. Cool on a wire rack. Store in the refrigerator.
1 PIECE 425 cal., 17g fat (8g sat. fat), 18mg chol., 267mg sod., 67g carb. (36g sugars, 2g fiber), 3g pro.

PEANUT BUTTER PRETZEL BARS

My secret to these rich no-bake bites? Pretzels in the crust. They add a salty crunch to the classic peanut butter and chocolate pairing.
—*Jennifer Beckman, Falls Church, VA*

PREP: 15 min. + chilling • **MAKES:** 4 dozen

- 1 pkg. (16 oz.) miniature pretzels, divided
- 1½ cups butter, melted
- 1½ cups peanut butter
- 3 cups confectioners' sugar
- 2 cups semisweet chocolate chips
- 1 Tbsp. shortening

1. Line a 13x9-in. baking pan with foil, letting the ends extend up the sides. Set aside 1½ cups pretzels for topping. In a food processor, pulse remaining pretzels until fine crumbs form. In a large bowl, mix butter, peanut butter, confectioners' sugar and the pretzel crumbs.

2. Press mixture into prepared pan. In a microwave, melt chocolate chips and shortening; stir until smooth. Spread over peanut butter layer. Break reserved pretzels and sprinkle over top; press down gently. Refrigerate, covered, until set, about 1 hour. Lifting with foil, remove from pan. Cut into bars.

1 BAR 201 cal., 13g fat (6g sat. fat), 15mg chol., 233mg sod., 22g carb. (12g sugars, 1g fiber), 3g pro.

READER REVIEW

"I made these for a holiday cookout. Before I could get the pan in the fridge, both daughters and my grandson had eaten four large pieces. It was a big hit even before it was ready to serve!"
— KBBRADFORD

GRILLED PEACHES & POUND CAKE

Store-bought cake makes this unique grilled dessert quick to prepare, and the rich, caramelized flavor will make it disappear fast.
—*Joy Pendley, Ortonville, MI*

TAKES: 20 min. • **MAKES:** 6 servings

3 medium peaches, sliced
1 Tbsp. balsamic vinegar
1 loaf (10¾ oz.) frozen pound cake, thawed
¼ cup packed brown sugar
2 Tbsp. butter, melted
3 cups vanilla ice cream

1. Brush peaches with vinegar and place in a grill wok or basket. Grill, uncovered, over medium heat for 10-12 minutes or until tender, stirring frequently.
2. Cut pound cake into 6 slices. In a small bowl, combine brown sugar and butter; brush over both sides of cake slices. Grill, uncovered, over medium heat for 1-2 minutes on each side or until light golden brown. Place cake slices on serving plates, and top with peaches and ice cream.
1 SERVING 413 cal., 20g fat (12g sat. fat), 112mg chol., 269mg sod., 55g carb. (39g sugars, 1g fiber), 6g pro

---

TEST KITCHEN TIP

If you do not have a grill wok or basket, use a disposable foil pan. Poke holes in the bottom of the pan with a meat fork to allow liquid to drain.

SMOKED WALNUT PIE
(PICTURED ON P. 204)

My husband loves to grill and use his smoker. I'd been trying to find new ways to use the smoker and thought of this recipe. It's our favorite pie—with all the same great flavors but just a hint of smoke! You can use pecans instead of walnuts if you like.
—*Courtney Stultz, Weir, KS*

PREP: 15 min. • **COOK:** 1 hour + cooling
MAKES: 8 servings

　 Dough for single-crust pie
3 large eggs
½ cup packed brown sugar
⅓ cup maple syrup
¼ cup butter, melted
¼ cup honey
1 tsp. vanilla extract
½ tsp. sea salt
1½ cups chopped walnuts

1. Preheat smoker to 250°. Add wood chips or pellets to smoker according to manufacturer's directions.
2. On a lightly floured surface, roll out dough to a ⅛-in.-thick circle; transfer to a 9-in. pie plate. Trim crust to ½ in. beyond rim of plate; flute edge. Refrigerate while preparing filling.
3. Whisk eggs and sugar until smooth. Add maple syrup, butter, honey, vanilla and salt. Stir in walnuts. Pour into crust.
4. Place in smoker; smoke until a knife inserted in the center comes out clean and crust is golden brown, 1-1¼ hours. Cool on a wire rack for 1 hour. Store in the refrigerator.
DOUGH FOR A SINGLE-CRUST PIE Combine 1¼ cups all-purpose flour and ¼ tsp. salt; cut in ½ cup cold butter until crumbly. Gradually add 3-5 Tbsp. ice water, tossing with a fork until dough holds together when pressed. Shape into a disk; wrap and refrigerate 1 hour.
1 PIECE 513 cal., 33g fat (13g sat. fat), 115mg chol., 353mg sod., 49g carb. (31g sugars, 2g fiber), 8g pro.

REFRESHING KEY LIME PIE

Everyone who has this pie tells me it's the best Key lime pie they have ever had!
—*Denise Gursky, Miami, FL*

PREP: 20 min. • **BAKE:** 15 min. + chilling
MAKES: 8 servings

1½ cups graham cracker crumbs
¼ cup sugar
⅓ cup butter, melted
2 cans (14 oz. each) sweetened condensed milk
4 large egg yolks
1 cup Key lime juice
　 Optional: Sweetened whipped cream and lime slices

1. Preheat oven to 375. In a small bowl, combine cracker crumbs, sugar and butter until crumbly. Press onto the bottom and up the side of an ungreased 9-in. pie plate. Bake until crust is lightly browned, 8-10 minutes. Cool on a wire rack while making filling.
2. In a large bowl, beat milk, egg yolks and lime juice on low for 2 minutes or until smooth and slightly thickened.
3. Pour into prepared crust. Bake until a knife inserted in the center comes out clean, 15-20 minutes. Cool on a wire rack for 1 hour. Refrigerate until chilled, about 3 hours. If desired, serve with whipped cream and lime slices.
1 PIECE 637 cal., 24g fat (13g sat. fat), 158mg chol., 321mg sod., 96g carb. (84g sugars, 1g fiber), 13g pro.

STRAWBERRY PRETZEL DESSERT

A salty pretzel crust nicely contrasts with the cream cheese and gelatin layers in this all-time favorite dessert.
—*Aldene Belch, Flint, MI*

PREP: 30 min. + chilling
MAKES: 16 servings

- 2 cups crushed pretzels (about 8 oz.)
- ¾ cup butter, melted
- 3 Tbsp. sugar

FILLING
- 2 cups whipped topping
- 1 pkg. (8 oz.) cream cheese, softened
- 1 cup sugar

TOPPING
- 2 pkg. (3 oz. each) strawberry gelatin
- 2 cups boiling water
- 2 pkg. (16 oz. each) frozen sweetened sliced strawberries, thawed
  Optional: Additional whipped topping and pretzels

1. Preheat oven to 350°. In a bowl, combine pretzels, butter and sugar. Press into an ungreased 13x9-in. baking dish. Bake for 10 minutes. Cool on a wire rack.

2. For the filling, in a small bowl, beat whipped topping, cream cheese and sugar until smooth. Spread over the pretzel crust. Refrigerate until chilled.

3. For topping, dissolve the gelatin in boiling water in a large bowl. Stir in sweetened strawberries; refrigerate until partially set.

4. Carefully spoon strawberry mixture over filling. Refrigerate until firm, 4-6 hours. Cut into squares. Serve with additional whipped topping and pretzels if desired.

1 PIECE 295 cal., 15g fat (10g sat. fat), 39mg chol., 305mg sod., 38g carb. (27g sugars, 1g fiber), 3g pro.

AIR-FRYER LEMON OREOS

I love fried Oreos at the county fair every summer. Since this version cooks up quickly in the air fryer, I can enjoy my favorite summer treat all year round! Lemon zest and lemon yogurt add a burst of flavor to the batter, and a dusting of powdered sugar makes for a pretty presentation.
—Jennifer Gilbert, Brighton, MI

PREP: 10 min. • **COOK:** 10 min./batch
MAKES: about 2 dozen

- 2 cups complete buttermilk pancake mix
- 5 Tbsp. sugar
- 2 Tbsp. grated lemon zest
- ¾ cup (6 oz.) lemon yogurt
- ½ cup 2% milk
- 1 large egg
- 2 tsp. clear vanilla extract
- 27 lemon creme Oreo cookies Confectioners' sugar, optional

1. Preheat air fryer to 350°. In a large bowl, combine the pancake mix, sugar and zest. In a separate bowl, combine yogurt, milk, egg and vanilla. Add to the dry mixture; whisk until smooth.
2. Line air-fryer basket with parchment. In batches, dip Oreos into batter, tapping off excess. Arrange Oreos in a single layer on parchment, 2 in. apart.
3. Cook until golden brown, 6-8 minutes. Repeat with the remaining Oreos. If desired, dust with confectioners' sugar. Serve warm.
1 COOKIE 130 cal., 4g fat (1g sat. fat), 8mg chol., 172mg sod., 21g carb. (11g sugars, 0 fiber), 2g pro.

🕐 5i

HONEY-RUM GRILLED BANANAS

These grilled bananas are the perfect dessert following a cookout. My family was skeptical at first, but they all tried them and everyone agreed they were delicious. I use coconut rum from the Bahamas.
—Lori Wendt, Mahomet, IL

TAKES: 15 min. • **MAKES:** 4 servings

- 2 Tbsp. rum
- 2 Tbsp. honey
- 1 tsp. ground cinnamon
- 4 medium firm unpeeled bananas Vanilla ice cream

1. In a small bowl, combine rum, honey and cinnamon; set aside. Cut bananas in half lengthwise, leaving the peel on.
2. Place bananas cut side down on grill. Cover and grill over medium heat for 3 minutes. Turn and brush with honey mixture. Cover and grill until tender, 5-6 minutes longer. Peel bananas. Serve immediately with ice cream.
1 BANANA 155 cal., 0 fat (0 sat. fat), 0 chol., 2mg sod., 36g carb. (23g sugars, 3g fiber), 1g pro.

SUMMER SQUASH POUND CAKE

This golden brown, tender pound cake is the perfect treat to make when you have an abundance of summer squash in your garden. It's not overly sweet, so it appeals to everyone.
—Lisa Brockwell, Necedah, WI

PREP: 20 min. • **BAKE:** 50 min. + cooling
MAKES: 12 servings

- ½ cup butter, softened
- 1¼ cups sugar
- 2 large eggs, room temperature
- 1 tsp. lemon juice
- ¼ tsp. almond extract
- 2½ cups all-purpose flour
- 1½ tsp. baking powder
- ¼ tsp. baking soda
- ¼ tsp. salt
- ½ cup sour cream or plain Greek yogurt
- 2 cups shredded yellow summer squash

GLAZE
- ¾ cup confectioners' sugar
- 2 to 3 tsp. water
- 1½ tsp. lemon juice

1. Preheat oven to 350°. Grease and flour a 10-in. fluted tube pan. In a large bowl, beat butter and sugar until crumbly. Add eggs, 1 at a time, beating well after each addition. Beat in lemon juice and extract.
2. In another bowl, whisk flour, baking powder, baking soda and salt; add to the creamed mixture alternately with sour cream, beating after each addition just until combined. Stir in squash.
3. Transfer batter to prepared pan. Bake until a toothpick inserted in center comes out clean, 50-55 minutes. Cool in pan 10 minutes before removing to a wire rack to cool completely.
4. Combine the glaze ingredients; pour over cake.
1 PIECE 310 cal., 11g fat (6g sat. fat), 54mg chol., 213mg sod., 50g carb. (29g sugars, 1g fiber), 4g pro.

RHUBARB STRAWBERRY COBBLER

Mom's yummy cobbler is a truly wonderful finale to any meal. This sweet-tart family favorite is brimming with berries and rhubarb and has a thick, easy-to-make crust.
—Susan Emery, Everett, WA

PREP: 20 min. • **BAKE:** 40 min.
MAKES: 8 servings

- 1⅓ cups sugar
- ⅓ cup all-purpose flour
- 4 cups sliced fresh or frozen rhubarb, thawed (½-in. pieces)
- 2 cups halved fresh strawberries
- 2 Tbsp. butter, cubed

CRUST
- 2 cups all-purpose flour
- ½ tsp. salt
- ⅔ cup canola oil
- ⅓ cup warm water
- 1 Tbsp. 2% milk
- 1 Tbsp. granulated or coarse sugar Vanilla ice cream, optional

1. Preheat oven to 425°. In a large bowl, mix sugar and flour. Add the fruit; toss to coat. Transfer to a greased 11x7-in. baking dish. Dot with butter.
2. For the crust, mix flour and salt. In a second bowl, whisk oil and water; add to the flour mixture, stirring with a fork until a dough is formed (dough will be sticky).
3. Roll out dough between 2 pieces of waxed paper into an 11x7-in. rectangle. Remove top piece of waxed paper; invert rectangle over filling. Gently peel off waxed paper. Brush pastry with milk; sprinkle with sugar.
4. Bake 40-50 minutes or until golden brown. If desired, serve with ice cream.
NOTE If using frozen rhubarb, measure rhubarb while still frozen, then thaw completely. Drain in a colander, but do not press liquid out.
1 SERVING 479 cal., 22g fat (4g sat. fat), 8mg chol., 181mg sod., 68g carb. (38g sugars, 3g fiber), 5g pro.

WATERMELON CUPCAKES

My granddaughter and I bake together each week. She was inspired by all of her mommy's flavored syrups, so we came up with this watermelon cupcake. If you have watermelon syrup, it can replace some of the lemon-lime soda in the cake batter and frosting, but the gelatin adds a lot of watermelon flavor on its own. If you are not going to pipe the frosting, you can reduce the amount of frosting by half.
—*Elizabeth Bramkamp, Gig Harbor, WA*

PREP: 30 min. • **BAKE:** 20 min. + cooling
MAKES: 2 dozen

- 1 pkg. white cake mix (regular size)
- 1 cup lemon-lime soda
- 3 large egg whites, room temperature
- ¼ cup canola oil
- 1 pkg. (3 oz.) watermelon gelatin
- 2 drops watermelon oil, optional

FROSTING
- 2 cups butter, softened
- 6 cups confectioners' sugar
- 1 pkg. (3 oz.) watermelon gelatin
- 5 to 6 Tbsp. lemon-lime soda
- 15 drops red food coloring
- 3 Tbsp. miniature semisweet chocolate chips

1. Preheat oven to 350°. Line 24 muffin cups with paper liners. In a large bowl, combine cake mix, soda, egg whites, oil, gelatin and, if desired, watermelon oil; beat on low speed 30 seconds. Beat on medium speed for 2 minutes. Transfer to prepared pans. Bake until a toothpick inserted in center comes out clean, 18-21 minutes. Cool in pans 10 minutes before removing to wire racks to cool completely.
2. For frosting, in a large bowl, combine butter, confectioners' sugar, gelatin, soda and food coloring; beat until smooth. Frost cupcakes. Sprinkle with chocolate chips. Store in the refrigerator.
1 CUPCAKE 385 cal., 19g fat (11g sat. fat), 41mg chol., 282mg sod., 54g carb. (46g sugars, 1g fiber), 2g pro.

CHOCOLATE CHUNK WALNUT BLONDIES

Put a stack of these beauties out at a potluck and you'll find only crumbs on your platter when it's time to head home. Everyone will be asking who made those scrumptious blondies, so be sure to bring copies of the recipe!
—*Peggy Woodward, Shullsburg, WI*

PREP: 15 min. • **BAKE:** 30 min. + cooling
MAKES: 2 dozen

- 1 cup butter, melted
- 2 cups packed brown sugar
- 2 tsp. vanilla extract
- 2 large eggs, room temperature
- 2 cups all-purpose flour
- ½ cup ground walnuts
- 1 tsp. baking powder
- ½ tsp. salt
- ⅛ tsp. baking soda
- 1 cup chopped walnuts, toasted
- 1 cup semisweet chocolate chunks

1. Preheat oven to 350°. Line a greased 13x9-in. pan with parchment, letting ends extend up sides; grease paper.
2. In a large bowl, mix butter, brown sugar and vanilla until blended. Add eggs, 1 at a time, whisking to blend after each addition. In another bowl, mix flour, ground walnuts, baking powder, salt and baking soda; stir into the butter mixture. Fold in walnuts and chocolate chunks.
3. Spread batter into prepared pan. Bake until a toothpick inserted in the center comes out clean, 30-35 minutes (do not overbake). Cool completely in pan on a wire rack. Lifting with parchment, remove from pan. Cut into bars. Store in an airtight container.
1 BAR 260 cal., 15g fat (7g sat. fat), 38mg chol., 140mg sod., 32g carb. (22g sugars, 1g fiber), 3g pro

ⓛ ⑤ⱼ
BALSAMIC-GOAT CHEESE GRILLED PLUMS

Make a real statement at your summer dinner party with this simple and elegant treat. Ripe plums are grilled, then dressed up with a balsamic reduction and sprinkled with tangy goat cheese.
—*Ariana Abelow, Holliston, MA*

TAKES: 25 min. • **MAKES:** 8 servings

- 1 cup balsamic vinegar
- 2 tsp. grated lemon zest
- 4 medium firm plums, halved and pitted
- ½ cup crumbled goat cheese

1. For glaze, in a small saucepan, combine vinegar and lemon zest; bring to a boil. Cook 10-12 minutes or until mixture is thickened and reduced to about ⅓ cup (do not overcook).
2. Grill plums, covered, over medium heat until tender, 2-3 minutes on each side. Drizzle with glaze; top with cheese.
1 PLUM HALF WITH 1 TBSP. CHEESE AND 2 TSP. GLAZE 58 cal., 2g fat (1g sat. fat), 9mg chol., 41mg sod., 9g carb. (8g sugars, 1g fiber), 2g pro. **DIABETIC EXCHANGES** ½ starch, ½ fat.

CHERRY BARS

Whip up a pan of these festive bars in just 20 minutes with staple ingredients and pie filling. Between the easy preparation and the pretty colors, they're destined to become a family favorite.
—*Jane Kamp, Grand Rapids, MI*

PREP: 20 min. • **BAKE:** 35 min. + cooling
MAKES: 5 dozen

- 1   cup butter, softened
- 2   cups sugar
- 1   tsp. salt
- 4   large eggs, room temperature
- 1   tsp. vanilla extract
- ¼   tsp. almond extract
- 3   cups all-purpose flour
- 2   cans (21 oz. each) cherry pie filling

GLAZE
- 1   cup confectioners' sugar
- ½   tsp. vanilla extract
- ½   tsp. almond extract
- 2   to 3 Tbsp. 2% milk

1. Preheat oven to 350°. In a large bowl, cream butter, sugar and salt until light and fluffy, 5-7 minutes. Add eggs, 1 at a time, beating well after each addition. Beat in extracts. Gradually add flour.
2. Spread 3 cups dough into a greased 15x10x1-in. baking pan. Spread with pie filling. Drop the remaining dough by teaspoonfuls over filling. Bake until golden brown, 35-40 minutes. Cool completely in pan on a wire rack.
3. For the glaze, mix confectioners' sugar, extracts and enough milk to reach desired consistency; drizzle over top.

1 BAR 112 cal., 3g fat (2g sat. fat), 21mg chol., 72mg sod., 19g carb. (9g sugars, 0 fiber), 1g pro.

CLASSIC TRES LECHES CAKE

A classic in Mexican kitchens for generations, this cake gets its name from the three types of milk— evaporated, sweetened condensed and heavy whipping cream—used to create a super moist and tender texture.
—Taste of Home *Test Kitchen*

PREP: 45 min. • **BAKE:** 20 min. + chilling
MAKES: 10 servings

- 4   large eggs, separated, room temperature
- ⅔   cup sugar, divided
- ⅔   cup cake flour
      Dash salt
- ¾   cup heavy whipping cream
- ¾   cup evaporated milk
- ¾   cup sweetened condensed milk
- 2   tsp. vanilla extract
- ¼   tsp. rum extract

TOPPING
- 1¼ cups heavy whipping cream
- 3   Tbsp. sugar
      Optional: Dulce de leche or sliced fresh strawberries

1. Place egg whites in a large bowl. Line the bottom of a 9-in. springform pan with parchment; grease the paper.
2. Preheat oven to 350°. In another large bowl, beat egg yolks until slightly thickened. Gradually add ⅓ cup sugar, beating on high speed until thick and lemon-colored. Fold in flour, a third at a time.
3. Add salt to the egg whites; with clean beaters, beat on medium until soft peaks form. Gradually add the remaining ⅓ cup sugar, 1 Tbsp. at a time, beating on high after each addition until sugar is dissolved. Continue beating until soft glossy peaks form. Fold a third of the whites into batter, then fold in remaining whites. Gently spread into prepared pan.
4. Bake until top springs back when lightly touched, 20-25 minutes. Cool 10 minutes before removing from pan to a wire rack to cool completely.
5. Place cake on a rimmed serving plate. Poke holes in the top with a skewer. In a small bowl, mix cream, evaporated milk, sweetened condensed milk and extracts; brush or pour slowly over cake. Refrigerate, covered, 2 hours.
6. For topping, beat cream until it begins to thicken. Add sugar; beat until peaks form. Spread over top of cake. If desired, top cake with dulce de leche or fresh strawberries just before serving.
1 PIECE 392 cal., 23g fat (14g sat. fat), 142mg chol., 104mg sod., 40g carb. (33g sugars, 0 fiber), 8g pro.

READER REVIEW

"Wow! This cake is delicious! I've always been hesitant to try a tres leche cake but this recipe was easy and worth it! We made this with gluten-free flour and dairy-free milks and it was so good!"
—LPHJKITCHEN

BEST EVER FRESH STRAWBERRY PIE

Next time you get a pint or two of perfectly ripe strawberries, make my favorite pie. It combines fresh berries and a lemony cream cheese layer. If you're in a hurry, you can use a premade pie shell.
—*Janet K Leach, Granger, WA*

PREP: 1 hour + chilling
COOK: 10 min. + chilling
MAKES: 8 servings

- 2 cups all-purpose flour
- 2 tsp. sugar
- ½ tsp. salt
- ⅔ cup shortening
- 1 Tbsp. white vinegar
- 4 to 5 Tbsp. 2% milk

FILLING
- 1 pkg. (8 oz.) cream cheese, softened
- ¾ cup confectioners' sugar
- 2 tsp. grated lemon zest
- ½ tsp. lemon extract

TOPPING
- 6 cups fresh strawberries, hulled (about 2 lbs.)
- ¾ cup sugar
- 1 Tbsp. cornstarch
- ¼ tsp. salt
- 1 cup water
- 1 pkg. (3 oz.) strawberry gelatin
- 1 tsp. butter

1. In a large bowl, mix flour, sugar and salt; cut in shortening until crumbly. Gradually add vinegar and milk, tossing with a fork until dough holds together when pressed. Shape into a disk; wrap and refrigerate 1 hour or overnight.
2. On a lightly floured surface, roll dough to a ⅛-in.-thick circle; transfer to a 9-in. deep-dish pie plate. Trim crust to ½ in. beyond rim; flute edge. Refrigerate 30 minutes. Preheat oven to 425°.
3. Line crust with a double thickness of foil. Fill with pie weights, dried beans or uncooked rice. Bake on a lower oven rack for 20-25 minutes or until edge is golden brown. Remove foil and weights; bake until the bottom is golden brown, 3-6 minutes longer. Cool completely on a wire rack.
4. For the filling, beat cream cheese, confectioners' sugar, lemon zest and extract until blended. Spread carefully onto the bottom of the crust. Refrigerate while preparing topping.
5. For topping, place strawberries in a large bowl. In a small saucepan, mix sugar, cornstarch, salt and water until blended; bring to a boil over medium heat, stirring constantly. Cook and stir until thickened and clear, 1-2 minutes longer. Remove from heat; stir in gelatin until dissolved. Stir in butter. Pour over strawberries, tossing gently to coat. Arrange over filling. Refrigerate 4 hours or until set.
NOTE Let pie weights cool before storing. Beans and rice may be reused for pie weights, but not for cooking.
1 PIECE 564 cal., 27g fat (10g sat. fat), 33mg chol., 359mg sod., 75g carb. (47g sugars, 3g fiber), 7g pro.

PEACH PANNA COTTA

This no-bake dessert is guaranteed to cool you off in the summer heat. I really enjoy the texture—rich and creamy panna cotta balanced by the sweet and pulpy texture of the peach puree.
—*Andrea Campbell, Los Angeles, CA*

PREP: 30 min. + chilling • **COOK:** 10 min.
MAKES: 8 servings

- 4 medium peaches, peeled and pitted
- 1 Tbsp. lemon juice
- 1 envelope (¼ oz.) unflavored gelatin
- 1 cup peach nectar, chilled

PANNA COTTA
- 1 envelope (¼ oz.) unflavored gelatin
- 1½ cups cold whole milk
- 1½ cups heavy whipping cream
- ⅓ cup sugar
- 1 tsp. grated lemon zest
- ½ tsp. salt
- ¼ tsp. vanilla extract
  Optional: Sliced peaches and fresh mint leaves

1. Place peaches and lemon juice in a blender or food processor. Cover and process until smooth.
2. In a microwave-safe bowl, sprinkle gelatin over the peach nectar; let stand 1 minute. Microwave on high for 30-40 seconds. Stir and let stand 1 minute or until gelatin is completely dissolved. Let stand 5 minutes. Stir in the pureed peach mixture. Pour into eight 8-oz. glass dessert dishes. Refrigerate until set, at least 3 hours.
3. For the panna cotta, in a small saucepan, sprinkle gelatin over milk; let stand 1 minute. Heat and stir over low heat until the gelatin is completely dissolved. Stir in cream, sugar, lemon zest, salt and vanilla.
4. Pour panna cotta mixture over peach gelatin layers. Refrigerate until set, at least 2 hours. If desired, garnish with peach slices and mint leaves.
1 SERVING 266 cal., 18g fat (11g sat. fat), 55mg chol., 185mg sod., 23g carb. (22g sugars, 1g fiber), 5g pro.

GINGER PLUM TART

Sweet cravings, begone: This free-form plum tart is done in only 35 minutes. Plus, it's extra-awesome when served warm.
—Taste of Home *Test Kitchen*

PREP: 15 min. • **BAKE:** 20 min. + cooling
MAKES: 8 servings

- 1 sheet refrigerated pie crust
- 3½ cups sliced fresh plums (about 10 medium)
- 3 Tbsp. plus 1 tsp. coarse sugar, divided
- 1 Tbsp. cornstarch
- 2 tsp. finely chopped crystallized ginger
- 1 large egg white
- 1 Tbsp. water

1. Preheat oven to 400°. On a clean work surface, unroll crust. Roll out to a 12-in. circle. Transfer to a parchment-lined baking sheet.
2. In a large bowl, toss plums with 3 Tbsp. sugar and the cornstarch. Arrange plums on crust to within 2 in. of edge; sprinkle with ginger. Fold crust edge over plums, pleating as you go.
3. In a small bowl, whisk egg white and water; brush over folded crust. Sprinkle with the remaining 1 tsp. sugar.
4. Bake until crust is golden brown, 20-25 minutes. Cool in pan on a wire rack. Serve warm or at room temperature.
1 PIECE 190 cal., 7g fat (3g sat. fat), 5mg chol., 108mg sod., 30g carb. (14g sugars, 1g fiber), 2g pro. **DIABETIC EXCHANGES** 1½ starch, 1 fat, ½ fruit.

NO-BAKE CHOCOLATE CHIP CANNOLI CHEESECAKE

I make this cheesecake in the summer for a flavorful and refreshing treat. I love the added bonus of not having to turn on the oven in hot weather.
—*Kristen Heigl, Staten Island, NY*

PREP: 25 min. + chilling
MAKES: 8 servings

- 1 pkg. (4 oz.) cannoli shells
- ½ cup sugar
- ½ cup graham cracker crumbs
- ⅓ cup butter, melted

FILLING

- 2 pkg. (8 oz. each) cream cheese, softened
- 1 cup confectioners' sugar
- ½ tsp. grated orange zest
- ¼ tsp. ground cinnamon
- ¾ cup part-skim ricotta cheese
- 1 tsp. vanilla extract
- ½ tsp. rum extract
- ½ cup miniature semisweet chocolate chips
  Chopped pistachios, optional

1. Pulse cannoli shells in a food processor until coarse crumbs form. Add sugar, cracker crumbs and melted butter; pulse just until combined. Press onto bottom and up side of a greased 9-in. pie plate. Refrigerate until firm, about 1 hour.
2. Beat the next 4 ingredients until blended. Beat in ricotta cheese and extracts. Stir in chocolate chips. Spread into the crust.
3. Refrigerate, covered, until set, about 4 hours. If desired, top with pistachios.
1 PIECE 548 cal., 36g fat (20g sat. fat), 88mg chol., 292mg sod., 51g carb. (38g sugars, 1g fiber), 8g pro.

TEST KITCHEN TIP

Cannoli shells can be found in select markets and bake shops. If you can't find them, substitute crumbled sugar cones or shortbread cookies, or go with a classic graham cracker crust.

MANGO ALMOND ICEBOX CAKE

This recipe was inspired by my friend who asked me to make a mango cake. It has a light, refreshing taste and is easy to prepare. You can also use fresh or unsweetened frozen strawberries if you prefer.
—*Rachel Simoneau, Danbury, CT*

PREP: 35 min. + chilling
MAKES: 12 servings

- 1 cup water
- ½ cup sugar
- ¼ tsp. almond extract
- 1 pkg. (16 oz.) frozen mango chunks, thawed, divided
- 4 oz. cream cheese, softened
- ½ cup confectioners' sugar
- ½ tsp. vanilla extract
- 2 cups heavy whipping cream
- 22 crisp ladyfinger cookies
- 1 pkg. (5 oz.) miniature meringue cookies, coarsely crushed
- 1 cup sliced almonds

1. Place water in a microwave-safe bowl; microwave on high 30 seconds. Stir in sugar and almond extract until sugar is dissolved; cool syrup completely.
2. Finely chop ¼ cup mango chunks; place in a large bowl. Add cream cheese, confectioners' sugar and vanilla extract; beat until blended. In another bowl, beat cream until stiff peaks form; fold into the mango mixture.
3. To assemble, line the bottom of a 9-in. springform pan with 11 ladyfingers; slowly drizzle with half of the syrup. Layer with half each of the cream mixture, meringue cookies, remaining mango and almonds in the order listed. Repeat layers, starting with remaining ladyfingers. Refrigerate, covered, for 8 hours or overnight. To serve, loosen side from pan with a knife; remove rim.
1 PIECE 389 cal., 22g fat (11g sat. fat), 71mg chol., 72mg sod., 45g carb. (38g sugars, 2g fiber), 5g pro.

TEST KITCHEN TIPS

To crush meringue cookies, place them in a large zip-top plastic bag and pound gently with a meat mallet.

To get the smoothest whipped cream, beat on medium speed, not high.

RHUBARB CUSTARD BARS

Once I tried these rich, gooey bars, I just had to have the recipe so I could make them for my family and friends. The shortbread-like crust and the rhubarb and custard layers inspire people to seek out rhubarb so they can fix a batch for themselves.
—*Shari Roach, South Milwaukee, WI*

PREP: 25 min. • **BAKE:** 50 min. + chilling
MAKES: 3 dozen

CRUST
- 2 cups all-purpose flour
- ¼ cup sugar
- 1 cup cold butter

FILLING
- 2 cups sugar
- 7 Tbsp. all-purpose flour
- 1 cup heavy whipping cream
- 3 large eggs, beaten
- 5 cups finely chopped fresh or frozen rhubarb, thawed and drained

TOPPING
- 6 oz. cream cheese, softened
- ½ cup sugar
- ½ tsp. vanilla extract
- 1 cup heavy whipping cream, whipped

1. Preheat oven to 350°. Combine the flour and sugar; cut in butter until the mixture resembles coarse crumbs. Press into a greased 13x9-in. baking pan. Bake for 10 minutes.

2. Meanwhile, for filling, combine sugar and flour in a large bowl. Whisk in cream and eggs. Stir in the rhubarb. Pour over crust. Bake at 350° until custard is set, 40-45 minutes. Cool.

3. For topping, beat cream cheese, sugar and vanilla until smooth; fold in whipped cream. Spread over top. Cover and refrigerate until firm enough to cut, about 1 hour. Cut into bars. Store in the refrigerator.

1 BAR 198 cal., 11g fat (7g sat. fat), 52mg chol., 70mg sod., 23g carb. (16g sugars, 1g fiber), 2g pro.

OLD-TIME BUTTERMILK PIE

This recipe is older than I am—and I was born in 1919! My mother and grandmother made this pie with buttermilk and eggs from our farm and set it on the tables at church meetings and social gatherings. I did the same and now our children make it too!
—*Kate Mathews, Shreveport, LA*

PREP: 15 min. • **BAKE:** 45 min. + cooling
MAKES: 10 servings

CRUST
- 1½ cups all-purpose flour
- 1 tsp. salt
- ½ cup shortening
- ¼ cup cold 2% milk
- 1 large egg, lightly beaten

FILLING
- ½ cup butter, softened
- 2 cups sugar
- 3 Tbsp. all-purpose flour
- 3 large eggs
- 1 cup buttermilk
- 1 tsp. vanilla extract
- 1 tsp. ground cinnamon
- ¼ cup lemon juice
- Optional: Whipped cream and fresh berries

1. Preheat oven to 350°. In a large bowl, mix flour and salt. Cut in shortening until crumbly. Gradually stir in milk and egg. On a lightly floured surface, roll dough to a ⅛-in.-thick circle; transfer to a 9-in. pie plate. Trim crust to ½ in. beyond rim of plate; flute edge.

2. For filling, in a large bowl, cream butter and sugar; beat in flour. Add the eggs, 1 at a time, beating well after each addition. Stir in buttermilk, vanilla, cinnamon and lemon juice; mix well. Pour into crust.

3. Bake until center is set, 45-50 minutes. Cool completely on a wire rack. Serve or refrigerate within 2 hours. If desired, top servings with whipped cream and fresh berries.

1 PIECE 448 cal., 21g fat (9g sat. fat), 100mg chol., 388mg sod., 59g carb. (42g sugars, 1g fiber), 6g pro.

TEST KITCHEN TIP
It is important not to over-bake this pie or the surface will crack as it cools. The center of the pie will still be slightly wobbly after baking but will set up as it cools.

MAMA'S COCONUT PIE

My mama showed me how to make this pie about 40 years ago, just as her mama showed her. Now I'm honored to teach it to my daughter.
—*Lisa Allen, Joppa, AL*

PREP: 20 min. • **BAKE:** 50 min.
MAKES: 8 servings

      Dough for single-crust pie
   1 cup sugar
   3 large eggs
   ½ cup buttermilk
   ½ cup unsalted butter, melted and
      cooled
   2 Tbsp. all-purpose flour
   1½ tsp. vanilla extract
      Dash salt
   1½ cups sweetened shredded coconut

1. Preheat oven to 325°. On a lightly floured surface, roll dough to a ⅛-in.-thick circle; transfer to a 9-in. pie plate. Trim to ½ in. beyond rim of plate; flute edge. Place pie plate on a rimmed baking sheet.
2. In a large bowl, beat sugar, eggs, buttermilk, butter, flour, vanilla and salt until blended. Stir in coconut. Pour into crust. Bake until top is light golden brown and the center is almost set, 50-60 minutes. Cool on a wire rack; serve or refrigerate within 2 hours.

DOUGH FOR SINGLE-CRUST PIE Combine 1¼ cups all-purpose flour and ¼ tsp. salt; cut in ½ cup cold butter until crumbly. Gradually add 3-5 Tbsp. ice water, tossing with a fork until dough holds together when pressed. Shape into a disk; wrap and refrigerate 1 hour.

1 PIECE 550 cal., 35g fat (23g sat. fat), 142mg chol., 318mg sod., 54g carb. (34g sugars, 1g fiber), 6g pro.

ROASTED STRAWBERRY SHEET CAKE

My Grandma Gigi loved summer berry cakes. Almost any time I'd call her during the warmer months, she'd invite me over to taste her latest masterpiece. This cake is an ode to her.
—*Kristin Bowers, Gilbert, AZ*

PREP: 1 hour • **BAKE:** 30 min. + cooling
MAKES: 24 servings

   4 lbs. halved fresh strawberries
   ½ cup sugar
CAKE
   1 cup butter, softened
   1½ cups sugar
   2 large eggs, room temperature
   2 tsp. almond extract
   3 cups all-purpose flour
   3 tsp. baking powder
   2 tsp. salt
   1 cup 2% milk
   ¼ cup turbinado (washed raw) sugar

1. Preheat oven to 350°. Place strawberries on a parchment-lined rimmed baking sheet. Sprinkle with ½ cup sugar and toss to coat. Bake until just tender, 35-40 minutes. Cool slightly.
2. Meanwhile, grease a 15x10x1-in. baking pan. Cream butter and sugar until light and fluffy, 5-7 minutes. Add eggs, 1 at a time, beating well after each addition. Beat in extract. In another bowl, whisk flour, baking powder and salt; add to the creamed mixture alternately with milk, beating well after each addition (batter may appear curdled).
3. Transfer batter to prepared pan. Top with 3 cups roasted strawberries; sprinkle with turbinado sugar. Reserve remaining strawberries for serving. Bake until a toothpick inserted in center comes out clean, 30-35 minutes. Cool completely in pan on a wire rack. Serve with reserved roasted strawberries.

1 PIECE 235 cal., 9g fat (5g sat. fat), 37mg chol., 329mg sod., 37g carb. (23g sugars, 2g fiber), 3g pro.

ZUCCHINI BROWNIES

A fast peanut butter and chocolate frosting tops these cakelike brownies. What a sweet way to use up your garden bounty!

—*Allyson Wilkins, Amherst, NH*

PREP: 20 min. • **BAKE:** 35 min.
MAKES: 1½ dozen

- 1 cup butter, softened
- 1½ cups sugar
- 2 large eggs, room temperature
- ½ cup plain yogurt
- 1 tsp. vanilla extract
- 2½ cups all-purpose flour
- ¼ cup baking cocoa
- 1 tsp. baking soda
- ½ tsp. salt
- 2 cups shredded zucchini

FROSTING

- ⅔ cup semisweet chocolate chips
- ½ cup creamy peanut butter

1. Preheat oven to 350°. In a large bowl, cream butter and sugar until light and fluffy, 5-7 minutes. Add eggs, 1 at a time, beating well after each addition. Beat in yogurt and vanilla. In another bowl, combine the flour, cocoa, baking soda and salt; gradually add to the creamed mixture. Stir in zucchini.

2. Pour batter into a greased 13x9-in. baking pan. Bake until a toothpick inserted in the center comes out clean, 35-40 minutes.

3. For frosting, in a small saucepan, combine chocolate chips and peanut butter. Cook and stir over low heat until smooth. Spread over warm brownies. Cool on a wire rack. Cut into bars.

1 BROWNIE 307 cal., 17g fat (8g sat. fat), 52mg chol., 283mg sod., 37g carb. (21g sugars, 2g fiber), 5g pro.

MANGO CREAM TART

This fresh, luscious tart makes me happy—but once I take a bite, it makes me even happier!
—*Jami Geittmann, Greendale, WI*

PREP: 30 min. • **BAKE:** 15 min. + cooling
MAKES: 10 servings

- 2 cups crumbled soft coconut macaroons (about 12 cookies)
- 1 cup ground almonds
- 3 Tbsp. butter, melted
- ½ cup heavy whipping cream
- 1 pkg. (8 oz.) reduced-fat cream cheese, softened
- ¼ cup plus 2 Tbsp. honey, divided
- 2 tsp. orange juice
- ¼ tsp. almond extract
- ¼ cup apricot preserves
- 2 medium mangoes, peeled and thinly sliced
- 2 Tbsp. lemon juice
- ½ cup sliced fresh strawberries
- ½ cup fresh blackberries

1. Preheat oven to 350°. Place cookies, almonds and melted butter in a food processor; process until blended. Press onto bottom and up side of an ungreased 11-in. fluted tart pan with removable bottom. Place pan on a baking sheet. Bake until golden brown, 12-14 minutes. Cool completely on a wire rack.
2. For filling, in a small bowl, beat whipping cream until soft peaks form. In another bowl, beat cream cheese and ¼ cup honey until combined. Beat in orange juice and extract. Fold in whipped cream. Spread over crust.
3. For glaze, in a small saucepan, mix preserves and remaining honey. Cook and stir over low heat until melted; press through a strainer.
4. Toss mangoes with lemon juice. Arrange mango slices over filling; add strawberries and blackberries to form the eyes and mouth. Brush with glaze. Store in the refrigerator.
1 PIECE 311 cal., 18g fat (9g sat. fat), 39mg chol., 155mg sod., 34g carb. (26g sugars, 3g fiber), 6g pro.

LEMON CHESS PIE

This luscious, lemony pie cuts beautifully and has a smooth texture. It's one of my favorites.
—*Hannah LaRue Rider, East Point, KY*

PREP: 15 min. • **BAKE:** 35 min. + chilling
MAKES: 8 servings

- 1 sheet refrigerated pie crust
- 4 large eggs
- 1½ cups sugar
- ½ cup lemon juice
- ¼ cup butter, melted
- 1 Tbsp. cornmeal
- 2 tsp. all-purpose flour
- ⅛ tsp. salt
  Confectioners' sugar, optional

1. Preheat oven to 350°. Unroll crust into a 9-in. pie plate; flute edge. In a large bowl, beat eggs for 3 minutes. Gradually add the sugar; beat until the mixture becomes thick and lemon-colored, about 2 minutes. Beat in lemon juice, butter, cornmeal, flour and salt.
2. Pour into crust. Bake until a knife inserted in the center comes out clean, 35-40 minutes. Cool on a wire rack for 1 hour. Refrigerate at least 3 hours before serving. If desired, garnish with confectioners' sugar.
1 PIECE 363 cal., 15g fat (7g sat. fat), 113mg chol., 219mg sod., 54g carb. (39g sugars, 0 fiber), 4g pro.

GRILLED RASPBERRY PEACH COBBLER

When we grill, we often like to fix the entire meal outdoors. We have several grills, but prefer to grill with charcoal. We also have a 4-foot smoker that can be used as a charcoal grill so we can grill meat at one end, vegetables in the middle and dessert on the far end using an indirect heat method. Feel free to substitute other fruits in this cobbler—you'll need about 6 to 7 cups of fresh or frozen fruit.
—Donna Gribbins, Shelbyville, KY

PREP: 25 min. • **GRILL:** 40 min.
MAKES: 10 servings

- 2 Tbsp. butter
- ¾ cup sugar
- 3 Tbsp. cornstarch
- 8 medium ripe peaches, peeled and sliced
- 2 pints fresh raspberries
- 3 Tbsp. lemon juice
- 2 tsp. vanilla extract
- 1½ tsp. grated lemon zest
BISCUITS
- 2 cups all-purpose flour
- ⅓ cup plus 2 Tbsp. sugar, divided
- 2 tsp. baking soda
- 1 tsp. grated lemon zest
- ½ cup cold butter, cubed
- ½ cup buttermilk
  Vanilla ice cream, optional

1. Thoroughly grease a Dutch oven on bottom and side with 2 Tbsp. butter. In a large bowl, mix sugar and cornstarch. Add peaches, berries, lemon juice, vanilla and lemon zest; toss to combine. Transfer to prepared pan.
2. In a small bowl, whisk flour, ⅓ cup sugar, baking soda and lemon zest; cut in the butter until mixture resembles coarse crumbs. Add buttermilk; stir just until moistened. Drop topping by tablespoonfuls over peach mixture. Sprinkle with remaining 2 Tbsp. sugar.
3. Grill, covered, over indirect medium-high heat until the filling is bubbly and the topping is golden brown, 40-45 minutes. Serve warm. If desired, serve with vanilla ice cream.
1 CUP 377 cal., 13g fat (7g sat. fat), 31mg chol., 368mg sod., 64g carb. (37g sugars, 6g fiber), 5g pro.

MAMAW EMILY'S STRAWBERRY CAKE

My husband loved his Mamaw's strawberry cake and thought no one could duplicate it. I made it, and it's just as scrumptious as he remembers!
—Jennifer Bruce, Manitou, KY

PREP: 15 min. • **BAKE:** 25 min. + cooling
MAKES: 12 servings

- 1 pkg. white cake mix (regular size)
- 1 pkg. (3 oz.) strawberry gelatin
- 3 Tbsp. sugar
- 3 Tbsp. all-purpose flour
- 1 cup water
- ½ cup canola oil
- 2 large eggs, room temperature
- 1 cup finely chopped strawberries
FROSTING
- ½ cup butter, softened
- ½ cup crushed strawberries
- 4½ to 5 cups confectioners' sugar

1. Preheat oven to 350°. Line the bottoms of 2 greased 8-in. round baking pans with parchment; grease parchment.
2. In a large bowl, combine cake mix, gelatin, sugar and flour. Add the water, oil and eggs; beat on low speed for 30 seconds. Beat on medium 2 minutes. Fold in chopped strawberries. Transfer to prepared pans.
3. Bake until a toothpick inserted in the center comes out clean, 25-30 minutes. Cool in pans 10 minutes before removing to wire racks; remove paper. Cool completely.
4. For frosting, in a small bowl, beat butter until creamy. Beat in crushed strawberries. Gradually beat in enough confectioners' sugar to reach desired consistency. Spread frosting between layers and over top and side of cake.
1 PIECE 532 cal., 21g fat (7g sat. fat), 51mg chol., 340mg sod., 85g carb. (69g sugars, 1g fiber), 4g pro.

TEST KITCHEN TIP

You'll be smitten with the nostalgic charm of this rich pink buttercream frosting, but for a change of pace, try icing the cake with whipped cream or whipped topping and serve with fresh berries. Save your prettiest strawberries for garnishing. Use second-tier berries for the cake interior and frosting.

PINK LEMONADE STAND CAKE

If you love a moist and creamy cake, this is it! Lemon juice and lemonade give the layers a tangy, citrusy touch, and the cream cheese frosting with sprinkles makes it extra pretty.

—*Lauren McAnelly, Des Moines, IA*

PREP: 50 min. • **BAKE:** 20 min. + cooling
MAKES: 12 servings

- 1 cup buttermilk
- 2 Tbsp. lemon juice
- 2 Tbsp. seedless strawberry jam, warmed
- 2 Tbsp. thawed pink lemonade concentrate
- 2 Tbsp. grenadine syrup
- 1 cup unsalted butter, softened
- 1¼ cups sugar
- 3 Tbsp. grated lemon zest
- 4 large eggs, room temperature
- ½ tsp. vanilla extract
- 2½ cups all-purpose flour
- 1 tsp. baking powder
- ½ tsp. baking soda
- ½ tsp. salt

FROSTING
- 1 cup unsalted butter, softened
- 1 pkg. (8 oz.) cream cheese, softened
- 1 Tbsp. grated lemon zest
- 4 cups confectioners' sugar
- ⅓ cup plus 3 Tbsp. thawed pink lemonade concentrate, divided
  Pink sprinkles

1. Preheat oven to 350°. Line bottoms of 3 greased 8-in. round baking pans with parchment; grease parchment.
2. In a small bowl, whisk the first 5 ingredients until blended. In a large bowl, cream butter, sugar and lemon zest until light and fluffy, 5-7 minutes. Add eggs, 1 at a time, beating well after each addition. Beat in vanilla. In another bowl, whisk flour, baking powder, baking soda and salt; add to the creamed mixture alternately with the buttermilk mixture, beating well after each addition.
3. Transfer the batter to prepared pans. Bake until a toothpick inserted in center comes out clean, 20-24 minutes. Cool in pans 10 minutes before removing to wire racks; remove parchment. Cool completely.
4. For frosting, in a large bowl, beat the butter, cream cheese and lemon zest until smooth. Gradually beat in confectioners' sugar and ⅓ cup lemonade concentrate. If necessary, refrigerate until spreadable, up to 1 hour.
5. Place 1 cake layer on a serving plate. Brush 1 Tbsp. lemonade concentrate over cake; spread with ½ cup frosting. Repeat layers. Top with remaining cake layer; brush remaining lemonade concentrate over top. Spread remaining frosting over top and side of cake.
6. Decorate with sprinkles. Refrigerate until serving.

NOTE To substitute for each cup of buttermilk, use 1 Tbsp. white vinegar or lemon juice plus enough milk to measure 1 cup. Stir, then let stand 5 min. Or, use 1 cup plain yogurt or 1¾ tsp. cream of tartar plus 1 cup milk.

1 PIECE 732 cal., 39g fat (24g sat. fat), 172mg chol., 291mg sod., 91g carb. (68g sugars, 1g fiber), 7g pro.

FOR CUPCAKES Make batter as directed; fill 24 paper-lined muffin cups three-fourths full. Bake in a preheated 350° oven for 16-19 minutes or until a toothpick comes out clean. Cool in pans 10 minutes before removing to wire racks to cool completely. Prepare frosting as directed, omitting 3 Tbsp. lemonade concentrate for brushing layers; pipe or spread frosting over tops. **Yield:** 2 dozen cupcakes.

DEVIL'S FOOD SNACK CAKE

My husband and his friends request this cake for camping trips because it's easy to transport. That makes it great for taking to potlucks too. You can add frosting if you wish, but it's fine without it!
—*Julie Danler, Bel Aire, KS*

PREP: 30 min. • **BAKE:** 35 min.
MAKES: 24 servings

- 1 cup quick-cooking oats
- 1¾ cups boiling water
- ¼ cup butter, softened
- ½ cup sugar
- ½ cup packed brown sugar
- 2 large eggs, room temperature
- ⅓ cup buttermilk
- 3 Tbsp. canola oil
- 1 tsp. vanilla extract
- ¾ cup all-purpose flour
- ¾ cup whole wheat flour
- 2 Tbsp. dark baking cocoa
- 1 Tbsp. instant coffee granules
- 1 tsp. baking soda
- ⅛ tsp. salt
- 1 cup miniature semisweet chocolate chips, divided
- ¾ cup chopped pecans, divided

1. Preheat oven to 350°. Place oats in a large bowl. Cover with boiling water; let stand for 10 minutes.

2. Meanwhile, beat the butter and sugars until crumbly, about 2 minutes. Add eggs, 1 at a time, beating well after each addition. Beat in buttermilk, oil and vanilla. Combine flours, cocoa, coffee granules, baking soda and salt. Gradually add to creamed mixture. Stir in the oat mixture, ½ cup chocolate chips and ⅓ cup pecans.

3. Pour into a greased 13x9-in. baking pan. Sprinkle with remaining chips and pecans. Bake until a toothpick inserted in center comes out clean, 35-40 minutes. Cool on a wire rack before cutting.

1 PIECE 174 cal., 9g fat (3g sat. fat), 23mg chol., 91mg sod., 22g carb. (13g sugars, 2g fiber), 3g pro. **DIABETIC EXCHANGES** 2 fat, 1½ starch.

SUMMER FUN

BRUNCH ON THE PATIO

When the weather is fine, treat your friends to a lovely midmorning get-together. Set up a breakfast table on the back patio and lay out a spread of amazing dishes—and a sweet morning cocktail too!

flatten. Fry in batches until golden brown on both sides, using remaining oil as needed. Drain on paper towels. Top with lox, and sour cream and chives if desired.

3 LATKES WITH ⅓ OZ. LOX 270 cal., 16g fat (2g sat. fat), 73mg chol., 610mg sod., 26g carb. (3g sugars, 2g fiber), 6g pro.

GARLIC-HERB BAGEL SPREAD

Our Test Kitchen staff mixed up this mouthwatering must-have, which is loaded with oregano, basil, garlic and feta. The flavorful combination is perfect with toasted bagels or crunchy breadsticks.
—Taste of Home *Test Kitchen*

TAKES: 10 min.
MAKES: 8 servings (1 cup)

- 3   oz. cream cheese, softened
- ⅓   cup sour cream
- ¼   cup crumbled feta cheese
- 2   garlic cloves, minced
- ½   tsp. each garlic powder, dried oregano and basil
      Bagels, split

In a small bowl, beat the cream cheese until smooth. Add the sour cream, feta cheese, garlic and seasonings; mix well. Toast bagels if desired; top with spread.
2 TBSP. 68 cal., 6g fat (4g sat. fat), 15mg chol., 71mg sod., 2g carb. (1g sugars, 0 fiber), 2g pro.

LATKES WITH LOX

Lox, a salty smoked salmon, is a year-round delicacy. This recipe, inspired by one from the *Jewish Journal*, uses lox as a topping for crispy latkes.
—Taste of Home *Test Kitchen*

PREP: 20 min. • **COOK:** 5 min./batch
MAKES: 3 dozen

- 2   cups finely chopped onion
- ¼   cup all-purpose flour
- 6   garlic cloves, minced
- 2   tsp. salt
- 1   tsp. coarsely ground pepper
- 4   large eggs, lightly beaten
- 4   lbs. russet potatoes, peeled and shredded
- ¾   cup canola oil

TOPPINGS
- 4   oz. lox
      Optional: Sour cream and minced fresh chives

1. In a large bowl, combine the first 5 ingredients. Stir in eggs until blended. Add potatoes; toss to coat.
2. Heat 2 Tbsp. oil in a large nonstick skillet over medium heat. Drop batter by ¼ cupfuls into oil; press lightly to

5. Sprinkle with sesame or poppy seeds if desired. Place 2 in. apart on greased baking sheets. Bake at 400° until golden brown, 20-25 minutes. Remove from pans to wire racks to cool.

1 BAGEL 237 cal., 9g fat (5g sat. fat), 38mg chol., 271mg sod., 33g carb. (3g sugars, 1g fiber), 5g pro.

SWEET & SPICY BACON

Chili powder, cayenne and curry add an unexpected flavor twist to this taste-tempting bacon. With a touch of cinnamon and maple syrup, the well-seasoned strips complement just about any breakfast or BLT.
—Taste of Home *Test Kitchen*

TAKES: 25 min. • **MAKES:** 4 servings

- 1   tsp. chili powder
- ⅛   tsp. cayenne pepper
- ⅛   tsp. curry powder
- ⅛   tsp. ground cinnamon
- 8   bacon strips
- 3   Tbsp. maple syrup

1. Combine the seasonings; sprinkle over both sides of bacon. Place on a rack in an ungreased 15x10x1-in. baking pan. Bake at 450° for 10 minutes.
2. Drizzle bacon with 1 Tbsp. syrup. Turn and drizzle with remaining syrup. Bake for 6-10 minutes longer or until browned. Remove to paper towels. Serve warm.

2 PIECES 115 cal., 6g fat (2g sat. fat), 11mg chol., 210mg sod., 11g carb. (10g sugars, 0 fiber), 4g pro.

HOMEMADE BAGELS

Instead of going to a baker, head to the kitchen and surprise your friends and family with homemade bagels. For variation and flavor, sprinkle the tops with cinnamon sugar instead of sesame and poppy seeds.
—Rebecca Phillips, Burlington, CT

PREP: 30 min. + rising • **BAKE:** 20 min.
MAKES: 1 dozen

- 1   tsp. active dry yeast
- 1¼   cups warm 2% milk (110° to 115°)
- ½   cup butter, softened
- 2   Tbsp. sugar
- 1   tsp. salt
- 1   large egg yolk, room temperature
- 3¾   to 4¼ cups all-purpose flour
        Optional: Sesame or poppy seeds

1. In a large bowl, dissolve yeast in warm milk. Add the butter, sugar, salt and egg yolk; mix well. Stir in enough flour to form a soft dough.
2. Turn onto a floured surface; knead until smooth and elastic, 6-8 minutes. Place in a greased bowl, turning once to grease top. Cover and let rise in a warm place until doubled, about 1 hour.
3. Punch dough down. Shape into 12 balls. Push thumb through centers to form a 1½-in. hole. Stretch and shape dough to form an even ring. Place on a floured surface. Cover and let rest for 10 minutes; flatten bagels slightly.
4. Fill a Dutch oven two-thirds full with water; bring to a boil. Drop bagels, 2 at a time, into boiling water. Cook for 45 seconds; turn and cook 45 seconds longer. Remove with a slotted spoon; drain well on paper towels.

CHEESE & CRAB BRUNCH BAKE

Who doesn't love an easy, cheesy seafood casserole that can be pulled together in 30 minutes, refrigerated overnight and baked up the next morning?
—*Joyce Conway, Westerville, OH*

PREP: 30 min. + chilling • **BAKE:** 50 min.
MAKES: 12 servings

2 Tbsp. Dijon mustard
6 English muffins, split
8 oz. lump crabmeat, drained
2 Tbsp. lemon juice
2 tsp. grated lemon zest
2 cups shredded white cheddar cheese
12 large eggs
1 cup half-and-half cream
1 cup 2% milk
½ cup mayonnaise
1 tsp. salt
½ tsp. cayenne pepper
½ tsp. pepper
2 cups shredded Swiss cheese
1 cup grated Parmesan cheese
4 green onions, chopped
¼ cup finely chopped sweet red pepper
¼ cup finely chopped sweet yellow pepper

1. Spread mustard over bottom half of muffins. Place in a greased 13x9-in. baking dish. Top with crab, lemon juice and zest. Sprinkle with cheddar cheese. Top with muffin tops.
2. In a large bowl, whisk eggs, cream, milk, mayonnaise, salt, cayenne and pepper. Pour over muffins; sprinkle with Swiss cheese, Parmesan cheese, onions and sweet peppers. Cover and refrigerate overnight.
3. Remove from refrigerator 30 minutes before baking. Cover and bake at 375° for 30 minutes. Uncover; bake until set, 20-25 minutes longer. Let stand 5 minutes before serving. If desired, top with additional chopped green onions.
1 SERVING 428 cal., 28g fat (13g sat. fat), 286mg chol., 844mg sod., 18g carb. (4g sugars, 1g fiber), 26g pro.

KALE SLAW SPRING SALAD

My parents and in-laws are retired and like to spend winters in Florida. This tangy spring salad brings the snowbirds back in time for our Easter celebration!
—*Jennifer Gilbert, Brighton, MI*

TAKES: 25 min. • **MAKES:** 10 servings

5 cups chopped fresh kale
3 cups torn romaine
1 pkg. (14 oz.) coleslaw mix
1 medium fennel bulb, thinly sliced
1 cup chopped fresh broccoli
½ cup shredded red cabbage
1 cup crumbled feta cheese
¼ cup sesame seeds, toasted
⅓ cup extra virgin olive oil
3 Tbsp. sesame oil
2 Tbsp. honey
2 Tbsp. cider vinegar
2 Tbsp. lemon juice
⅓ cup pureed strawberries
   Sliced fresh strawberries

1. Combine kale and romaine. Add the coleslaw mix, fennel, broccoli and red cabbage; sprinkle with feta cheese and sesame seeds. Toss to combine.
2. Stir together olive oil and sesame oil. Whisk in honey, vinegar and lemon juice. Add pureed strawberries. Whisk until combined. Dress salad just before serving; top with sliced strawberries.
1⅓ CUPS 192 cal., 15g fat (3g sat. fat), 6mg chol., 140mg sod., 12g carb. (7g sugars, 3g fiber), 4g pro. **DIABETIC EXCHANGES** 3 fat, 1 starch.

AT-HOME COFFEE BAR

No need to make an impromptu coffee run to satisfy your brunch guests. Re-create the experience of visiting your favorite coffee shop by setting up your own coffee bar stocked with all the essentials—a variety of sweeteners, flavored syrups, creamers and more!

RHUBARB STREUSEL MUFFINS

What a pleasure it is to set out a basket of these rhubarb muffins ... although the basket doesn't stay full for very long! With six children and two grandsons, I do a lot of baking. I adapted this recipe from a favorite coffee cake recipe.
—*Sandra Moreside, Regina, , SK*

PREP: 15 min. • **BAKE:** 25 min.
MAKES: about 1½ dozen

- ½ cup butter, softened
- 1 cup packed brown sugar
- ½ cup sugar
- 1 large egg, room temperature
- 2 cups all-purpose flour
- 1 tsp. baking powder
- ½ tsp. baking soda
- ⅛ tsp. salt
- 1 cup sour cream
- 3 cups chopped fresh or frozen rhubarb, thawed

TOPPING
- ½ cup chopped pecans
- ¼ cup packed brown sugar
- 1 tsp. ground cinnamon
- 1 Tbsp. cold butter

1. Preheat oven to 350°. In a large bowl, cream butter and sugars until light and fluffy, 5-7 minutes. Beat in egg. Combine flour, baking powder, baking soda and salt; add to creamed mixture alternately with sour cream, beating well after each addition. Fold in rhubarb.

2. Fill paper-lined or greased muffin cups three-fourths full. For topping, combine the pecans, brown sugar and cinnamon in a small bowl; cut in the butter until crumbly. Sprinkle over batter.

3. Bake until a toothpick inserted in the center comes out clean, 22-25 minutes. Cool for 5 minutes before removing from pans to wire racks. Serve warm.

NOTE If using frozen rhubarb, measure it while still frozen, then thaw completely. Drain in a colander, but do not press the liquid out.

1 MUFFIN 238 cal., 11g fat (5g sat. fat), 36mg chol., 149mg sod., 33g carb. (22g sugars, 1g fiber), 3g pro.

LEMON RICOTTA FRITTERS

These delicious fritters are golden brown outside and soft and cakelike inside, and have a lovely citrusy flavor. They're great served with jam or honey.
—*Tina Mirilovich, Johnstown, PA*

TAKES: 30 min. • **MAKES:** about 2 dozen

- 1 cup all-purpose flour
- 2 tsp. baking powder
- 1½ tsp. grated lemon zest
- Pinch salt
- 3 large eggs, room temperature
- 1 cup whole-milk ricotta cheese
- 3 Tbsp. sugar
- ½ tsp. lemon extract
- Oil for deep-fat frying
- Confectioners' sugar
- Honey or strawberry jam

1. In a large bowl, whisk flour, baking powder, lemon zest and salt. In another bowl, whisk eggs, cheese, sugar and extract. Add to the dry ingredients, stirring just until moistened.
2. In a deep cast-iron skillet or deep-fat fryer, heat oil to 375°. Drop the batter by tablespoonfuls, several at a time, into the hot oil. Fry until golden brown. 2-3 minutes. Drain on paper towels. Dust with confectioners' sugar. Serve warm with honey or jam.
1 FRITTER 60 cal., 3g fat (1g sat. fat), 24mg chol., 58mg sod., 5g carb. (2g sugars, 0 fiber), 2g pro.

READER REVIEW
"These are a delicious treat with coffee ... I add a pinch of nutmeg, and after drizzle with a touch of honey and powdered sugar. Fabulous!"
—LINDAKILEY, TASTEOFHOME.COM

ONION-GARLIC HASH BROWNS

Quick to assemble, these slow-cooked hash browns are one of my go-to sides. Stir in hot sauce if you like a bit of heat. I top my finished dish with a sprinkling of shredded cheddar cheese.
—*Cindi Boger, Ardmore, AL*

PREP: 20 min. • **COOK:** 3 hours
MAKES: 12 servings

- ¼ cup butter, cubed
- 1 Tbsp. olive oil
- 1 large red onion, chopped
- 1 small sweet red pepper, chopped
- 1 small green pepper, chopped
- 4 garlic cloves, minced
- 1 pkg. (30 oz.) frozen shredded hash brown potatoes
- ½ tsp. salt
- ½ tsp. pepper
- 3 drops hot pepper sauce, optional
- 2 tsp. minced fresh parsley

1. In a large skillet, heat butter and oil over medium heat. Add onion and peppers; cook and stir until crisp-tender. Add garlic; cook 1 minute longer. Stir in hash browns, salt, pepper and, if desired, pepper sauce.
2. Transfer to a 5-qt. slow cooker coated with cooking spray. Cook, covered, until heated through, 3-4 hours. Sprinkle with parsley just before serving.
½ CUP 110 cal., 5g fat (3g sat. fat), 10mg chol., 136mg sod., 15g carb. (1g sugars, 1g fiber), 2g pro. **DIABETIC EXCHANGES** 1 starch, 1 fat.

PEACHY KEEN WINE COCKTAIL

A bushel of peaches gave me a reason to create a wine cocktail. The fresh fruity taste makes it as perfect for a summer brunch as for an evening gathering.
—*Katie Ferrier, Houston, TX*

PREP: 15 min. • **COOK:** 15 min. + cooling
MAKES: 6 servings

- 2 cups sugar
- 1 cup water
- 1 large piece fresh gingerroot (about 3 in.), peeled and coarsely chopped

COCKTAIL
- ¼ cup orange liqueur
- 2 medium ripe peaches, peeled and halved
- 1 bottle (750 ml) white wine, chilled
  Ice cubes
- 1 to 1½ cups chilled ginger ale
  Optional: Fresh mint leaves and peach slices

1. In a large saucepan, combine sugar, water and ginger; bring to a boil. Reduce heat; simmer for 10 minutes. Let cool completely. Pour the syrup through a strainer into a covered container; discard ginger.
2. Place liqueur and ¼ cup ginger syrup in a blender. (Cover and refrigerate remaining syrup for another use.) Add the peaches; cover and process until smooth.
3. Transfer mixture to a 2-qt. pitcher; stir in wine. Serve over ice, topping with ginger ale. If desired, serve with mint and peach slices.
¾ CUP 188 cal., 0 fat (0 sat. fat), 0 chol., 6mg sod., 20g carb. (17g sugars, 1g fiber), 1g pro.

TIME FOR A PICNIC

Outdoor meals can be as casual or as fancy as you like! Head for the banks of a nearby lake or stream, a local park or state forest or just a shady spot in your backyard and enjoy the day with friends and family.

BACON & ASPARAGUS FRITTATA

This frittata is quick and easy, but it always wins me many compliments!
—*Gwen Clemon, Soldier, IA*

PREP: 10 min. • **COOK:** 25 min.
MAKES: 6 servings

- 12 oz. bacon
- 2 cups sliced fresh asparagus (cut in ½-in. pieces)
- 1 cup chopped onion
- 2 garlic cloves, minced
- 10 large eggs, beaten
- ¼ cup minced parsley
- ½ tsp. seasoned salt
- ¼ tsp. pepper
- 1 large tomato, thinly sliced
- 1 cup shredded cheddar cheese

1. In a 9- or 10-in. ovenproof skillet, cook bacon until crisp. Drain, reserving 1 Tbsp. drippings in pan. Over medium-high heat, add asparagus, onion and garlic to the pan; saute until the onion is tender. Chop or crumble the bacon; set aside a third. In a large bowl, combine the remaining bacon, eggs, parsley, salt and pepper.
2. Pour egg mixture into the skillet; stir. Top with tomato, cheese and reserved bacon. Cover and cook on medium-low until eggs are nearly set, 10-15 minutes.
3. Preheat broiler; place skillet 6 in. from heat. Broil until lightly browned, about 2 minutes.
1 PIECE 344 cal., 24g fat (10g sat. fat), 351mg chol., 738mg sod., 7g carb. (3g sugars, 2g fiber), 23g pro.

51 RHUBARB PUNCH

I love the tart taste of rhubarb, and this lively, beautiful punch makes a refreshing treat at any get-together.
—*Eleanor Martens, Rosenort, MB*

PREP: 10 min. • **COOK:** 20 min. + cooling
MAKES: 48 servings (12 cups syrup)

- 3 qt. diced fresh or frozen rhubarb
- 4½ cups sugar
- 3 qt. water
- 1 can (6 oz.) frozen orange juice concentrate, thawed
- 3 Tbsp. lemon juice
  Lemon-lime soda

In a heavy saucepan, bring the rhubarb, sugar and water to a boil. Boil 15 minutes; cool and strain. Stir in orange and lemon juices. Chill. For each serving, combine ¼ cup rhubarb syrup and ¾ cup soda; serve in a chilled glass.
1 CUP PREPARED PUNCH 164 cal., 0 fat (0 sat. fat), 0 chol., 20mg sod., 42g carb. (38g sugars, 1g fiber), 0 pro.

LIGHT STRAWBERRY-SPINACH SALAD

I'm always looking for new ways to use our fresh Washington-grown strawberries. This light spinach salad is one of my favorite ways to do so.
—*Perlene Hoekema, Lynden, WA*

TAKES: 20 min. • **MAKES:** 8 servings

- 2 Tbsp. sesame seeds
- 1½ lbs. fresh spinach
- ⅓ cup canola oil
- ⅓ cup red wine vinegar
- 1 Tbsp. sugar
- 2 tsp. minced green onion
- ½ tsp. paprika
- ¼ tsp. Worcestershire sauce
- 2 cups fresh strawberries, washed, hulled and halved

1. In a small skillet over medium heat, cook and stir sesame seeds until golden; remove and set aside.
2. Wash spinach thoroughly; dry on paper towels and tear into bite-sized pieces. Blend oil, vinegar, sugar, onion, paprika and Worcestershire sauce.
3. In a large bowl, mix together the spinach, strawberries, dressing and seeds. Serve immediately.
¾ CUP 127 cal., 10g fat (1g sat. fat), 0 chol., 113mg sod., 8g carb. (4g sugars, 2g fiber), 2g pro. **DIABETIC EXCHANGES** 2 fat, 1 vegetable.

CURRY CARROT DIP

The flavors of sweet carrots, mustard and curry blend deliciously in this appetizing dip. Raw veggies are the perfect partners.
—*Louise Weyer, Marietta, GA*

TAKES: 30 min. • **MAKES:** 1 cup

- 1 small onion, chopped
- 2 tsp. canola oil
- 4 medium carrots, sliced
- ⅓ cup water
- ¼ tsp. salt
- ¼ tsp. pepper
- ¼ tsp. curry powder
- 2 Tbsp. reduced-fat mayonnaise
- 2 tsp. prepared mustard
  Assorted raw vegetables

1. In a nonstick skillet, saute onion in oil. Add the carrots, water, salt, pepper and curry. Bring to a boil. Reduce heat; cover and simmer for 6 minutes or until the vegetables are tender. Uncover; cook for 8 minutes or until the liquid has evaporated. Cool.
2. Transfer to a food processor or blender; cover and process until smooth. Add mayonnaise and mustard; mix well. Serve with vegetables.
2 TBSP. 40 cal., 3g fat (0 sat. fat), 1mg chol., 133mg sod., 4g carb. (2g sugars, 1g fiber), 0 pro.

BLUEBERRY THIRST QUENCHER

I first enjoyed this cocktail at a Kentucky Derby party and fell in love with it. With its beautiful color and zesty flavor, it's very festive for a summer picnic or party, and everyone likes it.
—*Belinda Gibson, Dry Ridge, KY*

TAKES: 5 min. • **MAKES:** 9 servings

- 6 cups chilled blueberry juice cocktail
- 3 cups chilled lemon-lime soda
- 9 oz. blueberry-flavored vodka, chilled
  Crushed ice
- 1 cup fresh blueberries
  Sliced peeled mango, optional

In a large pitcher, combine juice, soda and vodka. Serve over ice; garnish with blueberries and, if desired, mango.
1 CUP 179 cal., 0 fat (0 sat. fat), 0 chol., 33mg sod., 30g carb. (29g sugars, 0 fiber), 0 pro.

ZUCCHINI PICO DE GALLO

I love veggies and fresh ingredients in the summer. I make big bowls of this salsa, which we eat with pretty much everything while fresh tomatoes are in season. My kids love it, though I leave out the jalapeno when making it for them.
—*Amy Gattuso, Denham springs, LA*

PREP: 20 min. + chilling
MAKES: 4½ cups

- 2 large tomatoes, chopped
- 1 medium zucchini, finely chopped
- 1 poblano pepper, seeded and chopped
- ½ cup chopped onion
- 1 seeded and diced jalapeno pepper, optional
- 2 Tbsp. minced fresh cilantro
- 2 garlic cloves, minced
- ½ tsp. salt
- ¼ tsp. pepper
- 3 Tbsp. lime juice

Combine the first 9 ingredients. Add lime juice; toss to coat. Cover and refrigerate at least 1 hour.
NOTE Wear disposable gloves when cutting hot peppers; the oils can burn skin. Avoid touching your face.
¼ CUP 10 cal., 0 fat (0 sat. fat), 0 chol., 68mg sod., 2g carb. (1g sugars, 1g fiber), 0 pro. **DIABETIC EXCHANGES** free food.

ARNOLD PALMER CUPCAKES

These fun cupcakes take a favorite Arnold Palmer recipe and turn it into dessert. Add a slice of lemon on top for a puckery finish.
—*Jesse Arriaga, Reno, NV*

PREP: 20 min. • **BAKE:** 25 min. + cooling
MAKES: 2½ dozen

- 1 cup butter, softened
- 2 cups sugar
- 3 large eggs, room temperature
- 1 Tbsp. grated lemon zest
- 2 tsp. lemon juice
- 3½ cups all-purpose flour
- 1 tsp. baking soda
- ½ tsp. baking powder
- ½ tsp. salt
- 2 cups sour cream

ICED TEA FROSTING

- 9 Tbsp. butter, softened
- 6¾ cups confectioners' sugar
- ¾ cup 2% milk
- ¾ cup iced tea mix with lemon and sugar

1. Preheat oven to 350°. In a large bowl, cream butter and sugar until light and fluffy, 5-7 minutes. Add eggs, 1 at a time, beating well after each addition. Beat in lemon zest and lemon juice. Combine the flour, baking soda, baking powder and salt; add to creamed mixture alternately with sour cream, beating well after each addition (batter will be thick).
2. Fill 30 paper-lined muffin cups with ¼ cup batter. Bake until a toothpick inserted in the center comes out clean, 25-30 minutes. Cool 10 minutes before removing from pans to wire racks to cool completely.
3. For frosting, combine butter and confectioners' sugar in a small bowl until light and fluffy, 5-7 minutes. In small bowl, stir together milk and iced tea mix until dissolved. Add to the butter mixture; beat until smooth. Frost cupcakes.
1 CUPCAKE 355 cal., 14g fat (8g sat. fat), 48mg chol., 182mg sod., 57g carb. (45g sugars, 0 fiber), 3g pro.

TEST KITCHEN TIPS

Not a fan of iced tea? Use powdered lemonade mix instead of tea mix in the frosting. Want a sheet cake? Pour batter into a 13x9-in. baking pan and bake until a toothpick inserted in the center comes out clean, about 30 minutes.

TIPS FOR PLANNING THE PERFECT PICNIC

The sun is shining, and flowers are blooming—that means it's time for a picnic!

Keep a picnic kit ready to go Stash paper plates, picnic-ready flatware, sunblock and a few outdoor games in a container. When not in use, slip it in your cooler for next time!

Choose a place Consider the banks of a nearby lake or stream, a local park or a shady spot in your own backyard! Plan a hike and bring the picnic with you. Stop when you get hungry or find a scenic spot to eat.

Don't forget the games! Don't forget the games! Make getting to the picnic a scavenger hunt. Leave clues or a "treasure" map for your family to find their way to the picnic destination. If kids will be joining you, try to pick a park with a playground nearby. Bring along board games, a bocce ball, a softball and a catcher's mitt or a Frisbee for some outdoor fun.

Set the mood for a romantic outing with a sunset picnic. If it's allowed, bring a few votive candles and a small bouquet of flowers to add to the ambience.

Pack two containers—a basket for tableware and nonperishable items and a cooler for cold food and beverages. When packing the cooler, first place ice on the bottom and along the sides. Then place the heaviest and most perishable foods on top of the ice. Fill in with lighter items.

Pack your basket in reverse order to make it easy to get at the items you need when you first arrive at your picnic site. Place nonperishable food on the bottom, then serving items and tableware, and the tablecloth on top.

If you're feeding a lot of people, bring two coolers. Since opening a cooler allows cool air to escape, use one for frequently used items such as beverages. Use the second for perishable foods such as meats and salads.

Have a dish that needs to be kept warm? Transport it in the cooking vessel for a laid-back feel (as we did with the frittata on p. 244). If the dish has a lid and handles, tie a clean dish towel through the handles to secure the lid.

Short on time? Outdoor eats don't always have to be made from scratch. Hit the deli bar and choose from among the salads and cold meats on offer. Supplement with crusty bread, fresh fruit and a wedge of cheese.

Save extra condiment packets from fast-food restaurants—the packs are ideal for easy outdoor meals.

Keep ants away by placing a plastic dish under the foot of each leg of the picnic table—then fill with water to create small-scale moats the ants can't cross!

Bring along plastic bags to cart home dirty dishes and silverware, and for garbage in case there are no trash barrels at the picnic site.

ALMOND-APRICOT CHICKEN SALAD

Here's a one-of-a-kind pasta salad that combines tender chicken, sweet apricots and crunchy vegetables. Plus, the lemony dressing can't be beat.
—Susan Voigt, Plymouth, MN

PREP: 20 min. + chilling
MAKES: 10 servings

- 1 pkg. (8 oz.) spiral pasta
- 1 pkg. (6 oz.) dried apricots, thinly sliced
- 3 cups coarsely chopped fresh broccoli
- 2½ cups diced cooked chicken
- ½ cup chopped green onions
- ½ cup chopped celery
- 1 cup sour cream
- ¾ cup mayonnaise
- 1 Tbsp. lemon juice
- 2 tsp. grated lemon zest
- 2 tsp. Dijon mustard
- 1½ tsp. salt
- ¾ tsp. dried savory
- ½ tsp. pepper
- ¾ cup sliced almonds, toasted

1. Cook pasta according to the package directions, adding apricots during last 4 minutes. Drain and rinse with cold water; place in a large bowl. Add the broccoli, chicken, green onion and celery.
2. In a small bowl, combine the next 8 ingredients. Pour over salad and toss to coat. Cover and chill until serving; fold in almonds.
1 SERVING 411 cal., 24g fat (6g sat. fat), 52mg chol., 524mg sod., 31g carb. (10g sugars, 4g fiber), 17g pro.

TUNA MACARONI SALAD

Pack this classic salad for a picnic or workplace lunch. For best results, keep the salad in the fridge overnight to allow flavors to blend.
—Taste of Home *Test Kitchen*

PREP: 20 min. + chilling
MAKES: 10 servings

2 cups uncooked elbow macaroni
1 cup mayonnaise
¼ cup sweet pickle relish
½ tsp. salt
¼ tsp. pepper
1 cup frozen peas, thawed
½ cup chopped sweet onion
½ cup chopped celery
1 can (5 oz.) light tuna in water, drained and flaked
3 hard-boiled large eggs, chopped

1. Cook macaroni according to the package directions; drain and rinse with cold water. Cool completely.
2. For dressing, combine mayonnaise, relish, salt and pepper. In a large bowl, combine peas, onion, celery, tuna, eggs and macaroni. Add dressing; gently toss to coat. Refrigerate until serving.
¾ CUP 255 cal., 18g fat (3g sat. fat), 69mg chol., 352mg sod., 16g carb. (3g sugars, 1g fiber), 7g pro.

TEST KITCHEN TIP

When planning a picnic, closely estimate how much food your group will eat to avoid waste. Unless they can be kept cold, leftovers of perishable items—such as this salad—should be thrown away.

ROOT BEER COOKIES

When it's too difficult to take along root beer floats on a picnic, take these cookies instead! I've found the flavor is even better the next day. The hard part is convincing my family to wait that long before sampling them.
—*Violette Bawden, West Valley City, UT*

PREP: 20 min.
BAKE: 10 min./batch + cooling
MAKES: 6 dozen

- 1 cup butter, softened
- 2 cups packed brown sugar
- 2 large eggs, room temperature
- 1 cup buttermilk
- ¾ tsp. root beer concentrate or extract
- 4 cups all-purpose flour
- 1 tsp. baking soda
- 1 tsp. salt
- 1½ cups chopped pecans

FROSTING
- 3½ cups confectioners' sugar
- ¾ cup butter, softened
- 3 Tbsp. water
- 1¼ tsp. root beer concentrate or extract

1. Preheat oven to 375°. Cream butter and brown sugar. Add the eggs, 1 at a time, beating well after each addition. Beat in the buttermilk and root beer concentrate. Combine flour, baking soda and salt; gradually add to the creamed mixture. Stir in pecans.
2. Drop by tablespoonfuls 3 in. apart onto ungreased baking sheets. Bake until lightly browned, 10-12 minutes. Remove to wire racks to cool.
3. Combine frosting ingredients; beat until smooth. Frost cooled cookies.
NOTE To substitute for each cup of buttermilk, use 1 Tbsp. white vinegar or lemon juice plus enough milk to measure 1 cup. Stir; let stand for 5 min. Or use 1 cup plain yogurt or 1¾ tsp. cream of tartar plus 1 cup milk.
1 COOKIE 130 cal., 6g fat (3g sat. fat), 17mg chol., 96mg sod., 18g carb. (12g sugars, 0 fiber), 1g pro.

ROASTED POTATO & GREEN BEAN SALAD

I made this salad to take advantage of seasonal potatoes, onions and green beans. It's a perfect twist on the tangy German potato salad my mom used to make.
—*Blair Lonergan, Rochelle, VA*

PREP: 15 min. • **BAKE:** 25 min.
MAKES: 7 servings

- 6 medium red potatoes, cut into 1-in. cubes
- 1 large red onion, cut into 1-in. pieces
- ¼ lb. fresh green beans, trimmed and halved
- 2 Tbsp. olive oil
- 8 bacon strips, cooked and crumbled

VINAIGRETTE
- 2 Tbsp. cider vinegar
- 1 Tbsp. minced fresh thyme or 1 tsp. dried thyme
- 1 Tbsp. lemon juice
- 1 Tbsp. Dijon mustard
- ½ tsp. salt
- ¼ tsp. pepper
- ¼ cup olive oil

1. Preheat oven to 425°. Place potatoes, onion and green beans in a greased 15x10x1-in. baking pan. Drizzle with oil; toss to coat.
2. Roast for 25-30 minutes or until tender, stirring every 10 minutes. Transfer to a large bowl; add bacon.
3. In a small bowl, whisk the first 6 vinaigrette ingredients. Gradually whisk in oil until blended. Pour over potato mixture; toss to coat. Serve warm or at room temperature.
¾ CUP 206 cal., 15g fat (3g sat. fat), 8mg chol., 393mg sod., 14g carb. (2g sugars, 2g fiber), 4g pro.

RHUBARB SOUR CREAM COFFEE CAKE

With a tart kick from fresh rhubarb, this coffee cake is an irresistible way to start the day—or end it!
—*Roberta Schauer, Williamsport, PA*

PREP: 20 min. • **BAKE:** 45 min. + cooling
MAKES: 12 servings

- ¾ cup butter, softened
- 1½ cups sugar
- 3 large eggs, room temperature
- 1½ tsp. vanilla extract
- 3 cups all-purpose flour
- 2 tsp. baking powder
- 1 tsp. baking soda
- ¾ tsp. salt
- 1 cup sour cream
- 3 cups chopped fresh or frozen rhubarb

TOPPING
- ½ cup packed brown sugar
- ¼ cup all-purpose flour
- 1 tsp. ground cinnamon
- ¼ cup cold butter

1. Preheat oven to 350°. In a large mixing bowl, cream butter and sugar until light and fluffy, 5-7 minutes. Add eggs, 1 at a time, beating well after each addition. Add vanilla; mix well.
2. Combine flour, baking powder, baking soda and salt. Add to creamed mixture alternately with the sour cream. Fold in rhubarb. Spread into a greased 13x9-in. baking dish.
3. For topping, in a small bowl, combine the brown sugar, flour and cinnamon. Cut in the butter until mixture resembles coarse crumbs; sprinkle over the top.
4. Bake until a toothpick inserted in the center comes out clean, 45-50 minutes. Cool on a wire rack.

1 PIECE 458 cal., 21g fat (13g sat. fat), 92mg chol., 483mg sod., 62g carb. (35g sugars, 2g fiber), 6g pro.

SMOKY BAKED BEANS

They'll be lining up for this saucy bean recipe full of that hard-to-capture campfire flavor. A combination of colorful calico beans makes it a pretty dish alongside many summer entrees.
—*Lynne German, Buford, GA*

PREP: 25 min. • **COOK:** 7 hours
MAKES: 16 servings

- 1 lb. bulk spicy pork sausage
- 1 medium onion, chopped
- 2 cans (15 oz. each) pork and beans
- 1 can (16 oz.) kidney beans, rinsed and drained
- 1 can (16 oz.) butter beans, rinsed and drained
- 1 can (15½ oz.) navy beans, rinsed and drained
- 1 can (15 oz.) black beans, rinsed and drained
- 1 can (10 oz.) diced tomatoes and green chiles, drained
- ½ cup hickory smoke-flavored barbecue sauce
- ½ cup ketchup
- ½ cup packed brown sugar
- 1 tsp. ground mustard
- 1 tsp. steak seasoning
- 1 tsp. liquid smoke, optional

1. In a large skillet, cook sausage and onion over medium heat until meat is no longer pink, breaking sausage into crumbles; drain.
2. In a 5-qt. slow cooker, combine the beans, tomatoes and sausage mixture. In a small bowl, combine the barbecue sauce, ketchup, brown sugar, mustard, steak seasoning and, if desired, liquid smoke. Stir into the bean mixture.
3. Cover and cook on low 7-8 hours or until heated through.

¾ CUP 244 cal., 6g fat (2g sat. fat), 10mg chol., 896mg sod., 39g carb. (15g sugars, 8g fiber), 11g pro.

JUNETEENTH

June 19th commemorates Emancipation Day, and families across the country gather in backyards, parks and picnic grounds to celebrate the occasion. On the menu—a tempting spread of southern soul food.

WATERMELON SALAD WITH CINNAMON PRETZEL CRUNCH

This is such a wonderful side dish during the hot summer, especially here in Texas. My family loves watermelon, fresh peaches and nectarines, and I made a pretzel crunch to give the salad a little bit of bite.
—*Joan Hallford, North Richland Hills, TX*

PREP: 20 min. + chilling
BAKE: 5 min. + cooling
MAKES: 10 servings

- 2 cups chopped seedless watermelon
- 2 cups fresh blueberries
- 1 medium peach, chopped
- 1 medium nectarine, chopped
- 1 large kiwifruit, peeled and chopped
- ½ cup sweet white wine or grape juice
- 3 Tbsp. sugar

CRUNCH
- 1 cup chopped miniature pretzels
- ½ cup packed brown sugar
- ½ cup butter, melted
- ½ cup chopped pecans
- ¼ tsp. ground cinnamon

1. Preheat oven to 425°. In a large bowl, combine the watermelon, blueberries, peach, nectarine and kiwi. Drizzle with wine and sugar. Toss to coat. Cover and refrigerate for 1 hour.
2. Meanwhile, in a small bowl, combine pretzels, brown sugar, butter, pecans and cinnamon; toss to coat. Spread the mixture evenly onto a parchment-lined 15x10x1-in. baking pan. Bake 5-7 minutes or until the mixture is bubbly and sugar is dissolved. Cool completely. Break into small chunks.
3. Just before serving, gently stir half of the pretzel mixture into the fruit. Top with the remaining pretzel mixture to serve.
¾ CUP 244 cal., 14g fat (6g sat. fat), 24mg chol., 146mg sod., 30g carb. (23g sugars, 2g fiber), 2g pro.

STRAWBERRY COOLER

This refreshing beverage is easy to double. Just make two batches ahead of time, and add ginger ale and ice when you're ready for more!
—*Judy Robertson, Southington, CT*

TAKES: 10 min. • **MAKES:** 8 servings

- 3 cups water
- 5 cups sliced fresh strawberries
- ¾ to 1 cup sugar
- ¼ cup lemon juice
- 2 tsp. grated lemon zest
- 1 cup ginger ale
  Crushed ice
  Additional strawberries, optional

In a blender, process the water, sliced strawberries, sugar, and lemon juice and zest in batches until smooth. Strain the berry seeds if desired. Pour mixture into a pitcher; stir in the ginger ale. Serve in chilled glasses over ice. If desired, garnish with strawberries.
1 CUP 116 cal., 0 fat (0 sat. fat), 0 chol., 3mg sod., 29g carb. (26g sugars, 2g fiber), 1g pro.

SMOKED BRISKET

This is always a crowd favorite—it really melts in your mouth!
—*Jodi Abel, La Jolla, CA*

PREP: 20 min. + chilling
GRILL: 8 hours + standing
MAKES: 20 servings

- 2 Tbsp. olive oil
- 1 fresh beef brisket (7 to 8 lbs.)

RUB
- 2 Tbsp. garlic powder
- 2 Tbsp. onion powder
- 2 Tbsp. chili powder
- 1 Tbsp. ground mustard
- 1 Tbsp. ground cumin
- 1 Tbsp. paprika
- 1 Tbsp. smoked sea salt

MOP SAUCE
- 2 cups beef broth
- ¼ cup olive oil
- 2 Tbsp. Worcestershire sauce
- 2 Tbsp. hickory-flavored liquid smoke

1. Brush oil over brisket. Combine the rub ingredients; rub over both sides of beef. Place brisket on a rimmed baking sheet. Cover and refrigerate overnight or up to 2 days. In a small saucepan, combine the mop sauce ingredients. Simmer 15 minutes, stirring occasionally. Refrigerate until ready to grill.
2. Soak hickory and mesquite chips or pellets; add to smoker according to manufacturer's directions. Heat to 225°. Uncover brisket. Place brisket in smoker fat side up; smoke for 2 hours. Brush generously with mop sauce; turn meat. Smoke 2 more hours; brush generously with mop sauce again. Wrap brisket securely in heavy-duty aluminum foil; smoke until a thermometer inserted in beef reads 190°, 4-5 hours longer.
3. Let beef stand 20-30 minutes before slicing; cut diagonally across the grain into thin slices.
4 OZ. COOKED BEEF 252 cal., 11g fat (3g sat. fat), 68mg chol., 472mg sod., 2g carb. (0 sugars, 1g fiber), 33g pro **DIABETIC EXCHANGES** 4 lean meat.

PEACH UPSIDE-DOWN CHEESECAKE

I make this recipe every summer when peaches are ripe. Each year I improve the dessert with slight changes—this version is the best one yet!
—*Kristin Renee Olbert, Richmond, VA*

PREP: 30 min. • **BAKE:** 65 min. + chilling
MAKES: 16 servings

- ¼ cup butter, melted
- ½ cup packed brown sugar
- 3 medium fresh peaches, divided
- 3 pkg. (8 oz. each) cream cheese, softened
- 1 cup sugar
- 1 cup sour cream
- 1 tsp. vanilla extract
- 4 large eggs, room temperature, lightly beaten

1. Preheat oven to 350°. Line bottom and side of a 9-in. round baking pan with parchment. Pour butter into the prepared pan; sprinkle with brown sugar. Slice 2 peaches and arrange in a single layer over the brown sugar.
2. In a large bowl, beat cream cheese and sugar until smooth. Beat in sour cream and vanilla. Add eggs; beat on low speed just until blended. Chop remaining peach; fold into batter. Spoon over peach slices. Place cake pan in a larger baking pan; add 1 in. of hot water to larger pan.
3. Bake until center is just set and top appears dull, 65-75 minutes. Remove cake pan from the water bath. Cool cheesecake on a wire rack 10 minutes. Loosen side from the pan with a knife. Cool 1 hour longer. Refrigerate overnight, covering when completely cooled. Invert onto a serving plate.
1 PIECE 309 cal., 22g fat (13g sat. fat), 101mg chol., 181mg sod., 25g carb. (24g sugars, 0 fiber), 5g pro.

THE BEST BABY BACK RIBS

I like to marinate racks of ribs before adding my zesty spice rub. Then I grill them to perfection. They always turn out juicy and loaded with flavor.
—*Lola Egle, Bella Vista, AR*

PREP: 10 min. + marinating
GRILL: 1 hour 20 min.
MAKES: 6 servings

- 2 racks baby back ribs (about 4½ lbs.)
- ¾ cup chicken broth
- ¾ cup soy sauce
- 1 cup sugar, divided
- 6 Tbsp. cider vinegar
- 6 Tbsp. olive oil
- 3 garlic cloves, minced
- 2 tsp. salt
- 1 Tbsp. paprika
- ½ tsp. chili powder
- ½ tsp. pepper
- ¼ tsp. garlic powder
     Dash cayenne pepper
     Barbecue sauce, optional

1. If necessary, remove thin membrane from ribs and discard. Combine the broth, soy sauce, ½ cup sugar, vinegar, olive oil and garlic. Place the ribs in a shallow baking dish; pour two-thirds of the marinade over top. Turn to coat; cover and refrigerate overnight, turning occasionally. Cover and refrigerate the remaining marinade.

2. Drain ribs, discarding marinade in dish. Combine the remaining ½ cup sugar, salt and seasonings; rub over both sides of ribs.

3. Grill ribs, covered, on an oiled rack over indirect medium heat for 30 minutes on each side.

4. Baste with the reserved marinade, or, if desired, barbecue sauce. Move ribs to direct medium heat and cook until pork is tender, turning and basting occasionally, 20-40 minutes longer.

1 SERVING 647 cal., 41g fat (13g sat. fat), 123mg chol., 2345mg sod., 30g carb. (29g sugars, 1g fiber), 37g pro.

BACON COLLARD GREENS

Collard greens are a staple of southern cuisine. This side dish is often eaten alongside smoked or salt-cured meats, such as ham hocks, pork or fatback.
—*Marsha Ankeney, Niceville, FL*

PREP: 25 min. • **COOK:** 55 min.
MAKES: 9 servings

- 2 lbs. collard greens
- 4 thick-sliced bacon strips, chopped
- 1 cup chopped sweet onion
- 5 cups reduced-sodium chicken broth
- 1 cup sun-dried tomatoes (not packed in oil), chopped
- ½ tsp. garlic powder
- ¼ tsp. salt
- ¼ tsp. crushed red pepper flakes

1. Trim thick stems from the collard greens; coarsely chop leaves. In a Dutch oven, saute bacon for 3 minutes. Add onion; cook until onion is tender and bacon is crisp, 8-9 minutes longer. Add greens; cook just until wilted.
2. Stir in remaining ingredients. Bring to a boil. Reduce heat; cover and simmer until greens are tender, 45-50 minutes.
¾ CUP 157 cal., 10g fat (4g sat. fat), 12mg chol., 651mg sod., 11g carb. (4g sugars, 5g fiber), 7g pro.

WHAT IS JUNETEENTH?

What's the history of Juneteenth? On June 19, 1865, after the end of the Civil War, Union troops arrived in Galveston, Texas. This is when the remaining enslaved people in Texas finally learned of their freedom—more than two years after the Emancipation Proclamation.

In 1872, a group of Black ministers and businessmen purchased land and created Emancipation Park in Houston for an annual gathering.

Over the years, Juneteenth spread throughout the South. But the day is becoming well known across the country, and many state and local governments recognize it as an official holiday.

How is Juneteenth observed? Friends and family gather to celebrate the legacy of resilience and acknowledge the ongoing struggle through marches, prayers and other remembrances. Participants picnic with a variety of soul food dishes, one of the nation's most identifiable culinary traditions—an ode to history and heritage.

The "red trinity"—barbecue, watermelon and a red beverage—is at the heart of the meal. But no Juneteenth menu is complete without side dishes and desserts like collard greens, potato salad, cornbread pudding, peach cobbler and banana pudding.

COLORFUL CORNBREAD SALAD

When my garden comes in, I harvest the veggies for potluck dishes. In the South, we think bacon and cornbread make everything better—even salad!
—Rebecca Clark, Warrior, AL

PREP: 30 min. + chilling
BAKE: 15 min. + cooling
MAKES: 14 servings

- 1   pkg. (8½ oz.) cornbread/muffin mix
- 1   cup mayonnaise
- ½   cup sour cream
- 1   envelope ranch salad dressing mix
- 1   to 2 Tbsp. adobo sauce from canned chipotle peppers
- 4   to 6 cups torn romaine
- 4   medium tomatoes, chopped
- 1   medium green pepper, chopped
- 1   medium onion, chopped
- 1   lb. bacon strips, cooked and crumbled
- 4   cups shredded cheddar cheese

1. Preheat oven to 400°. Prepare the cornbread batter according to package directions. Pour into a greased 8-in. square baking pan. Bake until a toothpick inserted in center comes out clean, 15-20 minutes. Cool completely in pan on a wire rack.
2. Coarsely crumble cooled cornbread into a large bowl. In a small bowl, mix the mayonnaise, sour cream, salad dressing mix and adobo sauce.
3. In a 3-qt. trifle bowl or glass bowl, layer a third of the cornbread and half each of the romaine, tomatoes, pepper, onion, bacon, cheese and mayonnaise mixture in the listed order. Repeat layers. Top with the remaining cornbread, and additional chopped tomato and bacon if desired. Refrigerate, covered, 2-4 hours before serving.
¾ CUP 407 cal., 31g fat (11g sat. fat), 61mg chol., 821mg sod., 18g carb. (6g sugars, 2g fiber), 14g pro.

PECAN PIE COBBLER

I couldn't find a recipe, so I took it upon myself to devise this amazing dessert that combines the ease of a cobbler and the rich taste of pecan pie. It tastes even better with some ice cream or whipped topping.
—Willa Kelley, Edmond, OK

PREP: 20 min. • **BAKE:** 30 min. + cooling
MAKES: 12 servings

- ½   cup butter, cubed
- 1   cup plus 2 Tbsp. all-purpose flour
- ¾   cup sugar
- 3   tsp. baking powder
- ¼   tsp. salt
- ⅔   cup 2% milk
- 1   tsp. vanilla extract
- 1½   cups coarsely chopped pecans
- 1   cup packed brown sugar
- ¾   cup brickle toffee bits
- 1½   cups boiling water
-      Vanilla ice cream, optional

1. Preheat oven to 350°. Place butter in a 13x9-in. baking pan; heat pan in oven until butter is melted, 3-5 minutes. Meanwhile, combine the flour, sugar, baking powder and salt. Stir in the milk and vanilla until combined.
2. Remove baking pan from oven; add batter. Sprinkle with pecans, brown sugar and toffee bits. Slowly pour the boiling water over top (do not stir). Bake, uncovered, until golden brown, 30-35 minutes.
3. Cool on wire rack for 30 minutes (cobbler will thicken upon cooling). Serve warm, with ice cream if desired.
1 SERVING 411 cal., 23g fat (8g sat. fat), 26mg chol., 327mg sod., 51g carb. (41g sugars, 2g fiber), 3g pro.

BANANA CRUMB PUDDING

Friends and family ask me to make my thick and creamy banana pudding for all occasions. They can't get enough of the wonderful flavor of the fruit and the vanilla wafer crumbs. You can also top the classic southern treat with meringue instead of whipped cream.
—Yvonnia Butner, Pinnacle, NC

PREP: 15 min. + chilling
COOK: 20 min. + cooling
MAKES: 15 servings

- 1 cup sugar
- ½ cup cornstarch
- 6 cups 2% milk
- 5 large egg yolks
- ¼ cup butter, cubed
- 2 tsp. vanilla extract
- 1 tsp. kosher salt
- 2 pkg. (11 oz. each) vanilla wafers
- 7 medium bananas

TOPPING
- 2 cups heavy whipping cream
- 6 Tbsp. sugar

1. In a large heavy saucepan, mix sugar and cornstarch. Whisk in milk. Cook and stir over medium heat until thickened and bubbly. Reduce heat to low; cook and stir 2 minutes longer. Remove from heat.
2. Whisk a small amount of the hot mixture into the egg yolks; return all to pan, whisking constantly. Bring to a gentle boil; cook and stir 2 minutes. Remove from heat. Stir in butter, vanilla and salt. Cool for 15 minutes, stirring occasionally.
3. Reserve 1 cup whole wafers and 1 banana for topping. Slice the remaining 6 bananas. Crush 2 cups wafers and set aside. In a 13x9-in. baking dish, place a single layer of whole wafers, filling gaps with crushed wafers. Layer with a third of the banana slices and pudding. Repeat layers twice. Press plastic wrap onto surface of pudding. Refrigerate, covered, overnight.
4. In a bowl, beat the heavy cream until it begins to thicken. Add sugar; beat until soft peaks form (do not overmix). Slice the remaining banana. Just before serving, remove plastic wrap and spread whipped cream over the pudding; top with the banana slices and reserved whole wafers.

¾ CUP 535 cal., 27g fat (13g sat. fat), 121mg chol., 370mg sod., 70g carb. (46g sugars, 1g fiber), 7g pro.

TEST KITCHEN TIP

Want to change things up? For an unexpected flavor, add 2 Tbsp. spiced rum at the same time you add the vanilla extract.

SOUTHERN BLACK-EYED PEAS

The secret to a good black-eyed peas recipe? Pork!

—Emory Doty, Jasper, GA

PREP: 20 min. + standing • **COOK:** 45 min.
MAKES: 6 servings

- 1 lb. dried black-eyed peas, sorted and rinsed
- 1 large onion, chopped
- 2 Tbsp. olive oil
- 2 oz. sliced salt pork belly, chopped
- 6 garlic cloves, minced
- 2 bay leaves
- 1 Tbsp. minced fresh thyme or 1 tsp. dried thyme
- ¼ tsp. crushed red pepper flakes
- ¼ tsp. pepper
- 1 carton (32 oz.) reduced-sodium chicken broth
- 2 smoked ham hocks

1. Place peas in a Dutch oven; add water to cover by 2 in. Bring to a boil; boil for 2 minutes. Remove from the heat; cover and let stand for 1 hour. Drain and rinse peas, discarding liquid; set aside.

2. In the same pot, saute onion in oil until tender. Add pork belly, garlic, bay leaves, thyme, pepper flakes and pepper; cook 1 minute longer.

3. Add the broth, ham hocks and peas; bring to a boil. Reduce heat; simmer, uncovered, for 35-40 minutes or until peas are tender, stirring occasionally and adding more water if desired.

4. Discard bay leaves. Remove ham hocks; cool slightly. Remove meat from bones if desired; finely chop meat and return to pot. Discard bones. If desired, top with additional fresh thyme.

¾ CUP 359 cal., 11g fat (3g sat. fat), 5mg chol., 788mg sod., 48g carb. (9g sugars, 14g fiber), 20g pro.

1 **PIECE** 639 cal., 30g fat (14g sat. fat), 123mg chol., 281mg sod., 87g carb. (67g sugars, 1g fiber), 7g pro.

MARINATED SWEET POTATO SALAD

My dad has been growing sweet potatoes for more than two decades. My brother and I have been partners in the operation for the last several years. This recipe, from our mom and our wives, is a terrific way to serve our favorite vegetable.
—*Tim Jack Edmondson, Vardaman, MS*

PREP: 40 min. + chilling
MAKES: 12 servings

- 8   medium sweet potatoes (about 4 lbs.)
- 1   cup tarragon vinegar
- ½   cup canola oil
- 1   Tbsp. honey
- 2   garlic cloves, minced
- 2   bay leaves
- ½   tsp. salt
- ¼   tsp. pepper
- ¼   tsp. dried oregano
- ¼   tsp. dried thyme
- 1   medium onion, thinly sliced
- 1   medium green pepper, julienned

1. Place sweet potatoes in a large saucepan or Dutch oven; cover with water. Bring to a boil. Reduce heat; cover and cook for 20-23 minutes or just until tender. Drain; cool slightly and peel.
2. Meanwhile, in a jar with a tight-fitting lid, combine the next 9 ingredients; shake well.
3. Cut potatoes in half lengthwise; cut potato halves into ¼-in. slices. Place in a large bowl. Add the onion and green pepper. Shake dressing; drizzle over potato mixture and gently toss to coat. Cover and refrigerate for at least 3 hours. Discard bay leaves.
¾ CUP 222 cal., 9g fat (1g sat. fat), 0 chol., 112mg sod., 33g carb. (15g sugars, 4g fiber), 2g pro. **DIABETIC EXCHANGES** 2 starch, 2 fat.

RED VELVET POUND CAKE

This delicious red velvet pound cake is the perfect combination of flavors. Make sure the cake has cooled before icing it, and for extra crunch, sprinkle some roasted pecans on top.
—*Robin Smith, Old Fort, NC*

PREP: 30 min. • **BAKE:** 70 min. + cooling
MAKES: 16 servings

- 1   cup butter, softened
- ½   cup shortening
- 3   cups sugar
- 6   large eggs, room temperature
- 2   bottles (1 oz. each) red food coloring
- 1   tsp. lemon extract
- 1   tsp. vanilla extract
- 3¼ cups all-purpose flour
- 1   Tbsp. baking cocoa
- ½   tsp. baking powder
- ½   tsp. salt
- ¾   cup 2% milk

ICING
- 1   pkg. (8 oz.) cream cheese, softened
- ¼   cup butter or margarine, softened
- ½   tsp. vanilla extract
- 3¾ cups confectioners' sugar
- ½   cup chopped pecans, toasted

1. Preheat oven to 325°. Grease and flour a 10-in. fluted tube pan; set aside.
2. In a large bowl, cream the butter, shortening and sugar until light and fluffy, 5-7 minutes. Add eggs, 1 at a time, beating well after each addition. Beat in food coloring and extracts (mixture may appear curdled). In another bowl, whisk flour, baking cocoa, baking powder and salt; add to the creamed mixture alternately with milk, beating after each addition just until combined.
3. Transfer to prepared pan. Bake until a toothpick inserted in center comes out clean, 70-75 minutes. Cool in pan 15 minutes before removing to a wire rack to cool completely.
4. In a large bowl, beat cream cheese and butter until creamy. Beat in vanilla. Gradually beat in confectioners' sugar until smooth. Spread over cake; sprinkle with pecans. Store in refrigerator.

FOURTH OF JULY

Celebrate Independence Day in the backyard with a colorful and tasty spread—from spicy appetizers to sweet, cool desserts, it's all about classic cookout food lashed with patriotic touches.

PATRIOTIC PEPPER PLATTER

Cream cheese-stuffed peppers are simple to make, easy to travel with and wonderful to eat at room temperature. This platter can be made all summer long for each red, white and blue holiday! The dish accommodates those who eat meat as well as those who don't. With or without the bacon, these peppers are delish!
—Tina Martino, Hewitt, NJ

PREP: 30 min. • **BAKE:** 25 min.
MAKES: 4 dozen

- 24   miniature sweet red peppers
- 1   pkg. (8 oz.) cream cheese, softened
- ½   cup grated Parmesan cheese
- 12   bacon strips
- 2   slices white cheddar cheese
- 1   jar (9½ oz.) pitted Greek olives, drained
      Crushed red pepper flakes, optional

1. Preheat oven 400°. Cut red peppers in half lengthwise and remove seeds; set aside. In a small bowl, beat cream cheese and Parmesan cheese until blended. Spoon into pepper halves. Cut bacon in half lengthwise. Wrap half-strips of bacon around 24 pepper halves; place in a greased 15x10x1-in. baking pan. Place unwrapped pepper halves in another 15x10x1-in. baking pan.
2. Bake until bacon is cooked and filling is bubbly, 25-30 minutes.
3. Meanwhile, using a star cookie cutter, cut stars out of cheese slices. Arrange peppers, olives and cheese stars on a serving platter to resemble an American flag. If desired, sprinkle bacon-wrapped peppers with red pepper flakes.
1 STUFFED PEPPER HALF 50 cal., 4g fat (2g sat. fat), 8mg chol., 162mg sod., 1g carb. (0 sugars, 0 fiber), 2g pro.

STRAWBERRY MELON FIZZ

Experimenting in the kitchen is so much fun. I came up with this fizzy drink by combining a recipe for a melon ball arrangement with one for a beverage.
—Teresa Messick, Montgomery, AL

TAKES: 30 min. • **MAKES:** 10 servings

- 2   cups sugar
- 1   cup water
- 5   fresh mint sprigs
- 1   qt. fresh strawberries, halved
- 2   cups cubed honeydew
- 1¾   cups cubed cantaloupe
      Ginger ale or sparkling white grape juice

1. In a large saucepan, combine the sugar, water and mint; bring to a boil. Reduce heat; simmer for 10 minutes. Remove from the heat; allow to cool completely. Discard mint.
2. Combine strawberries and melon. Just before serving, fill tall glasses with fruit and drizzle each with 1 Tbsp. syrup. Add ginger ale to each glass.
1 SERVING 194 cal., 0 fat (0 sat. fat), 0 chol., 7mg sod., 49g carb. (46g sugars, 2g fiber), 1g pro.

MAKE A STAR-SPANGLED SNACK PLATTER

Kick off your Independence Day celebration by setting out a board brimming with red, white and blue bites.

Red ... Take advantage of in-season produce like raspberries, strawberries and watermelon for bright crimson bursts. Maraschino cherries and red licorice are other options.

White ... We chose star-shaped crackers and bite-sized cubes of white cheddar cheese. Speckled cranberry Stilton and a wedge of blue cheese add touches of red and blue to a white background.

& Blue! Blueberries are the obvious choice, but figs, blackberries and grapes also have a blue hue.

Colorful Candies In addition to blueberry yogurt pretzels, select on-theme candies, like mini peanut butter cups in striped wrappers, blue M&M's and red, white and blue nonpareils.

Honey-Lime Yogurt Dip A bowl of this fruit dip anchors the board. To make it, combine 2 cups plain yogurt, ¼ cup honey, 2 Tbsp. lime juice and ½ tsp. grated lime zest. Chill until serving.

SUMMER STRAWBERRY SALAD WITH CHICKEN

I love the Strawberry Poppyseed Salad at Panera but can't always make it to the restaurant, so I created my own homemade version. It's quick, delicious and ready when I want it.
—*Diane Marie Sahley, Lakewood, OH*

TAKES: 15 min. • **MAKES:** 4 servings

- 1 pkg. (10 oz.) romaine salad mix (about 8 cups)
- 1 lb. sliced cooked chicken
- 1½ cups sliced fresh strawberries
- 1 cup pineapple tidbits, drained
- ½ cup mandarin oranges, drained
- ½ cup fresh blueberries
- ½ cup chopped pecans
- ½ cup poppyseed salad dressing

Arrange salad mix on 4 serving plates. Top with the chicken, strawberries, pineapple, mandarin oranges and blueberries. Sprinkle with pecans. Drizzle with dressing.
2 CUPS 557 cal., 31g fat (5g sat. fat), 111mg chol., 329mg sod., 34g carb. (25g sugars, 5g fiber), 37g pro.

TEST KITCHEN TIP

For more flavor and crunch, toast your pecans. Put the nuts in a dry skillet and cook over medium heat, tossing frequently, for about 5 minutes. Or spread them on a foil-lined rimmed baking sheet and bake at 350° for 5-10 minutes, stirring occasionally. When the nuts are done, immediately transfer them to a bowl to cool—then chop them and add them to your salad.

🕐 CHERRIES JUBILEE

Made with sweet or tart cherries doused in brandy, this simple dessert will be a blazing success! Created as a tribute to Queen Victoria's Diamond Jubilee, it's perfect for non-royal celebrations too!
—Taste of Home *Test Kitchen*

TAKES: 20 min. • **MAKES:** 2 cups

- ⅓ cup sugar
- 2 Tbsp. cornstarch
- ¼ cup cold water
- ¼ cup orange juice
- 4 cups fresh dark sweet cherries, pitted, or frozen pitted tart cherries, thawed
- ¼ tsp. grated orange zest
- ⅓ cup cherry brandy
- ¼ tsp. cherry extract, optional
  Vanilla ice cream and/or sliced pound cake

1. In a large saucepan, combine sugar and cornstarch. Stir the water and orange juice into the cornstarch mixture until smooth. Bring to a boil over medium heat, stirring constantly. Cook and stir until thickened, 1-2 minutes.
2. Stir in cherries and zest. Cook and stir until softened, about 5 minutes. Reduce heat to low; stir in brandy and extract, coating evenly. Carefully ignite.
3. Leaving pan on cooking surface, gently shake pan back and forth until flames are completely extinguished. Immediately serve over ice cream and/or pound cake.
¼ CUP 96 cal., 0 fat (0 sat. fat), 0 chol., 0 sod., 24g carb. (17g sugars, 1g fiber), 1g pro.

GRANDMA'S POTATO SALAD

This salad is a must for the Fourth of July feast. The red potatoes hold their shape and texture even after they are boiled.
—*Sue Gronholz, Beaver Dam, WI*

PREP: 1 hour + chilling
MAKES: 24 servings

- 6 lbs. medium red potatoes

DRESSING
- 1 cup water
- ½ cup butter, cubed
- ¼ cup white vinegar
- 2 large eggs
- ½ cup sugar
- 4½ tsp. cornstarch
- ¾ cup heavy whipping cream
- ¾ cup Miracle Whip

SALAD
- 1 small onion, finely chopped
- 2 green onions, sliced
- 1 tsp. salt
- ½ tsp. pepper
- 3 hard-boiled large eggs, sliced
   Paprika

1. Place potatoes in a stockpot and cover with water. Bring to a boil. Reduce heat; cover and cook until tender, about 20 minutes. Drain. When cool enough to handle, peel and slice potatoes; let cool completely.
2. For the dressing, in the top of a double boiler or metal bowl over barely simmering water, heat 1 cup water, butter and vinegar until butter is melted. In a small bowl, beat eggs; add sugar and cornstarch. Add to butter mixture; cook and stir until thickened, 5-7 minutes. Transfer to a large bowl; cool completely.
3. In a small bowl, beat cream until stiff peaks form. Stir Miracle Whip into cooled dressing mixture; fold in whipped cream.
4. Stir in the onion, green onions, salt and pepper. Add potatoes; toss lightly to combine. Refrigerate, covered, until chilled. To serve, top with hard-boiled eggs; sprinkle with paprika.
¾ CUP 197 cal., 10g fat (5g sat. fat), 58mg chol., 202mg sod., 24g carb. (6g sugars, 2g fiber), 4g pro.

SLOW-COOKED BAKED BEANS

My friend suggested this recipe when I needed a new dish to take to a barbecue. It was an incredible success, and I've been making it ever since.
—*Jodi Caple, Cortez, CO*

PREP: 50 min. + soaking • **COOK:** 9 hours
MAKES: 8 servings

- 1 lb. dried navy beans
- 2 cups water
- ½ cup dark molasses
- 5 slices salt pork belly (about 3 oz.), cut into ½-in. pieces
- 1 small onion, finely chopped
- 3 Tbsp. brown sugar
- 2 garlic cloves, minced
- 1 tsp. ground ginger
- ½ tsp. salt
- ½ tsp. ground mustard
- ½ tsp. pepper

1. Rinse and sort beans. Place in a large saucepan; add water to cover by 2 in. Let soak, covered, overnight. Drain and rinse beans, discarding liquid.
2. Return beans to saucepan; add water to cover by 2 in. Bring to a boil. Boil 15 minutes. Drain and rinse beans, discarding the liquid.
3. Transfer beans to a 4-qt. slow cooker. Stir in the remaining ingredients. Cook, covered, on low until beans are tender, 9-11 hours.
¾ CUP 463 cal., 20g fat (7g sat. fat), 19mg chol., 1429mg sod., 56g carb. (23g sugars, 9g fiber), 15g pro.

BLT MACARONI SALAD

A friend served this salad, and I just had to get the recipe. My husband loves BLT sandwiches, so this has become a favorite of his. It's nice to serve on hot and humid summer days, which we frequently get here in Virginia.
—*Hamilton Myers Jr., Charlottesville, VA*

TAKES: 30 min. • **MAKES:** 6 servings

- ½ cup mayonnaise
- 3 Tbsp. chili sauce
- 2 Tbsp. lemon juice
- 1 tsp. sugar
- 3 cups cooked elbow macaroni
- ½ cup chopped seeded tomato
- 2 Tbsp. chopped green onions
- 3 cups shredded lettuce
- 4 bacon strips, cooked and crumbled

In a bowl, combine the first 4 ingredients. Add the macaroni, tomato and onions; toss to coat. Cover and refrigerate. Just before serving, add lettuce and bacon; toss to coat.

¾ CUP 259 cal., 17g fat (3g sat. fat), 10mg chol., 287mg sod., 21g carb. (4g sugars, 2g fiber), 5g pro.

GOURMET BURGERS WITH SUN-DRIED TOMATO

This recipe brings together many of the flavors my family enjoys, complete with a surprise in the center of each burger. You can use almost any cheese—Gorgonzola, feta, smoked Gouda, blue or another family favorite.
—*Aaron Shields, Hamburg, NY*

PREP: 40 min. • **GRILL:** 10 min.
MAKES: 8 servings

- 1 jar (7 oz.) oil-packed sun-dried tomatoes
- 3 medium onions, halved and thinly sliced
- 3 Tbsp. balsamic vinegar
- ½ cup finely chopped red onion
- 2 Tbsp. dried basil
- 2 tsp. ground cumin
- 2 tsp. ground chipotle pepper
- ½ tsp. salt
- ¼ tsp. pepper
- 3 lbs. lean ground beef (90% lean)
- 1 cup crumbled goat cheese
- 8 hamburger buns, split
  Mixed salad greens, optional

1. Drain tomatoes, reserving ⅓ cup oil; set aside. In a large skillet, saute sliced onions in 3 Tbsp. of the reserved oil until softened. Add vinegar. Reduce heat to medium-low; cook, stirring occasionally, until deep golden brown, 30-40 minutes.

2. Meanwhile, chop sun-dried tomatoes and transfer to a large bowl. Add the red onion, seasonings and the remaining 7 tsp. reserved oil. Crumble beef over mixture and mix lightly but thoroughly. Shape into 16 thin patties. Place 2 Tbsp. goat cheese on the center of each of 8 patties. Top with the remaining patties and press edges firmly to seal.

3. Grill burgers, covered, over medium heat until a thermometer reads 160° and juices run clear, 5-7 minutes on each side.

4. Place buns, cut side down, on grill until toasted, 1-2 minutes. Serve burgers on buns with onions, and mixed greens if desired.

1 BURGER WITH 2 TBSP. ONIONS 596 cal., 32g fat (10g sat. fat), 123mg chol., 588mg sod., 36g carb. (7g sugars, 5g fiber), 42g pro.

5i
PATRIOTIC POPS

My kids love homemade ice pops, and I love knowing that the ones we make are good for them. We whip up a big batch with multiple flavors so they have many choices, but these red, white and blue ones are always a favorite!
—*Shannon Carino, Frisco, TX*

PREP: 15 min. + freezing
MAKES: 1 dozen

- 1¾ cups vanilla yogurt, divided
- 2 Tbsp. honey, divided
- 1¼ cups sliced fresh strawberries, divided
- 1¼ cups fresh or frozen blueberries, thawed, divided
- 12 freezer pop molds or 12 paper cups (3 oz. each) and wooden pop sticks

1. Place 2 Tbsp. yogurt, 1 Tbsp. honey and 1 cup strawberries in a blender; cover and process until blended. Remove to a small bowl. Chop the remaining strawberries; stir into the strawberry mixture.

2. Rinse and dry blender, then process 2 Tbsp. yogurt, the remaining 1 Tbsp. honey and 1 cup blueberries until blended; remove to another bowl. Stir in the remaining blueberries.

3. In each mold, layer 1 Tbsp. blueberry mixture, 2 Tbsp. yogurt and 1 Tbsp. strawberry mixture. Top with holders. (If using paper cups, top with foil and insert sticks through the foil.) Freeze until firm.

1 POP 55 cal., 1g fat (0 sat. fat), 2mg chol., 24mg sod., 11g carb. (10g sugars, 1g fiber), 2g pro. **DIABETIC EXCHANGES** 1 starch.

RED-WHITE-AND-BLUE BERRY DELIGHT

Loaded with fresh strawberries and blueberries, this luscious treat is perfect for any Fourth of July celebration!
—*Constance Fennell, Grand Junction, MI*

PREP: 25 min. + chilling
MAKES: 8 servings

- ½ cup sugar
- 2 envelopes unflavored gelatin
- 4 cups white cranberry-peach juice drink, divided
- 1 Tbsp. lemon juice
- 2 cups fresh strawberries, halved
- 2 cups fresh blueberries

CREAM
- ½ cup heavy whipping cream
- 1 Tbsp. sugar
- ¼ tsp. vanilla extract

1. In a large saucepan, combine sugar and gelatin. Add 1 cup cranberry-peach juice; cook and stir over low heat until gelatin is completely dissolved, about 5 minutes. Remove from the heat; stir in lemon juice and the remaining 3 cups cranberry-peach juice.
2. Place strawberries in an 8-cup ring mold coated with cooking spray; add 2 cups gelatin mixture. Refrigerate until set but not firm, about 30 minutes. Set aside the remaining gelatin mixture.
3. Stir blueberries into the remaining gelatin mixture; spoon over strawberry layer. Refrigerate overnight. Unmold onto a serving platter.
4. In a small bowl, beat cream until it begins to thicken. Add sugar and vanilla; beat until stiff peaks form. Serve with gelatin.
1 PIECE WITH 2 TBSP. WHIPPED CREAM
203 cal., 6g fat (3g sat. fat), 20mg chol., 12mg sod., 38g carb. (35g sugars, 2g fiber), 3g pro.

PULLED BBQ PORK

After years of vacationing on the North Carolina coast, I was hooked on their pork barbecue. The version I developed is a favorite at potlucks.
—*Joseph Sarnoski, West Chester, PA*

PREP: 15 min. • **COOK:** 10 hours
MAKES: 8 servings

- 2 medium onions, finely chopped
- 1 Tbsp. canola oil
- 6 garlic cloves, minced
- 1 tsp. crushed red pepper flakes
- 1 tsp. pepper
- 1 can (14½ oz.) diced tomatoes, undrained
- ¼ cup packed brown sugar
- ¼ cup cider vinegar
- 2 Tbsp. hot pepper sauce
- 1 Tbsp. Worcestershire sauce
- 1 tsp. ground cumin
- 1 boneless pork shoulder butt roast (3 to 4 lbs.)
- 8 kaiser rolls, split
  Sliced sweet pickles, optional

1. In a large skillet, saute onions in oil until tender. Add the garlic, pepper flakes and pepper; cook 1 minute longer. Stir in the tomatoes, brown sugar, vinegar, hot pepper sauce, Worcestershire and cumin. Cook over medium heat until heated through and sugar is dissolved.
2. Cut roast in half. Place in a 5-qt. slow cooker; pour sauce over top. Cook, covered, on low until meat is tender, 10-12 hours. Remove roast; cool slightly. Skim fat from cooking juices. Shred meat with 2 forks and return to the slow cooker. Heat through. With a slotted spoon, place ¾ cup meat mixture on each roll. If desired, top with pickles.
1 SANDWICH 518 cal., 21g fat (7g sat. fat), 101mg chol., 528mg sod., 44g carb. (12g sugars, 3g fiber), 36g pro.

FIREWORKS PARTY

Get ready for a sky-high celebration! Grab a blanket and a cooler—whether you're headed to the local park or a nearby rooftop, this fun spread is just what you need as you watch the show!

CHOCOLATE-COVERED STRAWBERRY SNACK MIX

I love chocolate-covered strawberries, but it's a treat you want to make only on special occasions. With a little experimenting, I've captured the same incredible flavor in a snack I can take anywhere. Everyone is always amazed when I pull these out at a picnic or tailgate, or on a car trip.
—*TerryAnn Moore, Vineland, NJ*

PREP: 15 min. + standing • **MAKES:** 2 qt.

- 6 cups Rice Chex
- 2 cups Chocolate Chex
- 1 cup semisweet chocolate chips
- ½ cup seedless strawberry jam
- 3 Tbsp. butter
- 1 tsp. almond extract
- 2 cups ground almonds
- 1 cup white baking chips
  Sprinkles, optional

1. In a large bowl, combine the cereals. In a microwave, melt the chocolate chips, jam and butter; stir until smooth. Add the extract. Pour over cereal mixture and toss to coat. Sprinkle with almonds; toss to coat.
2. Immediately spread onto waxed paper. In a microwave, melt white chips; stir until smooth. Drizzle over cereal mixture. If desired, add sprinkles. Let stand until set. Break into pieces. Store in an airtight container.
¾ CUP 443 cal., 24g fat (9g sat. fat), 11mg chol., 231mg sod., 55g carb. (33g sugars, 3g fiber), 7g pro.

CALIFORNIA ROLL WRAPS

I love the California rolls I get at sushi restaurants and wanted to get those flavors in a sandwich I could take to work. I started with the standard ingredients, then added a few others to come up with this hit.
—*Mary Pax-Shipley, Bend, OR*

TAKES: 20 min. • **MAKES:** 6 wraps

- ½ cup wasabi mayonnaise
- 6 whole wheat tortillas (8 in.), warmed
- 2 pkg. (8 oz. each) imitation crabmeat
- 1 medium ripe avocado, peeled and thinly sliced
- 1½ cups julienned peeled jicama
- 1 medium sweet red pepper, julienned
- 1 small cucumber, seeded and julienned
- ¾ cup bean sprouts

Divide the wasabi mayonnaise evenly among the 6 tortillas and spread to within ½ in. of edges. Layer with crabmeat, avocado, jicama, red pepper, cucumber and bean sprouts. Roll up tightly.
1 WRAP 365 cal., 18g fat (3g sat. fat), 10mg chol., 647mg sod., 39g carb. (2g sugars, 7g fiber), 13g pro. **DIABETIC EXCHANGES** 2 starch, 2 fat, 1 vegetable, 1 lean meat.

WATERMELON & BLACKBERRY SANGRIA

This recipe is deliciously pink! Living in the zinfandel wine country of northern California, I use our local fare in my recipes often. Our scorching summer months of July and August inspired this refreshing, light style of sangria. I like to garnish it with sprigs of mint or basil for personal flair. This easy recipe is perfect for entertaining.
—*Carolyn Kumpe, El Dorado, CA*

PREP: 5 min. + chilling
MAKES: 8 servings

- 1 bottle (750 ml) white zinfandel or rose wine, chilled
- ¼ cup watermelon schnapps liqueur
- 1½ cups cubed seedless watermelon (½-in. cubes)
- 1 medium lime, thinly sliced
- ½ to 1 cup fresh blackberries, halved
- 1 can (12 oz.) lemon-lime soda, chilled
  Ice cubes
  Fresh basil or mint leaves

In a large pitcher, stir together wine and schnapps; add watermelon, lime and blackberries. Chill at least 2 hours. Just before serving, stir in soda. Serve over ice. Garnish with basil or mint.
¾ CUP 119 cal., 0 fat (0 sat. fat), 0 chol., 10mg sod., 12g carb. (8g sugars, 1g fiber), 0 pro.

TEST KITCHEN TIP

For variety, try raspberry liqueur or peach schnapps instead of melon liqueur, and use fresh peaches and raspberries instead of watermelon and blackberries. Also, try adding fresh herbs— mint, basil, lemon balm, rosemary or lavender would be delicious.

FOCACCIA SANDWICHES

Slices of this pretty sandwich make any casual get-together more special. Add or change ingredients to your taste.
—*Peggy Woodward, Shullsburg, WI*

TAKES: 15 min. • **MAKES:** 2 dozen

- ⅓ cup mayonnaise
- 1 can (4¼ oz.) chopped ripe olives, drained
- 1 focaccia bread (about 12 oz.), split
- 4 romaine leaves
- ¼ lb. shaved deli ham
- 1 medium sweet red pepper, thinly sliced into rings
- ¼ lb. shaved deli turkey
- 1 large tomato, thinly sliced
- ¼ lb. thinly sliced hard salami
- 1 jar (7 oz.) roasted sweet red peppers, drained
- 4 to 6 slices provolone cheese

In a small bowl, combine mayonnaise and olives; spread over the bottom half of bread. Layer with the remaining ingredients; replace the bread top. Cut into 24 pieces; secure with toothpicks.
1 PIECE 113 cal., 6g fat (2g sat. fat), 13mg chol., 405mg sod., 9g carb. (1g sugars, 1g fiber), 5g pro.

SPICY SHRIMP SALSA

Radishes add wonderful crunch to this colorful salsa, and the jalapeno adds flavor without being too hot. This dip also makes a delicious topping for grilled fish.
—*Mary Relyea, Canastota, NY*

TAKES: 15 min. • **MAKES:** 2 cups

- ½ lb. cooked shrimp, peeled, deveined and chopped
- 1 large tomato, chopped
- ¼ cup finely chopped onion
- 3 radishes, chopped
- ¼ cup minced fresh cilantro
- 2 Tbsp. lime juice
- 1½ tsp. finely chopped seeded jalapeno pepper
- ¼ tsp. salt
  Baked tortilla chip scoops

In a small bowl, combine the first 8 ingredients. Refrigerate until serving. Serve with chips.
NOTE Wear disposable gloves when cutting hot peppers; the oils can burn skin. Avoid touching your face.
¼ CUP 38 cal., 1g fat (0 sat. fat), 43mg chol., 119mg sod., 2g carb. (1g sugars, 0 fiber), 6g pro. **DIABETIC EXCHANGES** 1 lean meat.

butter and sugar until light and fluffy, 5-7 minutes. Beat in eggs, 1 at a time. In another bowl, whisk 3¼ cups flour, baking soda and salt; gradually add to creamed mixture alternately with zucchini mixture, mixing well after each addition. Toss blueberries with the remaining 2 Tbsp. flour; fold into batter.
3. Transfer batter to prepared pan, spreading evenly (pan will be full). Bake 30-35 minutes or until light golden brown and a toothpick inserted in center comes out clean. Cool completely in pan on a wire rack.
4. In a small bowl, mix glaze ingredients until smooth; spread over top. Let stand until set.
NOTE If using frozen blueberries, use without thawing to avoid discoloring the batter.
1 SQUARE 270 cal., 8g fat (5g sat. fat), 36mg chol., 197mg sod., 47g carb. (33g sugars, 1g fiber), 3g pro.

BLUEBERRY ZUCCHINI SQUARES

I saw a recipe for bars using apple and lemon zest on a muffin mix box. I tried it from scratch with shredded zucchini and blueberries instead. It's a nifty combo!
—*Shelly Bevington, Hermiston, OR*

PREP: 30 min. • **BAKE:** 30 min. + cooling
MAKES: 2 dozen

- 2 cups shredded zucchini (do not pack)
- ½ cup buttermilk
- 1 Tbsp. grated lemon zest
- 3 Tbsp. lemon juice
- 1 cup butter, softened
- 2½ cups sugar
- 2 large eggs, room temperature
- 3¼ cups plus 2 Tbsp. all-purpose flour, divided
- 1 tsp. baking soda
- ½ tsp. salt
- 2 cups fresh or frozen blueberries

GLAZE
- 2 cups confectioners' sugar
- ¼ cup buttermilk
- 1 Tbsp. grated lemon zest
- 2 tsp. lemon juice
- ⅛ tsp. salt

1. Preheat oven to 350°. Grease a 15x10x1-in. baking pan; set aside.
2. In a small bowl, combine zucchini, buttermilk, lemon zest and lemon juice; toss to combine. In a large bowl, cream

LET THE FUN TIMES RING!

To pass time until the main event, try a game of ring toss! Line up bottles (full or empty) in a wooden crate, and get to tossing. Mason jar rings wrapped with yarn are an easy craft— and perfect for making soft landings. Fire away!

SUMMER FRESH PASTA SALAD

This fast and easy salad is a perfect use
for fresh seasonal vegetables. I usually
serve this salad with almond crackers
and sharp cheddar slices. So tasty!
—*Cathy Orban, Chandler, AZ*

PREP: 20 min. + chilling
MAKES: 12 servings

- 4 cups uncooked campanelle or
     spiral pasta
- 2 medium carrots, finely chopped
- 2 medium peaches, chopped
- 1 pouch (11 oz.) light tuna in water
- ½ cup sliced celery
- ½ cup julienned cucumber
- ½ cup julienned zucchini
- ½ cup fresh broccoli florets, chopped
- ½ cup grated red cabbage
- ½ tsp. salt
- ½ tsp. pepper
- 2 cups Caesar salad dressing

Cook pasta according to the package
directions for al dente. Drain; rinse with
cold water and drain well. Transfer to a
large bowl. Add carrots, peaches, tuna,
celery, cucumber, zucchini, broccoli,
cabbage, salt and pepper. Drizzle with
dressing; toss to coat. Refrigerate,
covered, at least 3 hours before serving.
¾ CUP 357 cal., 23g fat (4g sat. fat), 25mg
chol., 651mg sod., 26g carb. (5g sugars,
2g fiber), 10g pro.

ULTIMATE CLUB ROLL-UPS

Packed with meat, cheese and olives,
these roll-ups are always a hit at parties.
Experiment with different lunch meat
and salad dressing flavors.
—*Linda Searl, Pampa, TX*

TAKES: 25 min. • **MAKES:** 8 servings

- 3 oz. cream cheese, softened
- ½ cup ranch salad dressing
- 2 Tbsp. ranch salad dressing mix
- 8 bacon strips, cooked and crumbled
- ½ cup finely chopped onion
- 1 can (2¼ oz.) sliced ripe olives,
     drained
- 1 jar (2 oz.) diced pimientos, drained
- ¼ cup diced canned jalapeno peppers
- 8 flour tortillas (10 in.), room
     temperature
- 8 thin slices deli ham
- 8 thin slices deli turkey
- 8 thin slices deli roast beef
- 2 cups shredded cheddar cheese

1. In a small bowl, beat the cream
cheese, ranch dressing and salad
dressing mix until well blended. In
another bowl, combine the bacon,
onion, olives, pimientos and jalapenos.
2. Spread cream cheese mixture over
tortillas; layer with ham, turkey and
roast beef. Sprinkle with bacon mixture
and cheddar cheese; roll up.
1 ROLL-UP 554 cal., 29g fat (12g sat. fat),
80mg chol., 1802mg sod., 39g carb.
(2g sugars, 7g fiber), 27g pro.

READER REVIEW

*"Delicious, easy and they
looked professional! I omitted
the roast beef, used sandwich
toothpicks and cut these
wraps into thirds."*
—DEANNER, TASTEOFHOME.COM

CHOCOLATE CHIP-CHERRY CHUNK COOKIES

My grandma and mom created this dough, a mix of chocolate chips, cherries and spices. In summer, we use them to make ice cream sandwiches!
—*Wade Rouse, Fennville, MI*

PREP: 30 min.
BAKE: 10 min./batch + cooling
MAKES: about 4 dozen

½ cup plus 1 Tbsp. butter, softened
½ cup sugar
¼ cup packed dark brown sugar
1 large egg, room temperature
1 tsp. vanilla extract
1 tsp. maple flavoring
1½ cups all-purpose flour
5 tsp. baking cocoa
½ tsp. baking soda
¼ tsp. salt
1 cup semisweet chocolate chips
1 cup white baking chips
½ cup dried cherries or dried cranberries
¼ cup sweetened shredded coconut

1. Preheat oven to 350°. Cream butter, gradually adding sugars, until light and fluffy, 5-7 minutes. Slowly beat in egg, vanilla and maple flavoring.
2. In another bowl, sift together flour, baking cocoa, baking soda and salt. Gradually beat into the creamed mixture just until moistened (do not overbeat). Stir in semisweet chocolate and white baking chips, dried cherries and coconut.
3. Drop dough by tablespoonfuls 2 in. apart onto ungreased baking sheets. Flatten slightly. Bake until golden brown, 10-12 minutes. Cool on pans 5 minutes. Remove to wire racks to cool completely.
1 COOKIE 92 cal., 5g fat (3g sat. fat), 10mg chol., 49mg sod., 12g carb. (9g sugars, 0 fiber), 1g pro.

CHOCOLATE-DIPPED ICE CREAM CONE CUPCAKES

I created this recipe based on our family's love of chocolate-dipped ice cream cones—these sweet treats can get packed up and taken places ice cream cones can't!
—*Jennifer Gilbert, Brighton, MI*

PREP: 40 min. • **BAKE:** 15 min. + cooling
MAKES: 2 dozen

- 24 ice cream cake cones (about 3 in. tall)
- 1 pkg. French vanilla or yellow cake mix (regular size)

FROSTING
- 1 cup butter, softened
- ½ cup shortening
- 6 cups confectioners' sugar
- ¼ cup 2% milk
- 2 tsp. vanilla extract

GLAZE
- 4 cups semisweet chocolate chips
- ¼ cup shortening
  Colored sprinkles

1. Preheat oven to 350°. Grease 24 mini-muffin cups. Stand ice cream cones in additional mini-muffin cups.
2. Prepare cake mix batter according to package directions. Fill each greased muffin cup with 1 Tbsp. batter. Divide remaining batter among ice cream cones (scant 2 Tbsp. each).
3. Bake until a knife inserted in center comes out clean, 15-20 minutes. Cool in pans 5 minutes. Transfer both plain and cone cupcakes to wire racks; cool completely.
4. For frosting, beat the butter and shortening until blended. Gradually beat in confectioners' sugar, milk and vanilla on medium speed until soft peaks form.
5. To assemble, spread a small amount of frosting on the bottom of each plain cupcake; attach each to the top of a cone cupcake. Spread remaining frosting over tops of cupcakes, rounding each top to resemble a scoop of ice cream. Freeze until frosting is firm, 5-10 minutes.
6. For glaze, in a large metal bowl over simmering water, melt chocolate and shortening, stirring until smooth. Dip tops of cones in the chocolate mixture. Decorate with sprinkles. Let stand until set.

1 CONE 445 cal., 23g fat (10g sat. fat), 44mg chol., 224mg sod., 61g carb. (48g sugars, 2g fiber), 2g pro.

COLORFUL FRUIT KABOBS

These luscious fruit kabobs are perfect as a summer appetizer, snack or side dish. The citrus glaze clings well and keeps the fruit looking fresh.
—*Ruth Ann Stelfox, Raymond, AB*

TAKES: 15 min. • **MAKES:** 1 cup glaze

- Assorted fruit of your choice: Strawberries, seedless red grapes, sliced kiwifruit, sliced star fruit, kumquats, and cubes of cantaloupe, honeydew or pineapple
- ⅓ cup sugar
- 2 Tbsp. cornstarch
- 1 cup orange juice
- 2 tsp. lemon juice

Alternately thread fruit onto skewers; set aside. In a saucepan, combine the sugar, cornstarch and juices until smooth. Bring to a boil; cook and stir for 1-2 minutes or until thickened. Brush over fruit. Refrigerate until serving.

2 TSP. GLAZE 18 cal., 0 fat (0 sat. fat), 0 chol., 0 sod., 5g carb. (4g sugars, 0 fiber), 0 pro.

SUMMER BLOCK PARTY

At your next neighborhood bash, take inspiration from traditional fair food! These fun, portable treats are perfect for cooking out and carrying along as you mix and mingle with your neighbors.

FUNNEL CAKES

This funnel cake recipe is simpler to make than doughnuts, and it's just as good. Funnel cakes have been a favorite of ours since we came across them while we were living in the Ozarks.
—*Mary Faith Yoder, Unity, WI*

PREP: 15 min. • **COOK:** 5 min./batch
MAKES: 8 cakes

- 2   large eggs, room temperature
- 1   cup 2% milk
- 1   cup water
- ½   tsp. vanilla extract
- 3   cups all-purpose flour
- ¼   cup sugar
- 3   tsp. baking powder
- ¼   tsp. salt
-     Oil for deep-fat frying
-     Confectioners' sugar

1. In a large bowl, beat eggs. Add milk, water and vanilla until well blended. In another bowl, whisk flour, sugar, baking powder and salt; beat into egg mixture until smooth. In a deep cast-iron or electric skillet, heat oil to 375°.

2. For each cake: Cover the bottom of a funnel spout with your finger; ladle ½ cup batter into the funnel. Holding the funnel several inches above the oil, release your finger and move the funnel in a spiral motion until all the batter is released, scraping with a rubber spatula if needed.

3. Fry until golden brown, 2 minutes on each side. Drain on paper towels. Dust with confectioners' sugar; serve warm.

NOTE: The batter can be poured from a liquid measuring cup instead of a funnel.

1 FUNNEL CAKE 312 cal., 12g fat (2g sat. fat), 49mg chol., 287mg sod., 44g carb. (8g sugars, 1g fiber), 7g pro.

DEEP-FRIED COOKIES

My kids love this delicious, indulgent treat. I like to give the batter a kick by adding a pinch of cinnamon and a teaspoon of vanilla extract.
—*Margarita Torres, Bayamon, PR*

PREP: 10 min. + freezing • **COOK:** 15 min.
MAKES: 1½ dozen

18 wooden skewers
18 Oreo cookies
     Oil for deep-fat frying
 1 cup biscuit/baking mix
 1 large egg, room temperature
½ cup 2% milk
     Confectioners' sugar

1. On each of eighteen 4-in. wooden skewers, thread 1 cookie, inserting pointed end of skewer into filling. Freeze until firm, about 1 hour.
2. In a deep cast-iron skillet or deep fryer, heat oil to 375°. Place biscuit the mix in a shallow bowl. In another bowl, combine egg and milk; whisk into biscuit mix just until moistened.
3. Holding skewer, dip cookie into biscuit mixture to coat both sides; shake off excess.
4. Fry cookies, a few at a time, until golden brown, 1-2 minutes on each side. Drain on paper towels. Dust with confectioners' sugar before serving.
1 COOKIE 100 cal., 5g fat (1g sat. fat), 11mg chol., 123mg sod., 13g carb. (5g sugars, 1g fiber), 1g pro.

CORN DOGS

It's super easy to make homemade corn dogs that taste just like those at fairs.
—*Ruby Williams, Bogalusa, LA*

TAKES: 25 min. • **MAKES:** 10 servings

¾ cup yellow cornmeal
¾ cup self-rising flour
 1 large egg, room temperature, lightly beaten
⅔ cup 2% milk
10 pop sticks
10 hot dogs
     Oil for deep-fat frying

1. In a large bowl, combine cornmeal, flour and egg. Stir in milk to make a thick batter; let stand 4 minutes. Insert sticks into hot dogs; dip into batter.
2. In an electric skillet or deep-fat fryer, heat oil to 375°. Fry corn dogs, a few at a time, until golden brown, 6-8 minutes, turning occasionally. Drain on paper towels.
1 CORN DOG 316 cal., 23g fat (7g sat. fat), 45mg chol., 588mg sod., 18g carb. (2g sugars, 1g fiber), 8g pro.

WALKING BANANA PUDDING

This is goodness on the go! A sweet take on walking tacos, mobile banana pudding combines all the beloved ingredients, including the quintessential vanilla wafers, in single personal-size bags.
—Taste of Home *Test Kitchen*

PREP: 15 min. + chilling.
COOK: 20 min. + cooling
MAKES: 12 servings

½ cup sugar
2 Tbsp. cornstarch
⅛ tsp. salt
2½ cups 2% milk
2 large egg yolks, lightly beaten
1 Tbsp. butter
1 tsp. vanilla extract
12 pkg. (1 oz. each) miniature vanilla wafers
4 medium bananas, sliced
¾ cup frozen whipped topping, thawed

1. In a large heavy saucepan, mix sugar, cornstarch and salt. Whisk in the milk. Cook and stir over medium heat until thickened and bubbly. Reduce heat to low; cook and stir 2 minutes longer. Remove from heat.
2. In a small bowl, whisk a small amount of hot mixture into egg yolks; return all to the pan, whisking constantly. Bring to a gentle boil; cook and stir 2 minutes. Remove from heat. Stir in the butter and vanilla. Cool 15 minutes, stirring occasionally.
3. Transfer to a large bowl. Press plastic wrap onto the surface of the pudding. Refrigerate until cold.
4. Just before serving, cut open the packages of wafers. Spoon pudding into each package. Top with banana slices and whipped cream.
1 SERVING 267 cal., 10g fat (4g sat. fat), 43mg chol., 165mg sod., 42g carb. (27g sugars, 1g fiber), 3g pro.

PUDDING, PRONTO!

Don't have time to make homemade pudding? Whip up instant banana cream pudding or use store-bought banana-flavored pudding cups for these single-serving sweets.

FALAFEL CHICKEN BURGERS WITH LEMON SAUCE

This was the first recipe I created myself, and it's still a favorite. Use leftover falafel mix to bread fish, chicken and veggies or use in meatballs.
—*Nicole Mederos, Hoboken, NJ*

PREP: 35 min. • **COOK:** 10 min.
MAKES: 4 servings

4 frozen onion rings, optional
SAUCE
1 carton (5.3 oz.) fat-free lemon Greek yogurt
¼ tsp. ground cumin
¼ tsp. dill weed
⅛ tsp. salt
⅛ tsp. paprika

BURGERS
¼ cup minced fresh parsley
3 Tbsp. crumbled cooked bacon
3 garlic cloves, minced
¾ tsp. salt
¾ tsp. curry powder
½ tsp. pepper
¼ tsp. ground cumin
1 lb. ground chicken
1 pkg. (6 oz.) falafel mix
4 tsp. canola oil
4 sesame seed hamburger buns, split
1 cup fresh arugula or baby spinach
Optional: Sliced tomato and cucumber

1. If desired, prepare onion rings according to the package directions.
2. Meanwhile, in a small bowl, mix the sauce ingredients. In a large bowl, mix the first 7 burger ingredients. Add chicken; mix lightly but thoroughly. Shape into four ½-in.-thick patties. Place ½ cup falafel mix in a shallow bowl (save remaining mix for another use). Press the patties into the falafel mix, patting to help coating adhere.
3. In a large nonstick skillet, heat oil over medium-high heat. Add burgers; cook 4-5 minutes on each side or until a thermometer reads 165°. Serve the burgers on buns with sauce and arugula; if desired, add an onion ring, sliced tomato and cucumber slices to each.
1 BURGER 435 cal., 22g fat (5g sat. fat), 86mg chol., 1036mg sod., 33g carb. (9g sugars, 3g fiber), 32g pro.

BACKYARD BLOCKBUSTER

Jenga is the ultimate theme-appropriate game for a block party. The towering wooden block game is simple, inexpensive and endlessly entertaining. If you'd like, paint the plain brown pieces all different shades for a much-needed pop of color.

JALAPENO POPPER MEXICAN STREET CORN

One of the best things about summer is fresh sweet corn, and this recipe is a standout. We love its creamy dressing, crunchy panko coating and spicy jalapeno kick. If you're really feeling wild, sprinkle these with a bit of cooked and crumbled bacon!
—Crystal Schlueter, Northglenn, CO

TAKES: 30 min. • **MAKES:** 4 servings

- 4   ears fresh sweet corn
- 2   jalapeno peppers
- 3   Tbsp. canola oil, divided
- ¾ tsp. salt, divided
- ¼ cup panko bread crumbs
- ½ tsp. smoked paprika
- ½ tsp. dried Mexican oregano
- 4   oz. cream cheese, softened
- ¼ cup media crema table cream or sour cream thinned with 1 tsp. 2% milk
- 2   Tbsp. lime juice
     Ground chipotle pepper or chili powder
     Optional: Chopped fresh cilantro and lime wedges

1. Husk corn. Rub corn and jalapenos with 2 Tbsp. canola oil. Grill, covered, on a greased grill rack over medium-high direct heat until lightly charred on all sides, 10-12 minutes. Remove from heat. When the jalapenos are cool enough to handle, remove skin, seeds and membranes; chop finely. Set aside.
2. Sprinkle corn with ½ tsp. salt. In a small skillet, heat remaining oil over medium heat. Add panko; cook and stir until starting to brown. Add paprika and oregano; cook until crumbs are toasted and fragrant.
3. Meanwhile, combine cream cheese, crema, lime juice and remaining salt; spread over corn. Sprinkle with bread crumbs, jalapenos and chipotle pepper. If desired, sprinkle with cilantro and serve with lime wedges.

NOTE This recipe was tested with Nestle crema; look for it in the international foods section.

1 EAR OF CORN 339 cal., 26g fat (9g sat. fat), 39mg chol., 568mg sod., 25g carb. (8g sugars, 3g fiber), 6g pro.

LOADED PULLED PORK CUPS

Potato nests are simple to make and surprisingly handy for pulled pork, cheese, sour cream and other toppings. Make, bake, and collect the compliments.
—Melissa Sperka, Greensboro, NC

PREP: 40 min. • **BAKE:** 25 min.
MAKES: 1½ dozen

- 1   pkg. (20 oz.) refrigerated shredded hash brown potatoes
- ¾ cup shredded Parmesan cheese
- 2   large egg whites, beaten
- 1   tsp. garlic salt
- ½ tsp. onion powder
- ¼ tsp. pepper
- 1   carton (16 oz.) refrigerated fully cooked barbecued shredded pork
- 1   cup shredded Colby-Monterey Jack cheese
- ½ cup sour cream
- 5   bacon strips, cooked and crumbled Minced chives

1. Preheat oven to 450°. In a large bowl, mix hash browns, Parmesan cheese, egg whites and seasonings until blended. Divide the potato mixture among 18 well-greased muffin cups; press on the bottoms and up sides to form cups.
2. Bake until edges are dark golden brown, 22-25 minutes. Carefully run a knife around side of each cup. Cool 5 minutes before removing from pans to a serving platter. Meanwhile, heat pulled pork according to package directions.
3. Sprinkle cheese into cups. Top with pork, sour cream and bacon; sprinkle with chives. Serve warm.

1 HASH BROWN CUP 129 cal., 6g fat (3g sat. fat), 19mg chol., 439mg sod., 11g carb. (4g sugars, 0 fiber), 8g pro.

TOASTED COCONUT MILKSHAKES

I created this recipe as a reminder of my oldest brother, Brad, who was a picky eater who loved any dessert with coconut. It has a short list of ingredients, but it's certainly tall on coconut flavor!
—Laurie Hudson, Westville, FL

TAKES: 15 min. • **MAKES:** 4 servings

- ½ cup flaked coconut
- ⅔ cup coconut milk, stirred before measuring, then chilled
- ½ cup cream of coconut, stirred before measuring, then chilled
- 4   cups vanilla ice cream
     Sweetened whipped cream

1. In a small skillet, cook and stir the coconut over medium-low heat until toasted, 6-8 minutes. Let cool completely.
2. Place coconut milk, cream of coconut, ¼ cup toasted coconut and ice cream in a blender; cover and process until blended.
3. Pour into 4 glasses. Top with whipped cream; sprinkle with remaining coconut. Serve immediately.

1 CUP 502 cal., 30g fat (23g sat. fat), 58mg chol., 161mg sod., 54g carb. (51g sugars, 1g fiber), 6g pro.

5j
ORANGE CREAM POPS

For a lower-fat alternative to ice cream pops, try this citrus novelty. The tangy orange flavor will make your taste buds tingle, while the silky smooth texture offers cool comfort.
—Taste of Home *Test Kitchen*

PREP: 10 min. + freezing
MAKES: 10 pops

- 1   pkg. (3 oz.) orange gelatin
- 1   cup boiling water
- 1   cup vanilla yogurt
- ½   cup 2% milk
- ½   tsp. vanilla extract
- 10 freezer pop molds or 10 paper cups (3 oz. each) and wooden pop sticks

In a large bowl, dissolve gelatin in boiling water. Cool to room temperature. Stir in yogurt, milk and vanilla. Pour ¼ cup mixture into each mold or paper cup. Top molds with holders. If using cups, top with foil and insert pop sticks through foil. Freeze until firm.

1 POP 58 cal., 1g fat (0 sat. fat), 2mg chol., 41mg sod., 11g carb. (11g sugars, 0 fiber), 2g pro. **DIABETIC EXCHANGES** 1 starch.

SOUVLAKI PITA POCKETS

This is a favorite at our house, especially in summer. A quick trip to the market for very few ingredients results in gourmet-style Greek sandwiches we enjoy outdoors by the grill. A simple Greek salad on the side is a nice addition.
—*Becky A. Drees, Pittsfield, MA*

PREP: 20 min. + marinating
GRILL: 10 min. • **MAKES:** 6 servings

- 5   medium lemons, divided
- 4   Tbsp. olive oil
- 4   garlic cloves, minced
- 2   tsp. dried oregano
- ½   tsp. salt
- ¼   tsp. pepper
- 2   lbs. boneless skinless chicken breasts, cut into 1-in. pieces
- 6   whole pita breads
- 1   carton (8 oz.) refrigerated tzatziki sauce

Optional: Chopped tomatoes and cucumber, sliced red onion and fresh dill sprigs

1. Cut 3 lemons crosswise in half; squeeze juice from lemons. Transfer juice to a large bowl or shallow dish. Whisk in oil, garlic, oregano, salt and pepper. Add chicken; turn to coat. Refrigerate 1 hour.

2. Drain chicken, discarding marinade. Thinly slice remaining 2 lemons. On 12 metal or soaked wooden skewers, alternately thread chicken and lemon slices. Grill the kabobs, covered, over medium heat (or broil 4 in. from heat) until chicken is no longer pink, about 10 minutes, turning occasionally. Serve with pita bread, tzatziki sauce and toppings as desired.

1 PITA 369 cal., 8g fat (2g sat. fat), 90mg chol., 462mg sod., 34g carb. (2g sugars, 1g fiber), 37g pro. **DIABETIC EXCHANGES** 5 lean meat, 2 starch, 1 fat.

CHICKEN SKEWERS WITH COOL AVOCADO SAUCE

I'm always looking for lighter recipes to take on tailgate outings—and this one works fabulously for grilling. Just whip up the marinade, add the chicken and take it along to the pregame festivities.
—*Veronica Callaghan, Glastonbury, CT*

PREP: 25 min. + marinating
GRILL: 10 min.
MAKES: 16 skewers (¾ cup sauce)

- 1 lb. boneless skinless chicken breasts
- ½ cup lime juice
- 1 Tbsp. balsamic vinegar
- 2 tsp. minced chipotle pepper in adobo sauce
- ½ tsp. salt

SAUCE
- 1 medium ripe avocado, peeled and pitted
- ½ cup fat-free sour cream
- 2 Tbsp. minced fresh cilantro
- 2 tsp. lime juice
- 1 tsp. grated lime zest
- ¼ tsp. salt

1. Flatten chicken to ¼-in. thickness; cut lengthwise into sixteen 1-in.-wide strips. In a large bowl, combine the lime juice, vinegar, chipotle pepper and salt; add the chicken and turn to coat. Cover and refrigerate for 30 minutes.
2. Meanwhile, place sauce ingredients in a food processor; cover and process until blended. Transfer to a serving bowl; cover and refrigerate until serving.
3. Drain chicken, discarding marinade. Thread meat onto metal or soaked wooden skewers. On a lightly oiled rack, grill skewers, covered, over medium heat (or broil 4 in. from the heat) for 8-12 minutes or until chicken is no longer pink, turning frequently. Serve with sauce.

1 SKEWER WITH ABOUT 2 TSP. SAUCE
59 cal., 3g fat (0 sat. fat), 17mg chol., 74mg sod., 3g carb. (1g sugars, 1g fiber), 6g pro.
DIABETIC EXCHANGES 1 lean meat, ½ fat.

BEST TAILGATE EVER

Game day means it's time for a party! Tailgating can be as simple as a cooler of tasty dips and drinks, or a full spread with a grill, covered dishes and tents—and competition for the best dish is as fierce as anything on the field!

⏱ 5i BARBECUE SLIDERS

When company dropped in by surprise, all I had defrosted was sausage and ground beef. We combined the two for juicy burgers on the grill.
—B.J. Larsen, Erie, CO

TAKES: 25 min. • **MAKES:** 8 servings

- 1 lb. ground beef
- 1 lb. bulk pork sausage
- 1 cup barbecue sauce, divided
- 16 Hawaiian sweet rolls, split
  Optional: Lettuce leaves, sliced plum tomatoes and red onion

1. In a large bowl, mix beef and sausage lightly but thoroughly. Shape into sixteen ½-in.-thick patties.

2. Grill patties, covered, over medium heat or broil 4-5 in. from heat until a thermometer reads 160°, 3-4 minutes on each side. Brush with ¼ cup sauce during the last 2 minutes of cooking. Serve on rolls with remaining barbecue sauce; top as desired.

FREEZE OPTION Place patties on a waxed paper-lined baking sheet; cover and freeze until firm. Remove from pan and transfer to an airtight container; return to freezer. To use, grill frozen patties as directed, increasing time as necessary.

HEALTH TIP Make these with 90% lean ground beef and turkey breakfast sausage to save nearly 100 calories and more than half the fat per serving.

2 SLIDERS 499 cal., 24g fat (9g sat. fat), 96mg chol., 885mg sod., 47g carb. (23g sugars, 2g fiber), 24g pro.

⏱ 5i EASY BUFFALO CHICKEN DIP

Everyone will simply devour this savory and delicious dip with shredded chicken throughout. The spicy kick makes it perfect game-day food, and the recipe always brings raves.
—Janice Foltz, Hershey, PA

TAKES: 30 min. • **MAKES:** 4 cups

- 1 pkg. (8 oz.) reduced-fat cream cheese
- 1 cup reduced-fat sour cream
- ½ cup Louisiana-style hot sauce
- 3 cups shredded cooked chicken breast
  Assorted crackers

1. Preheat oven to 350°. In a large bowl, beat cream cheese, sour cream and hot sauce until smooth; stir in chicken.
2. Transfer to an 8-in. square baking dish coated with cooking spray. Cover and bake until heated through, 18-22 minutes. Serve warm with crackers.

3 TBSP. 77 cal., 4g fat (2g sat. fat), 28mg chol., 71mg sod., 1g carb. (1g sugars, 0 fiber), 8g pro.

LISA'S ALL-DAY SUGAR & SALT PORK ROAST

My family loves this tender and juicy roast, so we eat it a lot. The salty crust is so delicious mixed into the pulled pork.
—*Lisa Allen, Joppa, AL*

PREP: 15 min. + chilling
COOK: 6 hours 10 min.
MAKES: 12 servings

- 1 cup plus 1 Tbsp. sea salt, divided
- 1 cup sugar
- 1 bone-in pork shoulder butt roast (6 to 8 lbs.)
- ¼ cup barbecue seasoning
- ½ tsp. pepper
- ½ cup packed brown sugar
- 12 hamburger buns or kaiser rolls, split

1. Combine 1 cup sea salt and sugar; rub onto all sides of roast. Place in a shallow dish; refrigerate, covered, overnight.
2. Preheat oven to 300°. Using a kitchen knife, scrape salt and sugar coating from roast; discard any accumulated juices. Transfer pork to a large shallow roasting pan. Rub with the barbecue seasoning; sprinkle with pepper. Roast until tender, 6-8 hours.
3. Increase oven temperature to 500°. Combine brown sugar and the remaining 1 Tbsp. sea salt; sprinkle over cooked pork. Return pork to the oven and roast until a crisp crust forms, 10-15 minutes. Remove; when cool enough to handle, shred meat with 2 forks. Serve warm on buns or rolls.
FREEZE OPTION Freeze cooled meat with some of the juices in freezer containers. To use, partially thaw in refrigerator overnight. Heat through in a saucepan, stirring occasionally; add water if necessary.
1 SANDWICH 534 cal., 24g fat (9g sat. fat), 135mg chol., 2240mg sod., 33g carb. (14g sugars, 1g fiber), 43g pro.

DR PEPPER RIBS

These beautifully sweet and saucy ribs marinate in Dr Pepper overnight, which tenderizes the pork and adds a subtle soda flavor that pairs well with the spices in the homemade rub. After they bake low and slow, the ribs are finished with a Dr Pepper and barbecue sauce glaze.
—*Taste of Home Test Kitchen*

PREP: 15 min. + marinating
BAKE: 1 hour 55 min. • **MAKES:** 8 servings

- 6 lbs. pork baby back ribs, cut into 8 pieces
- 2 liters Dr Pepper, divided
- ⅓ cup packed brown sugar
- 2 Tbsp. chili powder
- 2 tsp. ground cumin
- 1 tsp. garlic powder
- 1 tsp. salt
- 1 cup barbecue sauce

1. Arrange ribs in a large shallow dish. Add Dr Pepper, reserving ¼ cup; turn to coat. Refrigerate remaining Dr Pepper. Cover and refrigerate ribs 8 hours or overnight. Drain ribs, discarding the marinade.
2. Preheat oven to 325°. In a small bowl, combine brown sugar, chili powder, ground cumin, garlic powder and salt; rub over ribs. Place ribs in a shallow roasting pan, bone side down. Bake, covered tightly with foil, until tender, 1½-2 hours.
3. Combine barbecue sauce and the remaining ¼ cup Dr Pepper. Brush half the sauce over ribs. Bake, uncovered, 25-30 minutes or until ribs are glazed, brushing occasionally with remaining sauce.
5 OZ. COOKED PORK 530 cal., 32g fat (11g sat. fat), 122mg chol., 844mg sod., 25g carb. (21g sugars, 1g fiber), 34g pro.

GRILLED CORN RELISH

This colorful relish is a great way to get kids to eat their veggies. It's an instant upgrade for hot dogs!
—*Ellen Riley, Murfreesboro, TN*

TAKES: 25 min. • **MAKES:** 2 cups

- 1 large sweet red pepper
- 2 medium ears sweet corn, husked
- 5 Tbsp. honey Dijon vinaigrette, divided
- 2 green onions, thinly sliced
- ½ tsp. coarsely ground pepper
- ¼ tsp. salt

1. Cut red pepper lengthwise in half; remove seeds. Grill red pepper and corn, covered, over medium heat 10-15 minutes or until tender, turning and basting occasionally with 3 Tbsp. vinaigrette.
2. Remove corn from cobs and chop red pepper; transfer to a small bowl. Add green onions, pepper, salt and remaining vinaigrette; toss to combine.
¼ CUP 42 cal., 1g fat (0 sat. fat), 0 chol., 157mg sod., 8g carb. (4g sugars, 1g fiber), 1g pro. **DIABETIC EXCHANGES** ½ starch.

FRESH TOMATO RELISH

My two grown sons actually eat this as a salad, but that's a bit too hot for me! The recipe's from my late husband's mother, and I haven't varied it over the years. I usually make a batch as soon as the first tomatoes of the season are ready.
—*Lela Baskins, Windsor, MO*

PREP: 30 min. + cooling
MAKES: about 6 pints

- 2 cups white vinegar
- ½ cup sugar
- 8 cups chopped tomatoes (about 11 large)
- ½ cup chopped onion
- 1 medium green pepper, diced
- 1 celery rib, diced
- ¼ cup prepared horseradish

- 2 Tbsp. salt
- 1 Tbsp. mustard seed
- 1½ tsp. pepper
- ½ tsp. ground cinnamon
- ½ tsp. ground cloves

1. In a large saucepan, bring vinegar and sugar to a boil. Remove from the heat; cool completely.
2. In a large bowl, combine remaining ingredients; add vinegar mixture and mix well. Spoon into storage containers, allowing ½ in. of headspace. Refrigerate up to 2 weeks or freeze up to 12 months. Serve with a slotted spoon.
2 TBSP. 9 cal., 0 fat (0 sat. fat), 0 chol., 151mg sod., 2g carb. (2g sugars, 0 fiber), 0 pro.

VIDALIA ONION RELISH

Burgers and brats get the star treatment with this sweet onion topping. Bourbon adds a lovely caramel note, and the crushed pepper flakes turn up the heat.
—*Janet Roth, Tempe, AZ*

PREP: 20 min. • **COOK:** 1 hour
MAKES: 3 cups

- 4 large sweet onions, chopped
- 2 Tbsp. canola oil
- 3 garlic cloves, minced
- ⅓ cup bourbon
- 4 plum tomatoes, peeled, seeded and chopped
- ½ cup golden raisins
- ¼ cup sugar
- ¼ cup packed dark brown sugar
- ¼ cup cider vinegar
- 1 tsp. mustard seed
- ½ tsp. salt
- ½ tsp. ground turmeric
- ½ tsp. ground mustard
- ½ tsp. crushed red pepper flakes
- ¼ tsp. pepper
  Cooked sausage or meat of your choice

1. In a large saucepan, cook onions in oil over medium heat 40-45 minutes or until onions are golden brown, stirring

occasionally. Add garlic; cook 1 minute longer. Remove from heat. Add bourbon, stirring to loosen browned bits from pan.
2. Stir in next 11 ingredients; bring to a boil. Reduce heat; simmer, uncovered, 15-20 minutes or until thickened. Store in airtight containers in the refrigerator up to 1 week. Serve with sausage or other meat.
2 TBSP. 65 cal., 1g fat (0 sat. fat), 0 chol., 56mg sod., 12g carb. (9g sugars, 1g fiber), 1g pro. **DIABETIC EXCHANGES** 1 starch.

TEST KITCHEN TIP

Grilling your dogs on site makes for the freshest taste, but there are other options if you don't have a grill ready. You can prep hot dogs in advance by slow-cooking, boiling, pan-frying or baking, then bring them along in a covered dish. If you're having a campfire, thread your hot dogs lengthwise onto a cooking fork, then rotate them over an open fire for 2-4 minutes or until heated through.

RELISH THE TOPPINGS

Set up a hot dog station with a variety of buns and condiments so guests can fashion their favorite frank.

FRESH TOMATO RELISH

VIDALIA ONION RELISH

GRILLED CORN RELISH

COKE COLA CAKE

We live in Coca-Cola country, and we all love a cake made with the soft drink. Our rich version does the tradition proud.
—Heidi Jobe, Carrollton, GA

PREP: 25 min. • **BAKE:** 25 min.
MAKES: 15 servings

- 2   cups all-purpose flour
- 2   cups sugar
- 1   tsp. baking soda
- ½   tsp. salt
- ½   tsp. ground cinnamon
- 1   can (12 oz.) cola
- 1   cup butter, cubed
- ¼   cup baking cocoa
- 2   large eggs, room temperature
- ½   cup buttermilk
- 1   tsp. vanilla extract

GLAZE

- 1   can (12 oz.) cola
- ½   cup butter, cubed
- ¼   cup baking cocoa
- 4   cups confectioners' sugar, sifted

1. Preheat oven to 350°. Grease a 13x9-in. baking pan.
2. In a large bowl, whisk the first 5 ingredients. In a small saucepan, combine cola, butter and cocoa; bring just to a boil, stirring occasionally. Add to the flour mixture, stirring just until moistened.
3. In a small bowl, whisk eggs, buttermilk and vanilla until blended; add to the flour mixture, whisking constantly.
4. Transfer batter to prepared pan. Bake 25-30 minutes or until a toothpick inserted in center comes out clean.
5. About 15 minutes before cake is done, prepare glaze. In a small saucepan, bring cola to a boil; cook 12-15 minutes or until liquid is reduced to ½ cup. Stir in butter and cocoa until butter is melted; remove from heat. Add confectioners' sugar; stir until smooth. Pour immediately over hot cake.

1 PIECE 491 cal., 20g fat (12g sat. fat), 74mg chol., 346mg sod., 78g carb. (63g sugars, 1g fiber), 4g pro.

CARAMELIZED HAM & SWISS BUNS

My next-door neighbor shared this recipe with me and I simply cannot improve it! You can make it ahead and cook it quickly when company arrives. The combo of poppy seeds, ham, cheese, horseradish and brown sugar makes it so delicious.
—Iris Weihemuller, Baxter, MN

PREP: 25 min. + chilling • **BAKE:** 30 min.
MAKES: 1 dozen

- 1   pkg. (12 oz.) Hawaiian sweet rolls
- ½   cup horseradish sauce
- ¾   lb. sliced deli ham
- 6   slices Swiss cheese, halved
- ½   cup butter, cubed
- 2   Tbsp. finely chopped onion
- 2   Tbsp. brown sugar
- 1   Tbsp. spicy brown mustard
- 2   tsp. poppy seeds
- 1½   tsp. Worcestershire sauce
- ¼   tsp. garlic powder

1. Without separating the rolls, cut rolls in half horizontally. Arrange bottom halves of rolls in a greased 9x9-in. baking pan. Spread cut side of roll bottoms with horseradish sauce. Layer with ham and cheese; replace top half of the rolls.
2. In a small skillet, heat butter over medium-high heat. Add onion; cook and stir until tender, 1-2 minutes. Stir in remaining ingredients. Pour over rolls. Refrigerate, covered, for several hours or overnight.
3. Preheat oven to 350°. Remove rolls from refrigerator 30 minutes before baking. Bake, covered, 25 minutes. Uncover and bake until golden brown, 5-10 minutes longer.

1 SANDWICH 315 cal., 17g fat (9g sat. fat), 61mg chol., 555mg sod., 29g carb. (13g sugars, 2g fiber), 13g pro.

CARAMEL BROWNIES

I love to cook. My family can't possibly eat all the sweets I whip up, so my co-workers are more than happy to help—particularly with these rich, chewy brownies that are full of gooey caramel, chocolate chips and crunchy walnuts.
—*Clara Bakke, Coon Rapids, MN*

PREP: 20 min. • **BAKE:** 50 min. + cooling
MAKES: 2 dozen

- 2 cups sugar
- 1 cup canola oil
- ¾ cup baking cocoa
- 4 large eggs, room temperature
- ¼ cup 2% milk
- 1½ cups all-purpose flour
- 1 tsp. salt
- 1 tsp. baking powder
- 1 cup semisweet chocolate chips
- 1 cup chopped walnuts, divided
- 1 pkg. (11 oz.) caramels
- ⅓ cup sweetened condensed milk

1. Preheat oven to 350°. In a large bowl, beat sugar, oil, cocoa, eggs and milk. In another bowl, combine flour, salt and baking powder; gradually add to the egg mixture until well blended. Fold in chocolate chips and ½ cup walnuts.
2. Spoon two-thirds of the batter into a greased 13x9-in. baking pan. Bake for 12 minutes.
3. Meanwhile, in a large saucepan, heat caramels and condensed milk over low heat until caramels are melted, stirring frequently. Pour over baked brownie layer. Sprinkle with remaining ½ cup walnuts.
4. Drop remaining batter by teaspoonfuls over caramel layer. Carefully swirl the brownie batter with a knife.
5. Bake until a toothpick inserted in center comes out with moist crumbs (do not overbake), 35-40 minutes longer. Cool completely on a wire rack.
1 BROWNIE 325 cal., 17g fat (3g sat. fat), 34mg chol., 170mg sod., 42g carb. (32g sugars, 1g fiber), 4g pro.

DEVILED EGGS WITH BACON

These yummy deviled eggs went over so well at our summer cookouts, I started making them for holiday dinners as well. Everyone likes the flavorful addition of crumbled bacon.
—*Barbara Reid, Mounds, OK*

TAKES: 30 min. • **MAKES:** 2 dozen

- 12 hard-boiled large eggs
- ⅓ cup mayonnaise
- 3 bacon strips, cooked and crumbled
- 3 Tbsp. finely chopped red onion
- 3 Tbsp. sweet pickle relish
- ¼ tsp. smoked paprika

Cut eggs in half lengthwise. Remove yolks; set whites aside. In a small bowl, mash yolks. Add the mayonnaise, bacon, onion and relish; mix well. Spoon or pipe filling into egg whites. Refrigerate until serving. Sprinkle with paprika.
1 STUFFED EGG HALF 67 cal., 5g fat (1g sat. fat), 95mg chol., 80mg sod., 1g carb. (1g sugars, 0 fiber), 4g pro.

READER REVIEW

"[When I make] these, the first half I omit the bacon for my vegetarian family and add a black olive so they know they are bacon free—then I add the bacon to the second half with a stuffed green olive on top to indicate they have bacon."
—MRPRISSY, TASTEOFHOME.COM

PIMIENTO CHEESE

I love pimiento cheese, but I've never made my own—this was a fun challenge! Serve cold on crackers or sandwiches. Drizzle with honey for added flavor; I used hot honey, which was great!
—*Darla Andrews, Boerne, TX*

TAKES: 10 min. • **MAKES:** 3 cups

- 1 pkg. (8 oz.) cream cheese, softened
- 2 green onions, chopped
- 2 Tbsp. mayonnaise
- ½ tsp. salt
- ½ tsp. onion powder
- ½ tsp. garlic powder
- ½ tsp. smoked paprika
- ¼ tsp. pepper
- 1 jar (4 oz.) diced pimientos, drained
- 2 cups shredded cheddar cheese
  Hot chile-infused honey, optional

Place the first 8 ingredients in a food processor. Process until smooth. Add cheddar cheese and pimientos. Pulse until combined. If desired, drizzle with honey before serving.
2 TBSP. 81 cal., 7g fat (4g sat. fat), 19mg chol., 147mg sod., 1g carb. (1g sugars, 0 fiber), 3g pro.

BBQ BRATS

In Wisconsin, brats are their own food group! We are always looking for new ways to cook them. This recipe is easy and a hit at any tailgate party or cookout, any time of year.
—*Jessica Abnet, DePere, WI*

PREP: 20 min. • **COOK:** 3 hours
MAKES: 10 servings

- 10 uncooked bratwurst links
- 1 bottle (12 oz.) beer or 1½ cups chicken broth
- 1 cup ketchup
- 1 cup honey barbecue sauce
- 10 hot dog buns, split
  Spicy brown mustard

1. Grill bratwursts, covered, on a greased rack over medium heat or broil 4 in. from heat 10 minutes, turning frequently. Transfer to a 5-qt. slow cooker.
2. In a large bowl, mix beer, ketchup and barbecue sauce; pour over bratwursts. Cook, covered, on low until cooked through, 3-4 hours. Place bratwursts in buns. Serve with mustard and, if desired, cooking liquid.
1 SERVING 480 cal., 27g fat (9g sat. fat), 64mg chol., 1659mg sod., 41g carb. (20g sugars, 1g fiber), 16g pro.

TEST KITCHEN TIP

If you prefer, you can brown the brats in a skillet on the stovetop, rather than grilling them, before transferring them to the slow cooker.

⑤ⁱ SLOW-COOKER BARBECUE PULLED PORK SANDWICHES

Foolproof and wonderfully delicious describes my barbecue pork recipe. Just four ingredients and a slow cooker make a fabulous dish with little effort from you.
—*Sarah Johnson, Chicago, IL*

PREP: 15 min. • **COOK:** 7 hours
MAKES: 6 servings

- 1 lemon-garlic pork loin fillet (about 1⅓ lbs.)
- 1 can (12 oz.) Dr Pepper
- 1 bottle (18 oz.) barbecue sauce
- 6 hamburger buns, split

1. Place pork in a 3-qt. slow cooker. Pour Dr Pepper over top. Cover and cook on low until meat is tender, 7-9 hours.
2. Remove meat; cool slightly. Discard cooking juices. Shred the meat with 2 forks and return to slow cooker. Stir in barbecue sauce; heat through. Serve on buns.
FREEZE OPTION Place individual portions of cooled meat mixture and juice in freezer containers. To use, partially thaw in refrigerator overnight. Microwave, covered, on high in a microwave-safe dish until heated through, stirring occasionally; add broth or water if necessary.
1 SANDWICH 348 cal., 8g fat (2g sat. fat), 45mg chol., 1695mg sod., 43g carb. (22g sugars, 2g fiber), 25g pro.

LEMONADE STAND

Let's make lemonade! Host a lemon-themed lawn party to keep your kids company as they charm walk-by customers with fresh-squeezed lemonade and some sweet-tart homemade treats.

FETA DIP

The base of this whipped feta dip is a fantastic blank canvas for different flavors. This version is flavored with garlic and lemon, but you might try other flavors such as roasted red pepper and Greek olive, or a spicy version with crushed red pepper flakes.
—*Dawn Parker, Surrey, BC*

TAKES: 10 min. • **MAKES:** 1⅓ cups

- 8 oz. feta cheese, crumbled
- ½ cup plain Greek yogurt
- 1 tsp. Greek seasoning
- 1 garlic clove, chopped
- ¾ tsp. grated lemon zest
- 1 Tbsp. extra virgin olive oil
  Fresh mint

Place the first 5 ingredients in a food processor; process until smooth. Spoon into serving dish; drizzle with olive oil and sprinkle with mint.
2 TBSP. 85 cal., 7g fat (4g sat. fat), 23mg chol., 311mg sod., 2g carb. (1g sugars, 0 fiber), 4g pro.

CRATE CREATION

For a simple centerpiece, load lemons in stacked milk crates. The wooden boxes evoke classic Americana—and show customers your lemonade doesn't come from a mix!

LEMONY CHICKEN SALAD

Every busy cook will appreciate the convenience of being able to prepare this refreshing salad ahead of time. And your family will enjoy a marvelous meal.
—*Joan Gatling, Bernalillo, NM*

PREP: 25 min. + chilling
MAKES: 8 servings

- ⅔ cup Miracle Whip or mayonnaise
- ⅔ cup sour cream
- 1 Tbsp. lemon juice
- 1½ tsp. grated lemon zest
- 1 tsp. salt
- ½ tsp. dried tarragon
- ¼ tsp. pepper
- 4 cups diced cooked chicken
- 1 cup thinly sliced celery
- 1 cup chopped green pepper
- 2 large red apples, cut into ½-in. pieces, optional
- ½ cup chopped onion
- ¼ cup minced fresh parsley
- 1 cup chopped walnuts

In a large bowl, combine the first 7 ingredients. Stir in chicken, celery, green pepper, apples if desired, onion and parsley. Cover and refrigerate for several hours. Stir in the walnuts just before serving.
1 CUP 333 cal., 23g fat (5g sat. fat), 83mg chol., 508mg sod., 8g carb. (4g sugars, 2g fiber), 24g pro.

LEMONADE 5 WAYS

These juicy spins on the traditional sipper are sure to hit the spot. Made with the same 3 basic components—lemon-flavored simple syrup, water and lemon juice—they're easy to stir up.

Berry: Substitute 1 cup strained pureed fresh berries (strawberries or raspberries) for 1 cup water when making the syrup.

Lavender: Add 1 tsp. dried lavender with the lemon zest in the syrup. Strain after cooling.

Ginger-Mint: Add 1 Tbsp. grated fresh ginger and ¼ cup fresh mint leaves with the lemon zest in the syrup. Strain after cooling.

Limeade: Substitute lime zest for lemon zest and limes for lemons.

Spike it! For an adults-only version, add 1 oz. bourbon or vodka to a tall glass of lemonade. Rim the glass with sugar for an extra-fancy cocktail.

OLD-FASHIONED LEMONADE

This sweet-tart lemonade is a traditional part of my Memorial Day and Fourth of July menus. Folks can't get enough of it.
—*Tammi Simpson, Greensburg, KY*

PREP: 10 min. • **COOK:** 5 min. + chilling
MAKES: 7 servings

- 1⅓ cups sugar
- 5 cups water, divided
- 1 Tbsp. grated lemon zest
- 1¾ cups lemon juice (about 10 large lemons)
  Ice cubes

1. In a large saucepan, combine sugar, 1 cup water and lemon zest. Cook and stir over medium heat until the sugar is dissolved, about 4 minutes. Remove from heat.
2. Stir in lemon juice and the remaining 4 cups water; refrigerate until cold. Serve over ice.

1 CUP 142 cal., 0 fat (0 sat. fat), 0 chol., 1mg sod., 37g carb. (35g sugars, 0 fiber), 0 pro.

BAKE-SALE LEMON BARS

The recipe for these tangy lemon bars comes from my cousin, who is famous for cooking up farm feasts.
—*Mildred Keller, Rockford, IL*

PREP: 25 min. • **BAKE:** 20 min. + cooling
MAKES: 15 bars

- ¾   cup butter, softened
- ⅔   cup confectioners' sugar
- 1½ cups plus 3 Tbsp. all-purpose flour, divided
- 3   large eggs
- 1½ cups sugar
- ¼   cup lemon juice
     Additional confectioners' sugar

1. Preheat oven to 350°. In a large bowl, beat butter and confectioners' sugar until blended. Gradually beat in 1½ cups flour. Press onto the bottom of a greased 13x9-in. baking pan. Bake 18-20 minutes or until golden brown.
2. Meanwhile, in a small bowl, whisk eggs, sugar, lemon juice and remaining 3 Tbsp. flour until frothy; pour over hot crust.
3. Bake 20-25 minutes or until the lemon mixture is set and lightly browned. Cool completely on a wire rack. Dust with additional confectioners' sugar. Cut into bars. Refrigerate leftovers.
1 BAR 247 cal., 10g fat (6g sat. fat), 62mg chol., 88mg sod., 37g carb. (26g sugars, 0 fiber), 3g pro.

TEST KITCHEN TIPS

For the best flavor, use fresh lemon juice. Better yet, add 1 tsp. grated lemon zest to the filling.

Line the pan with nonstick foil before baking, and the bars will come out easily when they're done.

BEET SALAD WITH LEMON DRESSING

I was looking for a recipe for pickled beets and saw one with lemon instead of vinegar. I immediately thought of making a tabbouleh-inspired salad with beets instead of tomatoes.
—*Ann Sheehy, Londonderry, NH*

PREP: 15 min. • **BAKE:** 1¼ hours
MAKES: 6 servings

- 3   medium fresh beets (about 1 lb.)
- 1   cup finely chopped English cucumber
- 6   green onions, thinly sliced
- ½   cup shredded carrot
- ½   cup chopped sweet yellow or red pepper
- ¼   cup finely chopped red onion
- ¼   cup finely chopped radish
- ¾   cup minced fresh parsley

DRESSING
- 3   Tbsp. olive oil
- 2   tsp. grated lemon zest
- 3   Tbsp. lemon juice
- 1   garlic clove, minced
- ¼   tsp. salt
- ¼   tsp. pepper

1. Preheat oven to 400°. Scrub beets and trim tops. Wrap beets in foil; place on a baking sheet. Bake until tender, 1¼-1½ hours. Cool slightly. Peel beets and cut into cubes.
2. Place the remaining vegetables and parsley in a large bowl. Whisk together the dressing ingredients; toss with the cucumber mixture. Gently stir in beets.
⅔ CUP 116 cal., 7g fat (1g sat. fat), 0 chol., 173mg sod., 13g carb. (8g sugars, 3g fiber), 2g pro. **DIABETIC EXCHANGES** 1½ fat, 1 vegetable.

⏱ WATERMELON WEDGES

I start looking forward to biting into this summery treat when snow is still on the ground here! Whenever I make this for my friends, they swoon. It's also my secret for getting my kids to eat their fruit.
—*Jami Geittmann, Greendale, WI*

TAKES: 25 min. • **MAKES:** 8 servings

- ½   cup plain Greek yogurt
- 1   Tbsp. minced fresh mint
- 1   Tbsp. honey
- 8   wedges seedless watermelon, about 1 in. thick
- 1   medium kiwifruit, peeled and chopped
- 1   tangerine, sliced
- ½   cup sliced ripe mango
- ½   cup fresh raspberries
- ¼   cup fresh blueberries
- ¼   cup pomegranate seeds
- 2   Tbsp. pistachios, chopped

In a bowl, combine yogurt, mint and honey. Arrange watermelon wedges on a platter; top each wedge with yogurt mixture, fruit and pistachios. If desired, top with additional honey and mint. Serve immediately.
1 WEDGE 103 cal., 2g fat (1g sat. fat), 4mg chol., 18mg sod., 21g carb. (18g sugars, 2g fiber), 2g pro. **DIABETIC EXCHANGES** 1½ fruit.

LEMONY TORTELLINI BACON SALAD

Summer meals really shouldn't be complicated. We love this simple salad on warm nights. Adding a glass of iced tea or lemonade on the side is just right.
—*Samantha Vicars, Kenosha, WI*

TAKES: 20 min. • **MAKES:** 4 servings

- 2 cups frozen cheese tortellini (about 8 oz.)
- 4 cups fresh broccoli florets
- ¾ cup mayonnaise
- 1 Tbsp. balsamic vinegar
- 2 tsp. lemon juice
- ¾ tsp. dried oregano
- ¼ tsp. salt
- 1 pkg. (5 oz.) spring mix salad greens
- 4 bacon strips, cooked and crumbled

1. In a large saucepan, cook tortellini according to the package directions, adding broccoli during the last 5 minutes of cooking. Meanwhile, in a small bowl, mix mayonnaise, vinegar, lemon juice, oregano and salt.

2. Drain tortellini and broccoli; gently rinse with cold water. Transfer to a large bowl. Add dressing; toss to coat. Serve over salad greens; sprinkle with bacon.

1 CUP SALAD WITH 2 CUPS GREENS 484 cal., 40g fat (7g sat. fat), 32mg chol., 693mg sod., 21g carb. (3g sugars, 4g fiber), 11g pro.

LEMON-GARLIC HUMMUS

Whipping up this smooth and creamy bean dip requires just five ingredients. It's a delicious alternative to traditional hummus, and is welcome at every party!
—*Kris Capener, Ogden, UT*

TAKES: 10 min. • **MAKES:** 1½ cups

- ¾ cup olive oil
- 2 cups canned garbanzo beans or chickpeas, rinsed and drained
- 3 Tbsp. lemon juice
- 2 tsp. minced garlic
- ½ tsp. salt
  Pita bread wedges or assorted fresh vegetables

In a food processor, combine the oil, beans, lemon juice, garlic and salt; cover and process until smooth. Transfer to a small bowl. Serve with pita wedges or vegetables.

¼ CUP 324 cal., 29g fat (3g sat. fat), 0 chol., 309mg sod., 14g carb. (2g sugars, 3g fiber), 3g pro.

TEST KITCHEN TIP

Homemade hummus tastes even better when the flavors have had a chance to blend and the mixture has firmed up a bit. Try letting it chill for 30 minutes before serving.

LEMONY ZUCCHINI BREAD

Flecks of zucchini give a third dimension to the popular lemon and poppy seed combination in this moist quick bread. My family loves this lemon zucchini bread at all times of the year.
—*Carol Funk, Richard, SK*

PREP: 25 min. • **BAKE:** 50 min. + cooling
MAKES: 2 loaves (16 pieces each)

- 4 cups all-purpose flour
- 1½ cups sugar
- 1 pkg. (3.4 oz.) instant lemon pudding mix
- 1½ tsp. baking soda
- 1 tsp. baking powder
- 1 tsp. salt
- 4 large eggs, room temperature
- 1¼ cups 2% milk
- 1 cup canola oil
- 3 Tbsp. lemon juice
- 1 tsp. lemon extract
- 2 cups shredded zucchini
- ¼ cup poppy seeds
- 2 tsp. grated lemon zest

1. Preheat oven to 350°. Grease two 9x5-in loaf pans; set aside. In a large bowl, combine the flour, sugar, pudding mix, baking soda, baking powder and salt. In another bowl, whisk the eggs, milk, oil, lemon juice and extract. Stir into the dry ingredients just until moistened. Fold in zucchini, poppy seeds and lemon zest.
2. Pour into prepared pans. Bake for 50-55 minutes or until a toothpick inserted in the center comes out clean. Cool for 10 minutes before removing from pans to wire racks to cool completely.

1 PIECE 187 cal., 8g fat (1g sat. fat), 28mg chol., 195mg sod., 25g carb. (12g sugars, 1g fiber), 3g pro.

2. Fill paper-lined muffin cups three-fourths full. Bake until a toothpick inserted in the center comes out clean, 18-22 minutes. Cool 10 minutes before removing from pans to wire racks to cool completely.

3. For frosting, in a small bowl, beat cream cheese, butter, lemon zest, vanilla and lemon juice until fluffy. Gradually beat in confectioners' sugar until smooth; stir in ¼ cup coconut. Frost cupcakes; sprinkle with the remaining ½ cup coconut. If desired, garnish with lemon slices.

1 CUPCAKE 327 cal., 18g fat (12g sat. fat), 85mg chol., 262mg sod., 37g carb. (26g sugars, 1g fiber), 4g pro.

⑤ LEMON ICEBOX CAKE

This easy cake, with its subtle lemon flavor and a pleasant crunch from the cookies, is a stunning centerpiece.
—*Peggy Woodward, Shullsburg, WI*

PREP: 20 min. + chilling
MAKES: 8 servings

- 3 cups heavy whipping cream
- 3 Tbsp. sugar
- 3 Tbsp. grated lemon zest
- 63 Maria cookies or Marie biscuits
  Lemon slices, optional

1. In a large bowl, beat the cream, sugar and lemon zest on high until stiff peaks form. Cut a small hole in the corner of a pastry bag. Fill with whipped cream.
2. On a serving plate, arrange 6 cookies in a circle. Place 1 cookie in the center. Pipe ⅔ cup whipped cream over cookies. Repeat the layers 8 times. Refrigerate overnight.
3. If desired, garnish with lemon slices.
1 PIECE 530 cal., 37g fat (23g sat. fat), 102mg chol., 158mg sod., 44g carb. (17g sugars, 2g fiber), 6g pro.

LEMON COCONUT CUPCAKES

Lemon plus coconut equals big smiles in this cupcake equation. The zesty gems are a hit with my family, friends neighbors.
—*Debra Henderson, Booneville, AR*

PREP: 20 min. • **BAKE:** 20 min. + cooling
MAKES: 15 cupcakes

- ¾ cup butter, softened
- 1 cup sugar
- 3 large eggs, room temperature
- 3 tsp. grated lemon zest
- ½ tsp. vanilla extract
- 1½ cups all-purpose flour
- ½ tsp. baking powder
- ½ tsp. baking soda
- ¼ tsp. salt
- ½ cup sour cream
- ½ cup sweetened shredded coconut

LEMON COCONUT FROSTING
- 4 oz. cream cheese, softened
- 2 Tbsp. butter, softened
- 1 tsp. grated lemon zest
- ¼ tsp. vanilla extract
- ¼ tsp. lemon juice
- 1¼ cups confectioners' sugar
- ¾ cup sweetened shredded coconut, divided
  Lemon slices, optional

1. Preheat oven to 350°. In a large bowl, cream butter and sugar until light and fluffy, 5-7 minutes. Add eggs, 1 at a time, beating well after each addition. Beat in lemon zest and vanilla. Combine flour, baking powder, baking soda and salt; add to the creamed mixture alternately with sour cream. Beat just until combined. Fold in coconut.

PICKLING

Sweet or spicy, these tasty concoctions make the most of summer fruits and veggies, and are great additions to salads, sandwiches, drinks and more. Plus, they add a beautiful finishing touch to a party table or picnic basket.

PICKLED DAIKON & CARROTS

This recipe is inspired by a pickle my family and I enjoyed at a local Asian restaurant. It is a delicious side to roasted meats as well as a tasty condiment on a burger or sandwich. You won't miss the high-fat dressing or mayonnaise.
—Lisa Keys, Kennett Square, PA

PREP: 20 min. + chilling
MAKES: 16 servings

- 1 medium daikon radish, peeled and julienned
- 1 cup julienned carrots
- 2 jalapeno peppers, seeded and thinly sliced
- ¾ cup water
- ¾ cup white vinegar
- ⅓ cup sugar
- 1 tsp. kosher salt
- 2 drops liquid smoke, optional

In a large bowl, combine daikon, carrots and jalapenos. In a saucepan, bring the water, vinegar, sugar, salt and, if desired, liquid smoke to a boil. Simmer until the sugar dissolves. Pour vinegar mixture over vegetables, ensuring the vegetables are submerged; cool. Transfer to jars if desired; cover tightly. Refrigerate, covered, at least 1 hour before serving. Store in the refrigerator up to 2 weeks, stirring occasionally.
NOTE Wear disposable gloves when cutting hot peppers; the oils can burn skin. Avoid touching your face.
¼ CUP 9 cal., 0 fat (0 sat. fat), 0 chol., 22mg sod., 2g carb. (1g sugars, 1g fiber), 0 pro. **DIABETIC EXCHANGES** 1 free food.

SPICY PICKLED STRAWBERRIES

I developed a unique and healthy recipe to feature my most-loved spring and summer fruit. My favorite way to serve these strawberries is as an appetizer with cheese.
—Roxanne Chan, Albany, CA

PREP: 10 min. + chilling
MAKES: 6 servings

- ½ cup rice vinegar
- 1 tsp. chili garlic sauce
- 1 tsp. toasted sesame oil
- ½ tsp. grated orange zest
- ½ tsp. black sesame seeds
- 1 green onion, minced
- 2 lbs. fresh strawberries, hulled

In a large bowl, combine the first 6 ingredients. Add strawberries and stir to coat. Refrigerate at least 1 hour. Transfer to jars if desired; cover tightly. Store in refrigerator up to 2 days.
¾ CUP 85 cal., 1g fat (0 sat. fat), 0 chol., 347mg sod., 19g carb. (14g sugars, 3g fiber), 1g pro.

PICKLED JALAPENO RINGS

I used to can Hungarian hot and mild peppers with my dad every year, but those are hard to find in California, so I started pickling jalapenos instead. These are better than any store-bought version.
—*Lou Kostura, Belmont, CA*

PREP: 15 min. + chilling
MAKES: 32 servings

- 1   lb. jalapeno peppers, sliced into rings
- 1   cup fresh dill sprigs
- 5   garlic cloves
- 1½ cups water
- ⅔   cup white vinegar
- 5   tsp. kosher salt
- 4   tsp. mixed pickling spices

In a clean 1-qt. glass jar, layer a quarter each of the jalapenos, dill and garlic; repeat, filling the jar. In a saucepan, bring water, vinegar, salt and pickling spices to a simmer until salt dissolves. Pour into jar to cover peppers; seal. Let stand until cool. Refrigerate for at least 7 days before serving, and up to 1 month.
NOTE Wear disposable gloves when cutting hot peppers; the oils can burn skin. Avoid touching your face.
2 TBSP. 5 cal., 0 fat (0 sat. fat), 0 chol., 180mg sod., 1g carb. (0 sugars, 0 fiber), 0 pro.

PICKLED CORN

When fresh corn is in season and you're overeating it straight off the cob, try pickling it instead!
—*Amanda Phillips, Portland, OR*

PREP: 15 min. + chilling
MAKES: 16 servings

- 4   medium ears sweet corn, husked
- 1   cup white vinegar
- ½   cup water
- ¼   cup sugar
- 2   garlic cloves, thinly sliced
- 1   tsp. salt
- ½   tsp. coarsely ground pepper
- 1   pinch crushed red pepper flakes

Cut corn from cobs; place in a large bowl. In a saucepan, combine vinegar, water, sugar, garlic, salt, pepper and pepper flakes. Bring to a boil; reduce heat and simmer until sugar dissolves, 1-2 minutes. Pour mixture over corn; cool. Transfer to jars if desired; seal tightly. Refrigerate at least 2 hours before serving. Store in the refrigerator up to 2 months.
½ CUP 24 cal., 0 fat (0 sat. fat), 0 chol., 19mg sod., 5g carb. (2g sugars, 1g fiber), 1g pro.

PICKLED BELL PEPPERS

Well received at potlucks, these colorful sliced peppers add zest to the menu—and they're a smart way to use peppers from the garden. I also like to make them as a zippy side for lunch or dinner at home.
—*Heather Prendergast, Sundre, AB*

PREP: 20 min. + chilling
MAKES: 16 servings (4 cups)

- 2 each medium sweet red, yellow and green peppers, julienned
- 1 large red onion, halved and thinly sliced
- 2 tsp. mixed pickling spices
- ½ tsp. celery seed
- 1 cup sugar
- 1 cup cider vinegar
- ⅓ cup water

1. In a large glass bowl, combine the peppers and onion. Place pickling spices and celery seed on a double thickness of cheesecloth. Gather corners of cloth to enclose seasonings; tie securely with string.
2. In a small saucepan, combine sugar, vinegar, water and spice bag. Bring to a boil; boil 1 minute. Transfer spice bag to the pepper mixture. Pour vinegar mixture over top; cool. Refrigerate, covered, 24 hours, stirring occasionally.
3. Discard spice bag. Transfer mixture to jars if desired; cover tightly. Refrigerate pickled peppers for up to 1 month.
¼ CUP 67 cal., 0 fat (0 sat. fat), 0 chol., 2mg sod., 17g carb. (15g sugars, 1g fiber), 1g pro.

TEST KITCHEN TIP

Serve these peppers with grilled steak or pork, toss them in a salad or use them to garnish a Bloody Mary.

SWEET & SPICY PICKLED RED SEEDLESS GRAPES

These flavor-packed grapes are distinctive and delicious on a fab antipasto, pickle or cheese tray.
—*Cheryl Perry, Hertford, NC*

PREP: 35 min. • **PROCESS:** 10 min.
MAKES: 4 pints

- 5 cups seedless red grapes
- 4 jalapeno peppers, seeded and sliced
- 2 Tbsp. minced fresh gingerroot
- 2 cinnamon sticks (3 in.), halved
- 4 whole star anise
- 2 tsp. coriander seeds
- 2 tsp. mustard seed
- 2 cups packed brown sugar
- 2 cups white wine vinegar
- 1 cup water
- 1 cup dry red wine
- 1½ tsp. canning salt

1. Pack grapes into 4 hot 1-pint jars to within 1½ in. of the tops. Divide jalapenos, ginger, cinnamon, star anise, coriander seeds and mustard seed among the jars.
2. In a large saucepan, combine brown sugar, vinegar, water, wine and canning salt. Bring to a boil; cook until the liquid is reduced to 3 cups, 15-18 minutes.
3. Carefully ladle hot liquid over the grape mixture in each jar, leaving ½-in. headspace. Remove air bubbles and adjust headspace, if necessary, by adding more hot liquid. Wipe rims. Center lids on jars; screw on bands until fingertip tight.
4. Place jars into canner, ensuring that they are completely covered with water. Bring to a boil; process for 10 minutes. Remove jars and cool.
NOTES The processing time listed is for altitudes of 1,000 feet or less. For altitudes up to 3,000 feet, add 5 minutes; 6,000 feet, add 10 minutes; 8,000 feet, add 15 minutes; 10,000 feet, add 20 minutes.
Wear disposable gloves when cutting hot peppers; the oils can burn skin. Avoid touching your face.
¼ CUP 32 cal., 0 fat (0 sat. fat), 0 chol., 7mg sod., 8g carb. (7g sugars, 0 fiber), 0 pro.

🅕 PICKLED RED ONIONS

Everyone should have a jar of these in their refrigerator at all times. I put them on everything and they keep for weeks. Any onion can be used, but red onions give you a nice pink color over time.
—*James Schend, Pleasant Prairie, WI*

PREP: 10 min. + standing
MAKES: 8 servings

- ¾ cup water
- ⅔ cup white wine or cider vinegar
- 2 tsp. sugar
- 1 tsp. kosher salt
- 1 medium red onion, thinly sliced
  Optional: Fresh rosemary, thyme or dill sprigs, whole black peppercorns, small dried chili or garlic clove

In a bowl, whisk together the first 4 ingredients until the sugar and salt dissolve. Place onions and desired optional ingredients into a large glass jar; pour vinegar mixture over onions. Seal and let stand at least 2 hours at room temperature. Refrigerate for up to 2 weeks.

1 SERVING 8 cal., 0 fat (0 sat. fat), 0 chol., 121mg sod., 2g carb. (1g sugars, 0 fiber), 0 pro. **DIABETIC EXCHANGES** 1 free food.

PICKLED RED ONION TIPS

What are some variations of this recipe? Start with the optional herbs listed to find a combination you like. If you want a little kick, add slices of jalapenos or red pepper flakes.

How can I use pickled red onions? They're fantastic on tacos, burrito bowls, salads and panini sandwiches.

MOM'S PICKLED CARROTS

My mother is the only other person I've known to make this recipe. In fact, when I take it to a potluck or picnic, no one has ever heard of pickled carrots. But once they try them, they are hooked.
—*Robin Koble, Fairview, PA*

PREP: 15 min. + chilling • **COOK:** 20 min.
MAKES: 6 cups

     2 lbs. carrots, cut lengthwise into
        ¼-in.-thick strips
  1½ cups sugar
  1½ cups water
  1½ cups cider vinegar
     ¼ cup mustard seed
     3 cinnamon sticks (3 in.)
     3 whole cloves

1. Place carrots in a large saucepan; add enough water to cover. Bring to a boil. Cook, covered, until crisp-tender, 3-5 minutes. Drain. Transfer carrots to a large bowl.
2. In another large saucepan, combine the remaining ingredients. Bring to a boil. Reduce heat; simmer, uncovered, for 20 minutes. Pour the mixture over the carrots. Refrigerate, covered, overnight to allow flavors to blend.
3. Transfer mixture to jars. Cover and refrigerate up to 1 month.
¼ CUP 30 cal., 0 fat (0 sat. fat), 0 chol., 170mg sod., 7g carb. (6g sugars, 1g fiber), 1g pro.

PICKLED CHERRY TOMATOES

These pickled cherry tomatoes really pop in your mouth. They stay beautifully bright and fresh tasting too.
—*Peggy Woodward, Shullsburg, WI*

PREP: 10 min. + chilling
MAKES: 6 cups

    20 oz. cherry tomatoes (about 2 pints)
      4 garlic cloves, halved
      2 tsp. whole peppercorns
     ½ tsp. mustard seed
      2 cups water
      2 cups cider vinegar
      3 Tbsp. salt
      2 Tbsp. sugar

Pierce the bottom of each cherry tomato with a skewer. In a large bowl, place tomatoes, garlic, peppercorns and mustard seed. In a saucepan, bring the water, vinegar, salt and sugar to a simmer until sugar and salt dissolve. Pour over tomatoes; cover. Let stand 2 hours. Transfer to jars if desired; seal tightly. Refrigerate 48 hours before serving, and up to 1 month.
¼ CUP 9 cal., 0 fat (0 sat. fat), 0 chol., 30mg sod., 2g carb. (2g sugars, 0 fiber), 0 pro.

51 PICKLED RED CABBAGE

This bright and tangy cabbage is so pretty! The color is gorgeous, and the cabbage maintains a nice crunchy texture. Try it on your favorite sandwich.
—Peggy Woodward, Shullsburg, WI

PREP: 10 min. + chilling • **MAKES:** 4 cups

- 4 cups shredded red cabbage (about ½ medium head)
- 2 garlic cloves, halved
- 1 tsp. whole peppercorns
- 1 cup water
- 1 cup cider vinegar
- 1 Tbsp. sugar
- 2 tsp. salt

In a large bowl, place cabbage, garlic and peppercorns. In a saucepan, bring water, vinegar, sugar and salt to a simmer until the sugar and salt dissolve. Pour over the cabbage; cover. Let stand 2 hours. Transfer to jars if desired; seal tightly. Refrigerate 48 hours before serving, and up to 1 month.

¼ CUP 5 cal., 0 fat (0 sat. fat), 0 chol., 5mg sod., 1g carb. (1g sugars, 0 fiber), 0 pro.

PICKLED RED CABBAGE TIPS

Can I use a different vinegar? If you don't have cider vinegar on hand, you can use white vinegar or red wine vinegar instead.

What can I serve with pickled red cabbage? It's delicious piled high on tacos (including fish tacos). Otherwise, keep it on hand for your favorite sandwiches.

PICKLED PEACHES

Fresh peach quarters soaked in vinegar, sugar and warm spices are a classic southern treat. Serve with ice cream, pound cake, roasted meat and veggies, or mix into your favorite salad greens.
—Nick Iverson, Denver, CO

PREP: 20 min. • **PROCESS:** 15 min.
MAKES: 12 servings

- 6 cinnamon sticks (3 in.)
- 24 whole peppercorns
- 18 whole cloves
- 2 tsp. thinly sliced fresh gingerroot
- 12 medium peaches, peeled, pitted and quartered
- 3 cups sugar
- 1 cup white vinegar
- 1 cup water

1. Divide cinnamon sticks, peppercorns, cloves and ginger slices among 6 hot 1-pint jars; add peaches.
2. In a large saucepan, bring the sugar, vinegar and water to a boil. Carefully ladle hot liquid over peaches, leaving ½-in. headspace. Remove air bubbles and adjust headspace, if necessary, by adding more of the hot mixture. Wipe rims. Center lids on jars; screw on bands until fingertip tight.
3. Place jars into canner with simmering water, ensuring they are completely covered with water. Bring to a boil; process for 15 minutes. Remove jars and cool.

NOTE The processing time listed is for altitudes of 1,000 feet or less. For altitudes up to 3,000 feet, add 5 minutes; 6,000 feet, add 10 minutes; 8,000 feet, add 15 minutes; 10,000 feet, add 20 minutes.

4 PIECES 78 cal., 0 fat (0 sat. fat), 0 chol., 0 sod., 19g carb. (17g sugars, 2g fiber), 1g pro.

PICKLED RAMPS

Pickling is a fantastic way to enjoy ramps beyond their short harvest season. Serve on sandwiches or mixed into salads.
—Taste of Home Test Kitchen

PREP: 15 min. + chilling • **MAKES:** 4 dozen

- 1 lb. ramps
- 2 bay leaves
- 5 whole allspice
- 1 tsp. mustard seed
- ½ tsp. whole peppercorns
- ¼ tsp. crushed red pepper flakes
- ¾ cup water
- ¾ cup white vinegar
- 3 Tbsp. sugar
- 2 tsp. kosher salt

1. Trim greens off ramps, save for another use. In a large bowl, place ramps, bay leaves, allspice, mustard seed, peppercorns and pepper flakes.
2. In a small saucepan, bring the water, vinegar, sugar and salt to a simmer until sugar and salt dissolve. Pour over the ramps; cover. Let stand 2 hours.
3. Transfer to jars if desired; seal tightly. Refrigerate for at least 48 hours before serving, and up to 1 month.

1 PICKLED RAMP 2 cal., 0 fat (0 sat. fat), 0 chol., 9mg sod., 0 carb. (0 sugars, 0 fiber), 0 pro. **DIABETIC EXCHANGES** 1 free food.

INDEX

P. 134

P. 40

P. 198

P. 264

P. 266